HIS EMINENCE AND
HIZZONER

ALSO BY MAYOR EDWARD I. KOCH

MAYOR: AN AUTOBIOGRAPHY
(Simon & Schuster, 1984)
POLITICS
(Simon & Schuster, 1986)

and

MAYOR EDWARD I. KOCH

HIS
EMINENCE
and
HIZZONER

A Candid Exchange

WILLIAM MORROW
and Company, Inc.
NEW YORK

Library of Congress Cataloging-in-Publication Data

O'Connor, John Joseph, 1920–
    His Eminence and Hizzoner : a candid exchange / John Cardinal
O'Connor and Mayor Edward I. Koch.
        p.   cm.
    Includes index.
    ISBN 0–688–07928–8
    1. Church and state—New York (N.Y.) 2. Church and state—
Catholic Church. 3. O'Connor, John Joseph, 1920– —Political and
social views. 4. Koch. Ed. 1924– . 5. New York (N.Y.)—Social
conditions. 6. New York (N.Y.)—Church history—20th century.
7. Catholic Church—New York (N.Y.) I Koch, Ed, 1924– .
II. Title.
BX1418.N5036 1989
974.7'1043—dc19   88-33078
                                                                         CIP

Printed in the United States of America

First Edition

1 2 3 4 5 6 7 8 9 10

BOOK DESIGN BY RICHARD ORIOLO

With deepest gratitude to
Monsignor Peter G. Finn
Ellen M. Stafford
Eileen M. White, J.D.
and all who helped me prepare the manuscript
and review it for publication.

—JOHN CARDINAL O'CONNOR

I dedicate this book to the City of New York and its
people, whom I fiercely love.

I conveyed that same thought in an epitaph I composed
in 1987 after recovering from a stroke. It said:

"He was fiercely proud of his Jewish faith. He
fiercely defended the City of New York and he fiercely
loved the people of the City of New York."

Bishop Edward Egan, then of the Archdiocese, paid me a
great compliment when he told me he loved my epitaph
"because there are so few people who are fierce about
anything."

—EDWARD I. KOCH

CONTENTS

CONTENTS

THE MAYOR
THE CARDINAL
and
ME

THE CARDINAL
WHY THIS BOOK

THE MAYOR

It was just one of many dinners I have had over the years with the prelate of the Catholic Archdiocese of New York. This night it was at the Cardinal's residence. Other times it had been on the porch at Gracie Mansion. Wherever or whenever it was held, I knew what to expect: a no-holds-barred discussion of the issues of the day. While our talks were always surrounded by good humor, we'd go straight to the point and speak frankly. I would be challenged, engaged—as would my staff. I had to be prepared, but there are few occasions I enjoy more.

This particular evening was to be forever memorialized. Between the ice cream and the coffee, Cardinal O'Connor turned to me to suggest that a book describing the challenges, travails and successes of the joint ventures between the Archdiocese of New York and the City of New York would make interesting reading.

Well, anytime someone suggests writing a book they have my complete attention. Of course, that's only after I've reminded them of how many weeks my first book spent on the *New York Times* best-seller list. The Cardinal's suggestion was really more than that, it was an offer to co-author a book with him. I jumped at the chance.

Little did I realize at the time how difficult it would be to reconcile the starkly contrasting styles of a Catholic political scientist-ethicist-admiral-archbishop-cardinal and a Jewish attorney-councilman-congressman-mayor from the Bronx. When all is said and done, they probably can't be reconciled. And it's more than just a matter of angels dancing on the head of a pin. We have different personalities, are of different faiths and backgrounds, and serve different institutional

13

interests. But the attempt at reconciliation and the contrasts it reveals will, I hope, make for refreshing, even rewarding reading.

I don't know what your expectation was when you picked up this book. What you'll get is insight into how two men try to address the needs and chart the future of one of the world's great cities. And New York City *is* a great city, a microcosm not just of the United States but of the whole world. Some 175 different races, religions or ethnic groups are represented among the 7.5 million people who live in our five boroughs. Every major incident that occurs anywhere or anytime on the face of our planet in one way or another reverberates in the city. We tout ourselves as the international center for communications, banking and finance and proudly, but correctly, believe the song that says "If you can make it here you can make it anywhere."

All cities have their problems. But our problems are of a dimension seen in few other places. And if it is going to happen anywhere, it will probably happen here first. We're at the cutting edge of urban problems. We're also at the cutting edge of solving them.

Drugs, homelessness, AIDS, broken homes, dropouts and poverty are the social plagues of our age. In the Reagan era the White House and its advocates have, in essence, turned their back on these problems, leaving the burden of dealing with them to the city halls of America. With limited resources we've not been able to meet every challenge or solve every problem. But in New York an enormous amount of energy from both the public and private sectors has been marshaled to say yes where Washington has said no, no, and no again.

The City of New York, much more than the State of New York, bears the principal responsibility for delivering the services necessary to address these ills. But no locality, regardless of its dedication, could be expected to meet the prodigious need unassisted. The state and federal governments do their parts through funding, though it's never enough. Government's involvement in meeting these needs goes back decades while the Church has been filling the void for centuries.

Because the need is so great and the undertaking so complex, the government and the Church have formed natural partnerships in many areas. While society has been well served when this occurs, there are those who believe that any merger of Church and State is dangerous to our liberty. Sad experience has taught us that such ideologues themselves represent a far greater danger to the liberty of the very constituencies they purportedly seek to protect.

What our forefathers crafted as a protection of religious freedom has, in some instances, been used as a weapon to deny those in need essential services on artificial grounds. It's just one more example of "lunacy in government," in which legal technicalities are considered more important than human needs. As you'll see in reading this book, lunacies in our time are regrettably abundant.

I'm sure you'll also discover that the Cardinal and I sometimes differ sharply in approaching problems. Where angels fear to tread, government is often obligated to go. His position is steeped in the doctrine of his Church. Mine is primarily informed by the secular law (and the rules of the political arena). It becomes provocative at the point where our two approaches intersect.

"The difference between the Cardinal and myself," I once told a CBS reporter, "is that he is in the business of saving souls and I am in the business of saving lives." By the nature of his profession he deals in the long term—"long" as in eternal—and the theoretical. Of course, he has his day-to-day concerns, including a huge number of archdiocesan programs to administer and worry about. I, on the other hand, am more interested in the here and now. I assume a pragmatic approach (perhaps, some would say, too pragmatic) in getting millions of people through the day, through the week and the rest of the year. Different time frames? Yes. Different commitments? Not as much as you might suspect.

But the contrast between the Cardinal and me is more than a question of style. It goes to the heart of the choice each of us made early in our lives—he to serve the Almighty, I to serve my city. But our shared goals of helping those most in need in New York provide the only framework necessary within which a mutually acceptable solution to almost any problem can be found. We both hope that in writing this book, we can help others discern the wisdom and benefits of this type of programmatic collaboration. To paraphrase that same song—if Church and State can make it here, they can make it anywhere.

My personal relationship with the Cardinal was cemented for all time when he singled me out for special mention in a humorous way in his first homily at St. Patrick's Cathedral. He borrowed a phrase I often use. In the middle of his speech he asked, "How'm I doing?" He then referred to his favorite mayor. He led the audience to believe he was referring to me, but unexpectedly he referred to the mayor of

Scranton, which is where the Cardinal used to live. He did it with great comedic flair.

After the ceremony, we all went to the back of the Cathedral to greet the Cardinal personally. I was standing behind Governor Cuomo. When the Cardinal greeted the governor he mistook him for me and said, "I have always wanted to meet you, Mayor Koch." It's hard to confuse me with Mario Cuomo; we don't look alike at all. But in any event it didn't matter, because the Cardinal and I quickly became good friends.

When the Cardinal was first designated, I was asked (and accepted with alacrity) to attend the ceremony at the Vatican. The Cardinal paid me a great honor by allowing me to be one of the four people who signed the document that gave him title to a church in Rome; each Cardinal is given such a church in addition to his Cathedral in his own city. At a dinner in Rome held in his honor on that occasion, he again singled me out when he spoke. He said, "Only in New York can two people who are constantly suing each other be such good friends." He was referring to the lawsuits, of which there were several, in which the City's position collided with that of the Church.

My special feeling about the Cardinal was enhanced during a scandal that involved the illegal acts of a handful of people in government. Early on I was overwhelmed with the revelations of corruption by the borough president of Queens, Donald Manes, and the Bronx county leader, Stanley Friedman, to cite just two. The Cardinal called me at Gracie Mansion on a Sunday.

He said, "Ed, I know that you are feeling terrible. I want you to know that you are in my prayers. I have full confidence in you as do the people of this city. They know that you are honest. I know that all of us are subject to being abused by those who work for us. I know what you are going through."

I said, "Thank you so much, Your Eminence. I cannot tell you how much your call means to me."

He said, "No, it is not important. I just wanted you to know that I am thinking of you."

I said, "It is very important. The Lubovitcher Rebbe did not call me and tell me of his support."

I hasten to add that this is not a reflection on the Lubovitcher Rebbe—the spiritual leader of one of the largest Hasidic Jewish communities—since it is not his style to get involved and he never calls me. Nor is it the style of most people to call. The Cardinal's call was the only one that I received from a religious spokesperson. Rabbi Morris Sherer—the president of Agudath Israel, a major charity organization in New York City that is run by Orthodox Jews—did call me after he heard me tell this story.

He said, "This is not the Lubovitcher Rebbe calling you. It's Morris Sherer. I want you to know that I support you."

I thanked him for calling and truly appreciated his thinking of me.

The Cardinal is a tough man. But I don't think he cares whether he is popular. When I say he doesn't care, I mean that he would not change a single position to gain popularity. He views his positions as long-held doctrines of the Church, two thousand years in their formulation, not to be changed on the basis of a vote.

In that respect, it is not surprising that Orthodox Jews identify with him as they do on a whole host of subjects, whether it is birth control, abortion or gay rights. They do not believe that religion should be subject to a popularity poll. I like to think that even though governing is not my religion, I view what I do in somewhat the same way. There are many things that I take positions on that cause me enormous problems from a political point of view.

The most recent and well-known incident was my criticism of Jesse Jackson during the campaign in the 1988 Democratic primary for president. An enormous number of people who are otherwise my loyal supporters were angry that I treated Jackson with tough questioning and verbal assaults. I considered it equal treatment for a major presidential contender comparable to the questioning and scrutiny to which other candidates like Gary Hart and Joe Biden were subject.

I have taken on sacred cows such as the newsstand vendors. I did so simply to regulate where they could be located, how close to the intersection they could be placed, and what they could and could not sell besides newspapers. The publishers of the papers were furious. I suspect that fear of lost revenue was what motivated the attacks rather than concern over the First Amendment, which was not being violated.

Finally, the regulation of street vendors, preventing ten or more peddlers from congregating on a corner and requiring that they be dispersed in a reasonable way throughout the business district, caused me to be attacked for wasting the city's energy, time and money. Yet when I undertook these mundane efforts, because I believed the government was required to do something about pedestrian traffic and prevent it from being impeded, I knew that it would make me unpopular.

However, I also am aware that very few things are ultimately worth antagonizing a substantial part of the electorate. An exception for me would be Jesse Jackson. I perceive him as a danger to many of the fundamental values I hold dear such as the security of Israel. I believe that they will be adversely affected by the ascendancy of Jackson's philosophy and its impact on the Democratic party and its policies on that subject, and I will not be silent.

But as for the Cardinal, because, as he says, he does not have to submit himself to the electorate every four years, nothing will deter him. Nor will he make any compromise on any principle and for that I admire him even more.

When the Cardinal went to Israel, he committed himself to visiting Jerusalem. He subsequently found out that would violate his instructions from the Vatican because of its protocol concerning nonrecognition of Jerusalem as the capital of Israel. He was attacked by the Jewish community after he admitted his gaffe. I was one of the few Jewish public officials who came to his defense. I said at the time, and would say it again, that he is not a free agent. The Church is not a democratic institution. The Cardinal's mandate is to carry out the wishes of the Pope and the doctrines of the Church. Therefore, to attack him for that is unfair, foolish and unavailing.

But in part as a result of my support for him, he found a way to meet with Teddy Kollek in Jerusalem. He carved out what he said was an exception since he was not meeting with the national government but rather with the mayor of the city. The logic failed me, but I did appreciate his calling me from Teddy Kollek's office in Jerusalem, where we had a three-way conversation.

I had already introduced the Cardinal to Teddy Kollek in a phone conversation during the time Kollek came to Gracie Mansion, the Sunday before the Cardinal went to Israel. I called the Cardinal and he spoke with Teddy Kollek. That created a bond among the three of us.

The Cardinal made another statement during the course of his trip. I believe he said it after his visit to Yad Vashem, which is the center in Israel dedicated to the commemoration of the deaths of six million Jews under Hitler. His statement concerned the "gift" that the Jews gave to the world by their suffering at the hands of Hitler. That statement was not understood by Jews because such a concept is bizarre for Jews.

Because I have attended so many Catholic funerals and have had discussions with so many Catholic prelates—the Cardinal, Bishop Mugavero, Bishop Sullivan and others—I understood the Catholic doctrine he was conveying by saying this. The Cardinal was referring to the doctrine of suffering as a mystical gift to God to help the entire world. It is an interesting concept but I would prefer not to be the vessel providing the gift. I am able to explain it though, and I recall on several occasions the Cardinal commenting that I was even better at explaining the concept than many Catholics, which was a nice compliment.

My concern for the Cardinal, who is clearly not interested in creature comforts, caused me to suggest that he add an outdoor garden for dining to his official residence. I have been a guest in his home on many occasions as he has been mine at Gracie Mansion. Gracie Mansion is a beautiful house with a vast lawn and gardens and a magnificent view of the river. The Cardinal's residence is, and I hope he will forgive me for saying so, very somber and formal and not too comfortable in appearance. I told him that he should have architects design an outdoor garden area. He said he didn't think it was possible since the building has been landmarked. I asked the commissioner of the Landmarks Commission to take a look at the site. I am told that the commissioner is having the matter evaluated. I hope someday to have dinner with the Cardinal in his newly created garden so as to make life a little pleasanter for him when he relaxes.

When I was hospitalized with what my doctors described as a trivial stroke, and I hasten to add it was trivial to them but not to me, one of the first people who came to visit was the Cardinal. I was in intensive-care because I was going in and out of seizures.

He said, "You are in my prayers every day. If you would like, I will pray for you in Hebrew."

I said, "No, I have already taken care of that. Please do it in Latin. I believe that God prefers listening to prayers in Latin, Greek or Hebrew." I may have said "only" listens to prayers in Latin, Greek or Hebrew but, on reflection, it is better to say "prefers." And, of course, I said this jocularly and he laughed.

My own Rabbi, Arthur Schneier, also came to see me.

He said, "It is important that you recite the special prayers for the sick asking to be healed. So recite after me."

Here he uttered the Hebrew prayer, which I will recite in English: "Heal me, God, and I shall be healed. Save me, God, and I shall be saved."

The Rabbi said, "When you leave the hospital, as you will, you must go as quickly as possible to the synagogue and thank God for saving you."

I promised him that I would do that and I did. I believe in the power of prayer. I believe that prayers of people like the Cardinal, Rabbi Schneier and others like Mother Teresa caused me to heal quickly and to leave the hospital in four days without paralysis of any kind or any diminution of my faculties. The doctors said that I was close to being paralyzed because the stroke affected an artery in my brain which they identified as chillingly close—they said hairsbreadth close—to the motor area of my brain.

I have known Mother Teresa for a number of years. She gets her way with everyone, including the Cardinal. No one knows if she is a saint, but many believe that she just might be the only living saint, so no one denies her wishes. I recall when she opened her first hospice for AIDS patients located in Greenwich Village. She did this when no one else was able to accomplish a similar goal. Without prior notice to anyone, she announced by calling people on that very day and saying that at 5:00 P.M. she was going to formally open the hospice. The Cardinal and I each had to cancel our prior engagements because neither of us could have failed to be there at her command. So even the Cardinal is a prisoner of this Yugoslavian-born Albanian nun, whose fame is worldwide and who brooks no dissent.

Mother Teresa said to me, "The patients [referring to those dying of AIDS] take my hands and place them on their sores. They demand that I touch them and then they look to see if I will cringe and, of course, I do not. They ask me for a ticket to heaven and I give it to them as they die, and I close their eyes for them."

The Catholic view, expressed by the Cardinal and by Mother Teresa on many occasions, is that the world in which we live cannot possibly be as good as the world to which we will go. That is not a view held by Jews. We do not know where we will go or even if there will be another world. I believe there will be, but there is no binding dogma to that effect. Jews are free to create their own fantasy. It may be because of my association with so many Catholics or my own desire that I picture another life, near physical in nature, for those eligible to enter heaven. And I believe in heaven and hell. But unlike Catholics, I prefer to delay the coming of the second act. I am really not interested in testing the theory of the world to come. But I do believe that it sustains Catholics in such a way that their funerals are much different from the funerals of Jews or many Protestants.

Jewish funerals I have attended are generally filled with tears, the families overwhelmed with grief. The Protestant funerals I have attended, in particular Episcopalian funerals, seem to me extremely devoid of feeling. The typical Episcopal funeral I have been present at features a violin concerto and a terse homily delivered without passion. Baptist funerals, however, resemble Jewish ones in their outpouring of emotion.

I have made arrangements for my own funeral, a fact that has been the subject of much criticism. A former deputy mayor of the city of New York, Lucille Rose, died last year. Before her death, she told her minister exactly how she wanted the service to be conducted. She even specified the hymns and the speakers. She had requested that I deliver a eulogy and of course I did. I feel it is appropriate to make such arrangements when you are able to do so. I later found out that Police Commissioner Ben Ward has also planned his funeral arrangements.

Without revealing my directions, which are in the hands of my lawyer, Allen Schwartz, and my Chief of Staff, Diane Coffey, I did announce publicly that I would like the Cardinal to speak at my funeral if he was disposed to do so.

I am told by Robert Wagner, Jr., who is the grandson of one of New York State's great senators and the son of former mayor of New York Robert Wagner, Sr., that my relationship with the Cardinal is unique. He said that it is far better than the relationship his father had with either Cardinal Cooke or Cardinal Spellman—and Mayor Wagner was a member of the Catholic laity, highly distinguished, and a former ambassador to the Vatican. Why our relationship is so unique I don't know, but it makes me proud.

THE CARDINAL

I hope that this book will help further dialogue on how the religious and political can relate to each other effectively in our pluralistic society. Relationships between Church and State, or (what are mistakenly perceived as the same) relationships between religion and politics, are unique in the United States. The mountain of literature which attempts valiantly to define them very probably suggests, instead, that they may well be indefinable. I do not pretend to be able to define them. The Mayor and I do, however, have a degree of experience, accrued in working together in a large city of exceptional diversities. It is largely this experience that prompts this book.

Ours has not been the lofty privilege of simply presenting respective positions to impartial listeners from the genteel pulpits of St. Patrick's Cathedral and City Hall. Each of us has felt obliged to win at least a *hearing* for our respective positions in the entire community, and to influence the community to adopt such positions as its own. We have had to compete with all the influences, propaganda, pressures and forces of the real world, of the megalopolis that is New York, and not infrequently with each other.

An editorial in *The New York Times* a couple of years ago reminded bishops of the United States that this is a hurly-burly world, and if they are going to have an impact on it, they have to expect to be battered around a little more than somewhat. Fair enough. That the same is true of public officeholders needs no comment. That's the reality of life in a democratic, pluralistic society. It is governed, in part, by the First Amendment. But neither that lofty law of the land nor any other provides a blueprint for the daily work of either churchman or politician. Nor does it protect either Church or State from body bruises. As he framed so many ideas so unmistakably, Harry Truman served us as well when he said: "If you can't stand the heat, get out of the kitchen."

What important issue is seriously addressed in our society without a great deal of tension and conflict? We needn't turn merely to the so-called "controversial" issues of abortion or homosexuality. There are endless others, many of them much less visible. On the surface, for example, one might not expect the need to house the homeless to be controversial. Nor is the *need*, in itself. But start to propose the *how* of housing the homeless and otherwise caring people of profound good-will begin shrieking at one another as if they were bitter enemies. Neither the elected official nor the churchman is exempt. The pastor of a parish can be a superb leader in the struggle for justice for the poor, but he may turn into a tiger at bay on behalf of his people if the City wants to open a residence for the homeless in *his* parish. An elected official can be equally ferocious, both in demanding that more be done about housing, and in protecting his constituents from having low-income housing built in *his* district.

How does one separate Church from State in such issues, or in any of the major issues that face society? When is "excessive entanglement" between Church and State involved?

Priests, sisters, brothers are expected to fight for human rights, civil rights, and whatever variations of rights may be of grave concern to their people. The Roman Catholic Church has joined with churches of many other persuasions in confronting the "system" and those public officials accused of perverting the system in places like the South Bronx. "We are taking charge," the resolution of South Bronx activists, is as politically explosive a battle cry as could be formulated. Right-minded people of every denomination and of none applaud, as well they should. Few people charge that fighting for decent housing, decent education and ridding tenements of rats and drug pushers is "meddling" in politics. Yet success in any battle is possible *only* through the political system. The Church *must* turn to the City and plead for help, demand help, insist privately, publicly and mightily that the City respond. For the Church not to do so would be to abdicate its moral responsibility. In the recent past the City has turned to the churches to clean up social messes that have defied municipal correction, as with the initial efforts in the 1970s to clean up Times Square.

When the Mayor critically needs facilities to take care of children who have been abandoned, or orphaned, or whose parents for whatever reason can't or won't take care of them, is he unduly entangling State with Church if he turns to the Church for help? Is he doing so if he contracts with the Church for such help, since it is a costly matter? When the Church agrees to help if, and only if, its own moral, spiritual or religious teachings and principles are respected, is the Mayor letting religion override politics if he accepts this position? Is he acting either unconstitutionally or unfairly?

Obviously, one could turn to the courts to resolve every conceivable difference. Not only would such an approach make tyrants of the courts; it would be virtually impossible. In this so-called litigious society, court dockets are packed. More important, no laws have yet been written that cover every conceivable issue into which both Church and State necessarily insert themselves as they attempt to carry out their obligations to the people.

It is only when churchman and officeholder are willing to be blackened and blued, willing to work for and fight for what they respectively believe to be the good of the people—even when it may mean fighting each other—that the democratic system can be forced to work. The very concept of democracy is fraught with ambiguities. It is *not* a smooth-working system. Only *people* can make it work, and then only those people willing to pay the price, in tension and conflict, in misunderstanding and perplexity.

This book is intended, then, as an account of how two people in a big city are trying to make the "system" work, with a tremendous amount of help from countless numbers of other people.

THE MAYOR
GOD *and* MAN
AT CITY HALL

THE CARDINAL
JURISDICTION
and
VALUES

THE MAYOR

I often speak at churches and synagogues. On Easter Sunday, 1985, I was invited to the Mt. Nebo Baptist Church in Harlem, where I said, "Nothing happens on this earth that wasn't ordained by God . . . while I know it was the people who elected me, it was God who selected me to be Mayor." My comments created a bit of controversy. But for the most part, the furor was the creation of headline writers, columnists and members of the liberal, even radical, clergy who oppose me politically. What I was saying was that I've not only been blessed by the Almighty with a wonderful family and my faith, but I've also been given the opportunity to use those blessings in public service. I don't believe the vast majority of people who believe in a Supreme Being would disagree that we are all meant to do what we can to help others.

In fact, I think what I said reflects the philosophy of my religion, of the Roman Catholic Church and of the parishioners at Mt. Nebo. I particularly appreciated the comments of Reverend William Gardner, pastor at Mt. Nebo, who said in answer to a reporter's question, "I certainly believe it is in God's providence to make one man mayor of our city. God uses us as his instruments. The time was right when Martin Luther King was born for the work he did, and I think the time is also right for Mayor Koch and the work he's doing." He's not at odds with my theology.

I was shocked, though, that some religious leaders got so hot under their clerical collars. Rabbi Marc Tanenbaum, for example, said that my comments were "an effort to appeal very directly, almost brazenly to churchgoing people and very conservative voters."

What an outrageous thing to say. Have we reached the time when an elected official isn't allowed to talk of God in or out of a church or synagogue? When those who express a deeply held religious feeling are pigeonholed and denounced as "conservative"? Is the worship of God now reserved only for priests, ministers and rabbis? If so, worship is being diminished in a time when it should be elevated.

My religion means a lot to me. I've described myself as being "fiercely proud of my Jewish faith." I've even said that I want those words as part of my epitaph. I say I'm "fiercely proud" of being Jewish. But there is a "shtetl" mentality among some Jews. That means, don't stick your head above the grass because if you do, some non-Jews will almost certainly come along and chop it off. If they chop off your head, they'll chop off others and soon all Jews will suffer. That's why some Jews like to keep a low profile.

As everyone must know, I've never held to the shtetl view and I'm certainly not known for my low profile. I personally believe that if you glory in and are fiercely proud of what you are and, specifically, what you are in relation to your faith, you help your faith grow and flourish. When he first heard of my "fierce" epitaph, Bishop Edward M. Egan, vicar for education at the New York Archdiocese, wrote that he was pleased the Mayor of New York has a "willingness to be fierce about the things in life which truly count." Not surprisingly, I was "fiercely" pleased with Bishop Egan's comment.

I think people respect the dedication, zeal and pride I bring to my faith, my job and the way I look at life. They know I'll stand up, speak my mind and not be afraid to face the tough issues or make the tough decisions. After so many years in public life, I think that's what the vast majority of people want. And it's certainly what they deserve in a democratic society. There are those who say it's best to downplay or, at least, not emphasize being Jewish. I always reply it's better to flaunt being Jewish. That's what I am and I'm proud of it. Why downplay it?

At the same time, I can't claim to be "fiercely observant," especially in terms of going to synagogue or adhering to dietary restrictions. I observe the High Holy Days and always show respect for those who adhere strictly to the articles of faith. For example, I would never engage in a public display of eating pork products. Everyone has to follow his or her conscience when it comes to the practice of religion and I follow mine.

28

Just as I respect those who are faithful to the tenets of my own religion, I also try to respect those who follow other faiths. What's wonderful about New York City is its diversity of racial, religious and ethnic groups. When I'm asked to attend a ceremony held by another faith—Christmas Eve at St. Patrick's Cathedral, the groundbreaking for a new mosque, Archbishop Manoogian's annual "One World Festival" or Easter Sunday at Mt. Nebo—I always try to be present. No matter who is mayor—Jewish or Catholic, Muslim or Buddhist—it's important for the city's highest elected official to pay respect to every faith in our city. It reminds people that though we may have different rituals, we all worship the same God under the protection of the same flag.

That said, I also believe that for years in New York it's been a negative for a politician to publicly say he or she believes in God. One is expected to honor the different faiths, but apparently not supposed to have a faith of one's own. Some people are simply so foolish as to believe that officials who say they believe in God somehow or other violate the constitutional separation of Church and State. Frankly, I think that's a stupid point of view.

This position is usually argued by people who call themselves "humanists"—a significant part of our population—who don't really believe in God. They believe in the existence of good, they believe in the existence of evil. But they don't believe in the existence of God. There are also very left-wing radicals who don't believe in anything except Karl Marx and possibly Sigmund Freud. I know good exists, I know evil exists and I also know God exists. There's no footnote or special rider attached to the First Amendment that says public officials can't believe in God or can't say they believe in God. What the Constitution does say is that government should take no action to establish a single religion. The corollary is that government should take no action to harm any religion either. Nothing precludes people from being religious and being in government, too. The name of God, after all, was invoked to bless our nation on July 4, 1776. He sustains us 213 years later.

And believe me, there are times when those in government are in need of religious sustenance. One of my most difficult moments was the corruption scandal that hit New York City during my third term. The citizens of New York certainly got firsthand exposure to the havoc corruption in government can wreak. Graft and corruption have been plaguing government for years, of course. Following the trial of people who engaged in a conspiracy to loot New York City's Parking Violations Bureau, Whitman Knapp, the presiding judge, said, "As long as people are people, I guess there will be some [corruption]". He's right, but government leaders must do all they can to prevent those who might be tempted from engaging in it.

Since the scandals broke, New York City has more than doubled the budget of our Department of Investigation, tightened up financial disclosure for city employees, pushed for a campaign-financing law, and taken a whole host of other steps to fight corruption. But as Judge Knapp suggests, until we can find a way to eradicate "original sin," there will inevitably be other instances of corruption in both the public and private sector.

The scandals my administration has confronted since former Queens Borough President Donald Manes was found bleeding in an apparent suicide attempt, late one January night in 1986 on the nearly deserted Grand Central Parkway, have seared my soul. Notwithstanding the fact that only seven of the hundreds, even thousands of people I have appointed during my eleven years as Mayor were indicted and another five left at my request because they committed ethical—not criminal—improprieties, that's twelve people too many. Usually it's easy for me to get up and go to work in the morning. During the heat of the scandals, there were times when I had to drag myself out of bed. But faith sustains, and I had faith not only in God but also in the ability of New York City to eliminate this stain on our municipal honor.

Naturally, the scandals have given my political opponents and critics in the press the chance for a field day. Even though they know it's an absurd fiction, some even dispense with the need to be intellectually honest and compare my administration to the widespread corruption of Boss Tweed and Mayor Jimmy Walker. What an outrage and how unfair.

Yes, twelve people of the many, many more I have appointed failed the people of New York and failed me. But do we indict an entire city government for the wrongdoing of a handful? I don't think that's fair. Some of the other indicted officials were independently elected. Until they were exposed, no one—and that includes the press—suspected they had engaged in illegal activity. But while they're elected independently of me, I'm held responsible by the press for their misdeeds. That's not fair either, but that's the way it is.

Forgiveness plays an important role in religion, but the truth is that I'll never forgive those who betrayed the City—people like Donald Manes, Stanley Friedman or Meade Esposito, who, while not a part of my administration, nonetheless cast shame upon it by their violations of the public trust. Nor will I ever forgive the wrongdoing of those I appointed. It's never pleasant to see people you know or have worked with bring shame upon themselves and their families. How does a mother explain to her children that daddy's going to jail for violating his public trust? It's a tragedy. But those who are found guilty of corruption ought to go to jail.

Frankly, government in New York City will never be the same again for any of us who have lived through the last four years. I'll never understand what turned these people onto a criminal path. Some probably deceived themselves into thinking that they weren't doing anything criminal. Others, such as Donald Manes and his cronies, had to be aware that what they were doing was criminal. They simply let greed dominate their actions. Perhaps some thought they were merely doing what everyone does. That's simply not true. The vast majority of public servants are honest, decent and hardworking people. As the saying goes, though, it takes just a few rotten apples to spoil a barrel.

That was brought home to me recently when I convened the inspectional forces from all City agencies at a meeting where commissioners and I could remind them of how important it is not just to be personally honest, but to turn in colleagues who are dishonest. I was aghast when the commissioners and I were greeted by a loud chorus of boos and hoots as we began the discussion. They booed with anonymity, but I was thunderstruck that they'd bring disgrace on themselves by trying to sabotage a frank discussion of honesty in government.

As I stood on stage I felt as though we were in the Circus Maximus performing before a raucous, bloodthirsty Roman audience. I had to restrain my anger in my comments to this mob. How close we are, I thought to myself, to the animals from which Darwin said we spring. The base animal instinct for blood seems to have evolved into a lust for larceny. What a disgraceful episode.

Obviously, we'll keep doing all we can to make sure our inspectional services—indeed, all City employees—are honest. But there's only so much we can do. After all, the desire to give in to temptation and engage in corruption is something best stifled in childhood, with education, love and the support of a mother, father and siblings who'll help a child find and stick to a straight and narrow path. Regrettably, our society seems to be losing sight of the importance of a strong moral education. Pity the poor child who grows up without that love and guidance. And pity too the mother and father who would be ashamed if any of their sons and daughters were among the group who see nothing wrong with booing an appeal for honesty and integrity.

The fact is that the law alone cannot create a safe and just society. We must have a source of moral guidance, as well. That's why I never shy away from expressing support for religious faith. Does that conflict with my obligations as a public official? I don't think it does. There was no conflict between John F. Kennedy, President, and John F. Kennedy, Catholic, or Jimmy Carter, President, and Jimmy Carter, "born again" Christian. There's no conflict between Ed Koch, Mayor, and Ed Koch, "fierce" though not necessarily observant Jew. If there were, I'd resolve it in favor of my public office, or I'd resign.

I have often been criticized for not keeping a firm line between my Jewish faith and my support for the state of Israel. During the mayoral campaign in 1977, I publicly gave President Carter a letter alerting him to the danger of inviting the Soviet Union to a peace conference on the Middle East. As an American citizen and a Jew, the safety of both America and Israel is of primary importance to me. I was trying to change Jimmy Carter's point of view. I later heard from others that Moshe Dayan believed my letter helped change history. He said it caused Carter to step back and not ask the Soviet Union to a peace conference on the Middle East. Now, that's a letter worth delivering.

In this country the fact that you advance the interest of the racial, ethnic or religious group of which you're a part doesn't make you dis-loyal, even though that interest may not reflect the view of the State Department, or of the majority. You're allowed to advance the inter-ests of another nation in public discussion and at the polls. Of course you can't always be sure that what you do will have the desired result. President Carter was embarrassed when I gave him the letter and some observers suggested he might take revenge by putting the lid on federal aid to New York City. (He didn't.) But what was I supposed to do, sell out my principles for a mess of pottage? More than a million Jews live in New York City. Their co-religionists in Israel were at risk. Should I have refused to fight for a safe and secure Israel in hope of getting federal funds for New York City? No way.

Let me suggest a parallel. Following an idea by the Reverend Leon

Sullivan, the City of New York has undertaken one of the largest programs anywhere in the country to divest from companies doing business in South Africa. People of every race, religion and ethnic group supported the bill which I introduced to begin divestment. The bill passed, even though critics of divestment, including Secretary of Transportation Elizabeth Dole, argued that it would exclude some noncompliant companies from our bidding procedures, reduce competition and thereby raise the amount of money bidded projects would cost.

Clearly, this bill would cost the City money. But when it came to the principle of opposing apartheid, the potential cost to the City was irrelevant to the citizens of New York. On moral issues, most people believe that principle is more important than pottage.

So religion—call it moral involvement if you will—plays a key role in the life of New York City. This is not to suggest that various religious institutions or organizations always see eye to eye. In particular, the City has had sharp disagreements with the Archdiocese of New York over questions of public policy. Cardinal O'Connor has said that the situation sometimes reminds him of the dispute between King Henry II of England and his friend (and later Archbishop of Canterbury) Thomas Becket. Cardinal O'Connor even hints I may feel the same frustration Henry felt when he asked, "Will no one rid me of this troublesome priest?" While I'm sure the Cardinal doesn't believe things have gone quite that far, he does seem reluctant to see his Church enter into arrangements with the City. I understand his concern. Many times through the centuries the Church has been the victim of secular power. When Henry VIII sought a divorce and learned that the Vatican wouldn't grant him one, he vented his anger on the Roman Catholic Church. I can see why Cardinal O'Connor believes that, like oil and water, Church and State don't mix.

I think there are two paramount reasons why we separate Church and State.

One is to prevent the establishment of an official state church, which existed in England and which still exists in some countries today. The constitution of Argentina, for example, provides that only a Roman Catholic can be president. That's fine for Catholics. But it's not so good for Protestants, Jews or members of any other faith. Until the provision is eliminated, non-Catholics will never really be full partners in Argentinian society. On the other hand, in a society like ours, which is founded on the principle that all men and women are created equal, no one faith should be superior to others.

The other reason is to allow religion to be practiced freely without undue government interference. It's a fragile balance that isn't always maintained. But it's essential to our society and, I believe, the intent of our Constitution that we try to do so. But it is extremely difficult for government to pursue policies that promote religious worship without giving specific religions State sanction.

Trying to achieve this delicate balance doesn't mean that Church and State can't work together side by side. I don't, for example, believe that contractual relations between Church and State are doomed to failure. Look at the programs operated by the Archdiocese under contract to the City and you'll find they're a sound formula for success. The Archdiocese operates outstanding programs, doing a job that's as good as or better than our secular contractors. The City-Church relationship is intended to avert disaster, not cause it.

As the Cardinal suggests, though, when too fine a point is put on the separation of Church and State, the results can at the least be ridiculous and at worst disastrous. Look at the U.S. Supreme Court's 1985 decision placing new restrictions on parochial schools' receiving federal remedial-education funds. The Court feared the funds might be used to religiously indoctrinate students at public expense.

The Court made the decision even though it couldn't cite a single instance of this happening during the seventeen years since Congress established the program. The majority erroneously assumed that the average student is unable to distinguish between remedial reading taught by a public-school teacher and the Scriptures taught by a parochial-school teacher. I give students more credit than that and believe that, in this case, the Court put legal niceties before educational necessities. That *can* be a prescription for disaster.

Cardinal O'Connor cites a specific example to suggest that the City's intervention in Church affairs can diminish its ability to serve the poor. "In my judgment," he says, "the Church's goal of better meeting the needs of the poor is not only consonant with its mission as a Church, but in the best interests of the poor in a city in which the poor tend to be grossly ignored. I see this goal as of a higher order than the perfectly legitimate goal of the Landmarks Commission to maintain the current skyline."

He's referring to the air-rights issue involving St. Bartholomew's

Episcopal Church on Park Avenue. St. Bart's wanted to sell the air rights above its building at the highest price possible. The City Landmarks Commission objected and said, "St. Bartholomew's is part of our architectural heritage and we won't see it destroyed." St. Bart's replied, "But we can use the proceeds to serve the poor. That's a higher order of priority than the skyline." The difficulty comes out of trying to determine who has the right to decide how the priorities are determined and then met, Church or State?

Almost every religious leader in this City—Jewish and Catholic, Protestant and Muslim—will probably say that more ought to be done for the homeless. They'll hold press conferences, write letters, give speeches, demanding that the City do more.

So, a few years ago, as part of our efforts to do more, the City of New York imposed a moratorium on the sale and conversion of single-room-occupancy hotels, a major, but declining, resource for homeless individuals. It seemed to be the right thing to do and, indeed, enjoyed the support of most religious leaders in the city.

As I recall, one of the buildings to be covered by the moratorium was owned by the Episcopal Church of New York. Episcopal Bishop Paul Moore is one of those religious leaders who frequently condemns the City's policies and programs for the homeless. Guess what? He called me up to urge that we exclude one of his buildings from the moratorium so that it could be sold, demolished, and a skyscraper built in its place. In that case, spiritual advancement clearly took a backseat to secular gain, though I'm sure that gain would undoubtedly be used for a laudable purpose.

An adjacent building was owned by the Archdiocese and covered by the moratorium. It too was up for sale and similarly would have earned millions of dollars for the Roman Catholic Church. The Cardinal called me after hearing of Bishop Moore's request and said, to his great credit, that he wanted no special privilege conferred on the property owned by the Archdiocese.

It's really a question of balancing interests. The Church has an obligation to serve and to help the poor. It does a good job of that. It also has an obligation to celebrate the joys and rituals that are an essential part of its religion. Some of its riches are used to clothe and feed the masses in the here and now and some of its riches are used to celebrate the Mass and life hereafter. It's a question of balancing spiritual and secular obligations.

The same is true of a city. If you take the position that a legitimate concern for the poor and others who are not so poor transcends every other concern, then you'd fund programs and services that serve the poor to a maximum, but leave every other service high and dry. The poor would benefit. But everyone else would suffer.

You'd put almost all of our police officers in poor neighborhoods like the Lower East Side, Central Brooklyn or the South Bronx, for example, and you would remove them from middle-class neighborhoods with less of a crime problem, like Brooklyn Heights or Riverdale. You'd probably also spend far more money on welfare and nothing on the Metropolitan Museum of Art or the Bronx Zoo. But doesn't a trip to a zoo or a visit to a museum satisfy a need of great dimension in this city? I think so.

And, of course, logically you'd have to favor doing away with zoning laws altogether. To maximize revenues, you'd say build to the sky. In a city like New York, where there's limited land, you'd remove zoning restrictions that protect neighborhoods of one- and two-family homes. "Turn them into apartment houses" would be the order of the day. And new tax revenues in the billions would flow into the city treasury.

You'd have a richer city, but not a better one. There'd be no parks, no playgrounds, no trees. Block after block would be transformed into canyon after canyon. The city's pocketbook would bulge. But its spirit would sag. It's trite, but it's true—whether in a church or in a city, neither men nor women live by bread alone.

I once said that in matters involving disputes between the Church and the State, people ought to follow the biblical injunction and render unto Caesar the things that are Caesar's and unto God the things that are God's. The exact meaning of this phrase has been the subject of scholarly and political debate for centuries. I know the Cardinal is uncomfortable when, as he says, he finds himself "interpreted as being equated with Jesus," the son of God. But, as Mayor, I don't have any problem being equated with Caesar. (Except maybe on the Ides of March.) "Caesar," in this case, is just another way of saying "government." I agree that the distinction is not always an easy or, indeed, useful one.

I don't believe you can condemn religious leaders for holding views they believe are consistent with the doctrines or teaching of their churches. It's their right to hold that moral belief. At the same time, you have to be careful that these religious or moral beliefs don't impinge upon civil law.

For example, I don't believe homosexual behavior is a sin. In fact, it's probably either the result of genetics or determined at an early age by cultural upbringing. You can't condemn someone for that. Indeed, it's the sexual preference of some 10 percent of our adult population. While I don't believe that every form of sexual behavior is acceptable—for example, pedophilia and incest are immoral and unacceptable—I believe homosexuality is acceptable in our society.

And I'll do all within my power to make sure that those who are homosexual are not victimized or discriminated against because they are homosexual, just as I try to prevent discrimination against people because of their race, religion, ethnic origin, sex, age or handicap. They're protected under the law and my job is to enforce that law, no matter what the view may be of those in opposition for religious or other reasons.

I recognize the problems that exist between Church and State, but we both have much to gain by helping each other. A few years ago there was some controversy because I asked churches and synagogues to help the city shelter the homeless. I don't feel this was such a surprising request. Taking care of the homeless has always been a mission of religious institutions. Caesar got into the act much later, well after the churches did. I was simply reminding them of this traditional role.

The City of New York provides shelter for all who request it. No one is turned away. But I do think it would be helpful to everyone—to the City and, more important, to the men and women to be sheltered—if the churches and synagogues opened their doors to provide beds to those in need. But when I made that request I was condemned by some religious leaders, including that friend of the homeless, Bishop Paul Moore. On the first anniversary of my request, the Reverend William Sloane Coffin of Riverside Church said, "Personally, I hate to see churches, synagogues and mosques become havens in a heartless world, because by caring for victims of that world we increase its heartlessness." Rabbi Marc Tanenbaum said, "Opening our doors to the homeless is like putting Band-Aids on terrible wounds."

I have to admit I was shocked by their reactions. But fortunately, other religious leaders came forward and opened their churches and synagogues to the homeless. Indeed, more than one hundred churches and synagogues opened their doors and their hearts. We asked them to give special attention to homeless people who are vulnerable—for example, the "shopping bag ladies" who never seek help from a City shelter, but might from a priest, minister or rabbi. I appreciate the tremendous efforts of the many churches and synagogues that came forward to help.

There are times when Church and State also share responsibility for upholding the law. In recent months a number of Roman Catholics who are gay have stood up and turned their backs on the altar during Sunday Mass in St. Patrick's. They're upset because they believe they're not fully recognized as members of the Church. There are probably others in St. Patrick's who feel that the protests disrupt their opportunity to worship. The difficult question is this: Should the police step in and remove the protestors?

I believe the same standard that applies to any private property applies to churches. If disorder erupts and the owner of the property requests the police to restore order, the police should do it. Under the law, interrupting a church service intentionally is disorderly conduct. And if the reports were accurate and the protestors used the old "half moon," albeit clothed, technique to show their contempt, it's certainly offensive. Ultimately, it's up to the court to decide whether conduct that prompts an invitation to the police is disorderly.

Obviously, there's a very large issue at stake here. In fact, I'm sympathetic to the cause of gays who feel the Church has abandoned them. But I'm not going to get involved in criticizing doctrine. The Church has a right to its doctrine as do the Orthodox Jews who take exactly the same position as Roman Catholics on gay rights and homosexuality. Personally, I disagree with both positions. But religious doctrine is religious doctrine. It's an issue for members of that church or synagogue—not the State—to debate and resolve. But sometimes the State does become involved in the debate.

In one case, a Sunday service at St. Patrick's was disrupted. The priest in charge asked the police to remove the demonstrators. I believe he was concerned that violence might erupt between those who supported the protestors and those who supported the Church's position. The priest asked the protestors not to interfere with the Mass and warned that if they did they would be removed. Not until the protestors went outside, sat down in the street and blocked the sidewalk did the police make arrests. It seems to me to have been a perfectly appropriate exercise of police power. You can picket peacefully, but you can't bring the city to a halt.

When I heard what happened I called Cardinal O'Connor. "Your Eminence," I said, "you ought to say to the demonstrators, as I would say to them, that if you want to change the doctrine of a church or synagogue—for example, the ban on women priests in the Catholic Church or on women rabbis in all but the Reform branch of Judaism—it's going to take a long time. It takes hundreds or thousands of years to establish religious doctrine. So it's going to take at least dozens, even hundreds of years to reform that doctrine. If you can't wait those dozens or hundreds of years, you should go out and form your own religion."

There are limits to what constitutes disruption, of course. If the protestors had stood up for the whole service and thereby prevented people behind them from seeing what was taking place at the altar, they should be removed. But if they stood only briefly, I think that's acceptable under our system. Of course its up to the courts, not me, to judge. In this instance, it was a regular occurrence that obviously tended to disrupt each and every service.

To avoid escalating incidents, sometimes the police don't enforce the law. This year, for example, about one thousand gays rallied on the Upper West Side to protest violence against gays. I met with gay leaders that same afternoon on the same issue and, in fact, had been invited to the rally. But I had other commitments and could not attend. That evening about midnight I received a telephone call reporting that many of the protestors had sat down in the street, were blocking traffic, and wouldn't leave until the police commissioner or I came down to meet with them. I called the captain in charge. "I told him we couldn't get in touch with you," he said. "Don't tell them that," I replied. "Tell them that you got in touch with me and I said hell could freeze over and I'm not coming. Tell them they're not going to get their way by violating the law or disrupting the city. I'm happy to meet with a group as I did this very afternoon. But I will never meet as a result of illegality."

"I can't arrest them all," he answered. "There are a thousand of them." "I'm not telling you to arrest any of them," I said. But I thought to myself, what he should do is wait for the crowd to thin and then arrest as many as he can. I didn't give him the advice. But that's exactly what the captain did. As a matter of fact, when the crowd was told I would not be dropping by but would meet with a small group in the future, the crowd dispersed. Only ninety-six desk summonses had to be issued and four people were arrested.

My perspective on such incidents was actually developed as a result of the riots that broke out in San Francisco following the assassinations of Mayor George Moscone and Supervisor Harvey Milk. Thousands of angry gay demonstrators attacked City Hall and, as I recall, they burned at least twenty police cars. When I saw the incident on television, I was shocked. "How in the world could police officers stand by and allow police cars to be torched?" I asked Bob McGuire, who was then my police commissioner. "You wouldn't let that happen here, would you?" "I certainly would," he replied, "if the choice was between property damage or violence with injuries and a riot we couldn't control."

On reflection, I decided he was right. You make a decision based on whether protecting police cars would have resulted in harming or shooting people. In San Francisco, a more aggressive police response could have seriously harmed hundreds of people. Since human life is more important than property, you're probably best advised to avoid a bloody confrontation that, frankly, you probably couldn't handle anyway. If the confrontation's manageable, fine. If not, don't provoke it any further. Just bide your time and let things cool down.

To help reduce unnecessary conflict, our society needs values we all hold in common. Cardinal O'Connor believes government should help configure society in such fashion that its values are institutionalized. I agree completely. After all, one reason our public-school system was established was to ensure that the various waves of immigrants into the United States would have the skills necessary to compete in the economy and to learn the values of our society.

Obviously, we shouldn't impose the values of a particular faith on all members of society. That would be a violation of the separation between Church and State. But my own view is that there are values that are universally accepted, regardless of whether the values are religious or secular. For example, no one believes people should be allowed to rob, rape or commit murder with impunity. Most of these universal values are incorporated in the Ten Commandments. If the Ten Commandments had not been written in the Bible, society would probably have evolved most of them on its own simply because a society must have rules for people to live by. Otherwise, as the philosopher Thomas Hobbes warned, it's a war of all against all and a rather nasty, short and brutish existence. If you violate the rules, you have to be punished. Some people will be punished twice. Once by the State. Once by God. My concern is the responsibility of the State to take action.

Let me cite what happened to Gary Hart. He is reported to have committed adultery. He broke one of the Ten Commandments. In normal circumstances this would be a matter between him, his wife, and the Almighty. We don't live in a theocracy and government has no place in the bedroom. The Church believes its values are eternal truths. Other faiths feel the same way. My own personal feeling is that eternal truths do exist, but I don't think the State should ever take the position of imposing the eternal truths of one faith over the eternal truths of another. In America, society has rights, but so do individuals.

Now, Gary Hart was pursued by the press for his indiscretion and the outcry ultimately forced him to withdraw as a candidate for president. When he reentered the race, he was treated as a laughingstock and lost miserably. Was it the act of adultery that brought such a critical response from a sophisticated American public? I don't think so. Most people today believe adultery is no one's business, except for those immediately involved. My initial feeling was that had his adultery been discreet yet reported by the press, it would have been the press that would have been more sullied than he. Indeed, at the outset I made critical comments about the press because of the way they snooped into his private life.

But that all changed as a result of two things Gary Hart did. First, he dared the press to follow him around. And follow him they did. The implication, of course, was that he had nothing to hide. But when he threw down the gauntlet and the press picked it up, it was the beginning of the end.

While the press probably went too far, Hart went even farther. He allowed his adulterous relationship to become what I believe Catholic clergy refer to as a public scandal. You remember the photograph of Gary Hart on the *Monkey Business* cruise with Donna Rice sitting on his knee. The American public has become more accepting on such matters. Ronald Reagan proves a divorced man can become president. But people don't want to see decent, civil and moral behavior held up to public scorn, especially if the person doing the scorning is running for president. The public will put up with only so much monkey business and no more.

The Ten Commandments are about as close to immutable truths and values as we are likely to get. But as the life-styles of those governed by those Commandments change, so too does our interpretation of them. The Bible, for example, decrees the punishment for adultery and any other unacceptable carnal acts to be death by stoning. Today, even those most intemperate on the issue of adultery wouldn't advocate physical punishment, let alone death, unless it's the death of a political career.

Public standards may have changed, but churches and religious leaders still play an important role in the political life of New York City. I make every effort to ensure that all religious groups and institutions are treated equally, regardless of their politics. For example, the City of New York awarded a housing rehabilitation contract to the Abyssinian Baptist Church in Harlem. The pastor is the Reverend Calvin Butts, who happens to be one of my harshest and—I believe—most unfair critics. When Abyssinian Baptist submitted an application detailing which buildings it wanted to renovate and what the cost and benefits to the surrounding community would be, the application was evaluated by an open and objective process. The City's review committee—I was not involved—judged the application to be one of the best, and the contract was awarded. Even though Reverend Butts is a political opponent of mine, who has expressed support for Louis Farrakhan, the rehabilitation contract was awarded on merit. Matters such as this should not be determined on the basis of political or philosophical viewpoints.

Some religious groups, of course, advocate ideas and principles that are abhorrent to the concepts of fairness and justice. Let's say there's a group that operates an orphanage where children are put in different buildings according to race. Should we cut off public aid only to the segregated building? No. We should use our leverage and make it clear that if they discriminate in any of their practices, they're not going to receive our financial help. Do what you will with your money. But do what we require with ours. And if you use ours with yours, yours becomes subject to our conditions. I would never honor someone who is known to be biased against people of another race, religion or ethnic group. That only brings dishonor on us all. What I'm trying to say is that when it comes to a substantive decision on the merits of one group's plan to deliver services versus those of other groups, you have to look at the issue objectively. Who'll do the best job? Not whether he or she, in the eyes of God or anyone else, is a good person.

Questions of good and evil are moral questions, and they have a place in both political and religious life. Sometimes spiritual and secular viewpoints come into conflict. One incident that comes to mind is Kurt Waldheim's audience with Pope John Paul at which, at least from appearances, his sins as an officer in the German army are forgiven. I spoke out at the time of Waldheim's audience with His Holiness. But I didn't express my full view. On the one hand I thought, well, why shouldn't the Pope meet with a miscreant of his Church who has violated moral law and give him absolution. After all, it's the nature of priests and certainly of popes to forgive the sins of their parishioners.

On the other hand, I regret that the Pope did not take the occasion to denounce Waldheim for his involvement with the Nazis and hold him responsible for what he did. Then, if it was deemed appropriate, his sins could be forgiven. I'm certain that not every sin can or should be forgiven by a priest or a rabbi. There are sins that can only be forgiven, at least in the Jewish religion, by those against whom the sin is committed. God may forgive Waldheim. I don't think his victims ever will.

I want to make it clear that Pope John Paul is a man for whom I have great respect. If he has some game plan vis-à-vis the Waldheim affair that the rest of us don't understand, I think it would be helpful if he revealed it. If Hitler had lived, would the Pope have forgiven him? I recognize that what Waldheim did was not on the order of what Hitler did. Waldheim was a retail murderer. Hitler was wholesale. As far as I'm concerned, neither deserves forgiveness.

If I am occasionally critical of religious leaders, there are also times when they are critical of me. During my 1988 pilgrimage to the Shrine of Our Lady of Knock in Ireland, Cardinal O'Connor took exception to my remarks about the British presence in Northern Ireland. He had every right to be critical. There's no question it was both wrong and stupid for me to suggest that recent improvements in Northern Ireland by the British government in the areas of civil rights, housing and employment for Catholics can make up for the more than eight hundred years of oppression the people of Ireland have suffered at the hands of the British. You just can't equate the two in the same breath and I'm sorry I tried to without conveying the necessary nuances.

At the same time, though one of us has spiritual obligations and the other has secular ones, both of us are committed to pursuing the truth. For twenty-five years I've said that the British should get out of Ireland. Nothing I saw during the pilgrimage causes me to change that view. But I did see things that would lead me to believe that the British government is seeking to make improvements in housing, employment and political representation. By calling attention to that "truth," I thought I might encourage the British to be even more responsible and, thereby, hasten the day of their departure.

Speaking of that pilgrimage, I spent more than fourteen hours at Masses celebrated by the Cardinal. Someone asked me what was going through my mind as I sat in the pew. Well, I'm not sure, but I remember thinking, I'll have to learn more Latin. And I think I will: just as soon as I learn more Hebrew.

THE CARDINAL

"Will no one rid me of this troublesome priest?" Thus does King Henry II rage aloud in the presence of his knight henchmen concerning Thomas Becket, Archbishop of Canterbury. The knight henchmen dutifully take the hint, and Becket is assassinated in his own cathedral. The date is December 29, 1170.

Thomas Becket was canonized a saint by Pope Alexander III within three years. King Henry II did penance at his tomb. Readers of Chaucer's *Canterbury Tales* will recall that the tales were told by pilgrims on their annual April journey from London to Canterbury some two hundred years later, to pray at Becket's tomb.

Times have changed, at least in the West. However troublesome the Archbishop of the Archdiocese of New York[1] might ever be to the Mayor of New York, it is improbable that the Mayor's deputies would arrange an assassination in St. Patrick's Cathedral. That is a very good thing. It facilitates dialogue.

The change in times, however, has not invalidated the instructional worth of the Henry II–Thomas Becket affair, neatly presented in T. S. Eliot's *Murder in the Cathedral.* Both Church and State can continue to learn from it.

The essential elements are few. Henry II and Thomas were the closest of friends. Henry appointed Thomas his Chancellor of State, and Thomas used this immensely powerful position to serve the King well.

---

1. The Archdiocese of New York comprises three of the five boroughs of the City of New York—Manhattan, Bronx, Richmond (Staten Island)—and the counties of Westchester, Rockland, Putnam, Dutchess, Orange, Ulster and Sullivan. The boroughs of Brooklyn and Queens are in the Diocese of Brooklyn.

The death of Theobald, Archbishop of Canterbury, created an extraordinary opportunity for Henry to rule State and Church simultaneously. Warned to the contrary by Thomas himself, who foresaw the trouble ahead, the King appointed Thomas Archbishop of Canterbury, expecting to use him as his access to total power. Once consecrated archbishop, however, Thomas resigned the state chancellorship, against Henry's fierce protest, and devoted himself completely to his new role in the Church. He changed his entire life, abandoning his extravagant living, giving himself to prayer and fasting, and wearing a hair shirt.

Henry would probably have ignored what he would have considered Thomas's spiritual idiosyncrasies, had Thomas knuckled under when Henry began moving in on the Church. It was a question of *jurisdiction*—who held the authority over matters of Church or State—and Thomas advised the bishops to resist Henry's effort to take over the spiritual courts of the day. An infuriated Henry drew up the "Constitutions of Clarendon," in which he bestowed upon himself a wide variety of powers traditionally held by the bishops, thus extending his jurisdiction over what was once exclusively the domain of the Church.

Thomas was tempted to compromise, then recovered both his integrity and common sense. Openly defying Henry, he exiled himself to France for six years. Eventually frightened that Thomas's friends had increased in number and strength, Henry asked him to return. A token reconciliation followed, but Thomas's decision to excommunicate certain bishops who had thrown in their lot with Henry was apparently too much for the King. It was then that he wondered aloud who would dispose of Thomas once and for all.

The Mayor of New York is not a King Henry II, in power, in temperament or in murderous intent. The current Archbishop of New York is certainly not a Thomas Becket, in courage, in capability or in proclivity for penitential shirts. Still, it seems to me that the Becket–Henry II affair epitomizes one of the most basic of all Church-State issues: the question of *jurisdiction*. Who has authority over what.

Jurisdiction is the key issue, for example, in a case (see pp. 000ff) commonly referred to as the Wilder Case.[2] It involves a long-standing suit brought by the American Civil Liberties Union (ACLU) against

2. *Wilder v. Bernstein*, 848 F. 2d 1338 (2nd Cir. 1988)

46

the City of New York regarding contracts the city makes with private agencies for child care. The Archdiocese of New York and other religious groups have been assisting the City of New York for a century by providing child care the City has not had the facilities to provide. The ACLU has argued that agencies operated by these religious groups must be required to engage in certain practices and refrain from others, if they are to receive City contracts. The Archdiocese of New York and some other religious agencies have rejected such demands, arguing that to yield to them would be to abdicate to the State what the Church believes to be its own proper jurisdiction over Church-sponsored agencies, a right recognized for more than a hundred years by the courts, as by political leaders.

Church-sponsored agencies and programs have always conformed to a variety of reasonable City regulations unquestionably within the City's jurisdiction. They continue to conform without resistance. The Church accepts the City's jurisdiction over sanitation, fire hazards, food distribution, for example. Why, then, does the Church balk concerning other requirements the City has recently begun to mandate? The answer is clear. In virtually every case in which we find the Church resisting the City, there are moral, spiritual, or religious considerations at issue, matters over which the Church agencies claim jurisdiction the City has acknowledged up until now. In the case at hand concerning child care, the Church is helping the City carry out the City's responsibility to take care of neglected and dependent children. If the City will not allow Church-sponsored agencies to administer their programs according to their own principles or philosophy, then the City perforce must take care of these children itself. If the Church is to be expected to assist, the Church must be free to do so without sacrificing its own teachings and practices, that is, without yielding its jurisdiction to the City.

At the same time, of course, the Church's commitment to child care means more than merely assisting the City. The Church assumes responsibility for meeting children's needs that the City cannot or will not meet. These are "transcendent" needs, moral, spiritual, religious. These are needs the Church met long before City contracts were dreamed of. Such needs fall beyond the jurisdiction of the City. The Church cannot and will not permit the City to determine how these "transcendent" needs under the *Church's* jurisdiction can be met. The Church, therefore, must be free to meet these transcendent needs of children in its care, while simultaneously fulfilling other requirements of municipal law. This is a classic case of dual jurisdiction, with both Church and City having authoritative roles to play. It is a classic case, as well, of "Render to Caesar the things that are Caesar's and to God the things that are God's."

It is not at all that the Church restricts its help to those who will accept its teachings. Catholic social service is extended to many on a purely humanitarian basis. In the Archdiocese of New York, for instance, our parishes maintain approximately one hundred shelters for the homeless. People come and go, with no questions asked and certainly no "proselytizing" attempted. Church-sponsored "soup kitchens" operate on the same basis. The Church conforms with governmental regulations in carrying out such activities. Were government to require the Church to betray its own teachings in some way, however, as the price for being allowed to provide even humanitarian help to the poor, the Church would have to resist, whether or not government funding were involved.

The point in citing such examples is simply to demonstrate how critical is the issue of *jurisdiction* in Church-State relations. One could almost say that Church and State can work together harmoniously for the good of all society only to the degree that issues of jurisdiction are cooperatively resolved. Conversely, conflict will ensue and society will be deprived whenever such issues remain unresolved or are settled in a manner prejudicial to either Church or State. For this reason, the Archdiocese of New York and the City of New York are constantly confronted with the need to resolve jurisdictional issues satisfactorily. Failures past and present must be discussed honestly if the New York experience is to prove helpful elsewhere. It is clear that some jurisdictional problems have defied solution, either because of an incapability to resolve them or an unwillingness to do so, for whatever reasons. Some of the pain of this book will inevitably lie in confronting, or at least describing, both incapability and unwillingness frankly.

Another critical question that bears importantly on the relationships between Church and State is that of the respective *purposes* of Church and State. This involves the respective values they are committed to and their very reasons for existence, quite apart from each other. Clearly, this question, though related to the issue of jurisdiction, has a life uniquely its own.

The purposes of any State, the values to which it is primarily committed, are many and varied, proportioned in part to varying political philosophies. The purposes of the United States are spelled out in the Constitution itself: "to form a more perfect Union, establish Justice, insure domestic Tranquility, provide for the common defense, promote the general Welfare, and secure the Blessings of Liberty to ourselves and our posterity." It is an oversimplification, of course, but for our purposes it suffices to say that state, county, city and other forms of local government have these same purposes on a smaller scale, to be achieved in different ways.

Whatever may have been the frequently debated religious sentiments of the Founding Fathers, I am certainly not interested in arguing that they established the Republic in order to ensure the eternal salvation of those fortunate enough to be its citizens. Except for a constitutional provision to ensure against establishing a state religion and guaranteeing the free exercise thereof, the Constitution of the United States busies itself with *temporal* matters, the stuff of the here and now. Such is equally true of the governing documents of all other forms of purely civil entities in our land. They concern themselves with *this* world, not with a world beyond.

The State is geared primarily to *this* life, the Church is focused primarily on the *next*. Of course, we believe that a well-ordered State will at least provide a climate conducive to permitting its citizens to go freely about the business of "saving their souls." Those who live the life the Church intended will in turn contribute significantly to the well-being of the State. But the *primary* purposes of the State, its primary values, are not those of the Church, and vice versa. There is hardly a more certain formula for disaster than to confuse the primary mission of the State with that of the Church, or that of the Church with the State's.

The purposes of the Church, the values to which it is primarily committed, are spelled out for our day in documents of the Second Vatican Council called by Pope John XXIII and begun in October of 1962. It brought together in Rome most of the three thousand Roman Catholic bishops in the world, who eventually designed sixteen documents, approved and published by Pope Paul VI in 1965, which define and govern the Church and its activities in our day. The Council was intended to "update" the Church—not to change what for the Church is unchangeable, but to apply its teachings to our day in understandable terms.[3]

3. During 1987 and 1988, we conducted an extensive study program in parishes of the Archdiocese to help people become more familiar with the teachings of the Second Vatican Council, found in sixteen documents and much more commonly referred to than read!

A knowledge of the Council's documents is indispensable for anyone who wants to know what the Church teaches in contemporary
terms, even about *itself*. The Constitution of the United States largely
defines our purpose and many of our values as a nation. The Church
also defines its purpose and many of its values in constitutions. These
are the Vatican II documents called, respectively, "Dogmatic Constitution of the Church"[4] and "Pastoral Constitution on the Church in
the Modern World."[5] The latter states:

> While helping the world and receiving many benefits from it, the
> Church has a single intention: that God's kingdom may come and
> that the salvation of the whole human race may come to pass.
> (GS 45)

In both documents cited above, and in various other documents of
the Council, Christians are reminded of their obligations to help make
the world a better place, and to carry out their civic responsibilities,
but the documents make clear that the Church exists primarily to help
them get to heaven.

Even the Council document called the "Decree on the Apostolate
of Lay People,"[6] which spells out the Church's *secular* responsibility,
particularly as it is to be carried out by laypersons, tells us very
straightforwardly:

> The mission of the Church concerns the salvation of human beings,
> which is to be achieved by faith in Christ and by his grace. (AA 6)

And the Pastoral Constitution asserts:

> Christ . . . gave his Church no proper mission in the political, eco-
> nomic or social order. The purpose which He set before her is a
> religious one. (GS 42)

The Council does not mean here that Christians have no obligations in justice and charity to help advance the legitimate ends of the
State and the temporal welfare of others. By "proper," the Council
means that the Church was not established for this purpose above all.
The Church must teach faith in Christ, administer the sacraments and

---

4. *Lumen Gentium*, Vatican II, November 21, 1964
5. *Gaudium et Spes* (GS), Vatican II, December 7, 1965.
6. *Apostolicam actuositatem* (AA), Vatican II, November 18, 1965

help in the achievement of related *spiritual* goals. It is to such values that the Church is primarily committed. There are many agencies apart from the Church that address themselves exclusively and "properly" to the *temporal* goals of the State.

I really believe we must understand these two issues, the question of jurisdiction and the question of purposes and values, if we are to have more than a superficial knowledge of why Church and State come into conflict, or of how the two might work together for the good of all. When we don't understand these issues—or don't want to—we tend to exchange all sorts of allegations about bigotry, prejudice, discrimination and who's imposing whose morality on whom, as a substitute for understanding. Our passions, emotions, convictions and downright tempers (not always free of dramatically contrived histrionics), take charge, and the temptation for all parties involved to go into high dudgeon becomes overwhelming. A few less-than-sympathetic news reports and a well-timed haughtily patronizing editorial or two may provide just the fuel the fire needs to rage out of control. Smoke gets in everyone's eyes, so that no one any longer sees the issues clearly.

Representatives of both Church and State, the public at large, and the media could contribute more effectively to conflict resolution by recognizing that the root of a conflict may not necessarily lie in mere perverseness or arrogance. Legitimate questions of jurisdiction, or "turf," or legitimate differences concerning respective goals and values may be at issue.

It should shock no one that the Church is jealous of its turf. We are not purely spiritual beings. We all have bodies. The Church is not merely a spiritual entity; it is concretized in this world of time and space. Even the most spiritually devout want to be able to worship in a church *building*, for example, preferably heated in winter, with a roof in reasonable condition. Church-sponsored schools require buildings. The same is true for Church hospitals, nursing homes, child-care institutions and the like. All of these constitute essential turf, if the Church—any church—is to carry out certain useful functions in this world.

In carrying out many of these functions, the Church is simultaneously supporting certain legitimate values to which the *State* is properly dedicated. In the pursuit of these ends and as a vital member of the body politic, therefore, the Church is entitled to an appropriate share of that body's resources. It is contributing to the body's goals and advancing its values. Conflict can be avoided or resolved, and constructive relationships developed, only if the State is willing to recognize the Church's right to share State resources, since it is doing or contributing to the State's work and conforming to the State's legitimate requirements concerning safety, health and similar matters.

The Church has clearly demonstrated both its willingness and its competence to help the State meet the legitimate needs and aspirations of the people by actually doing so for a very long time. In doing so, the Church has established certain institutional approaches to society's values.[7] Our society, for example, values quality health care. The Church has not simply contributed to such, but has "institutionalized" this value (long before many governments) by pioneering in providing quality-care hospitals, nursing homes, child-care institutions and other institutional settings requiring extensive and continuing allocations of resources. Here in New York City, for instance, there were only two hospitals in existence (New York Hospital and Bellevue) when St. Vincent's Hospital was opened by the Sisters of Charity in 1849. This was five years before Florence Nightingale began her work, when the existing hospitals were described as "a last refuge for the harmless poor, in which they could die with a minimum of inconvenience to those around them."

When Rose Hawthorne Lathrop, daughter of Nathaniel Hawthorne, opened St. Rose's Home in Manhattan in 1890, virtually no one was taking care of the cancerous poor. The first cancer hospital in the United States, now Memorial–Sloan Kettering, had opened only six years before. The cancerous were dreaded as lepers, and the poor were the worst of outcasts until Rose Hawthorne saw their need and met it, with absolutely no discrimination regarding religion, race, color or any other characteristics. Today, the Catholic Church in the Archdiocese of New York sponsors a strong Catholic Health Care Alliance. A medical college, eighteen Catholic hospitals, nine nursing homes, fifteen child-care institutions and a variety of ancillary and specialized activities help meet the health-care needs of the Archdiocese and the broader community. (More about such in a later chapter.)

7. Professor Harold Lasswell makes the point brilliantly that in order to meet the legitimate needs and aspirations of its people, a government must "institutionalize" its people's values, that is, support those values institutionally by appropriate allocations of resources. For example, it would be absurd to say that a government recognizes the value of education for its people, if it provides no schools. (See Harold D. Lasswell, *Politics: Who Gets What, When, How* (New York: Meridian Books, 1958.)

Mention is made of these institutionalized facilities only as illustrative of ways in which the Church assumes responsibility to institutionalize the maintenance of certain of society's values, meeting or helping government to meet people's needs. The Church is, in some ways, therefore, quite as interested as is the political system in *Who Gets What, When, How*. As the Church meets the needs that *it* believes must be met—needs regarding which government may or may not assume responsibility—and helps government meet the needs on its own agenda, Church and State encounter questions of jurisdiction.

The running battle waged between St. Bartholemew's Episcopal Church on Park Avenue and the Landmarks Commission provides a good illustration. As I understand the issue, St. Bartholemew's proposed to reallocate resources and use of its facilities to advance its work among the poor. The Landmarks Commission has argued in favor of maintaining the current skyline. This is a jurisdictional question that runs into a question of goals, or commitment to values. I have read many reports of heated arguments involving the St. Bartholemew's issue that have nothing to do with either jurisdiction or purpose or values; such reports often seem to me to be both uncharitable and unjust.

It seems to me that the Church has the right to determine how best to achieve the goals to which it is committed and, therefore, how best to allocate its resources. The Church's goal of meeting the needs of the poor is consonant with its mission as "Church." This goal must then be weighed against the legitimate goal of the Landmarks Commission to maintain the current skyline. I introduce the entire issue simply as an example of a "turf" conflict, with turf defined in this case in both a narrow and a broad sense, the latter involving both jurisdiction and goals or values. Clearly, it's in everyone's best interest if such a conflict can be harmoniously resolved outside of court. If not, court action may well be merited.

Countless jurisdictional and value-oriented issues greeted me upon my arrival in New York in March of 1984. Though an enthusiastic adopted son of New York, I was unfamiliar with its back roads, how situations blossom as they do, and with the New York "Who's Who." Decisions, some crucial, had to be made immediately upon my arrival. Some could be delayed. Certain of the former were to prove to affect my relationship with the State for a long time. Their implications continue to affect a broad spectrum of activities, and certainly influence my decision-making today.

Which brings up the whole decision-making process. I don't know how the Mayor makes serious decisions, but, whatever may be the popular fancy, I spend a great deal of time, perhaps even too much time, in consultation. I confer with the Priests Council (an advisory body of some thirty-nine priests, half of whom are elected by their peers, some of whom serve ex officio, with still others appointed by me), the six members of the Archdiocesan College of Consultors, three Councils of Women Religious, the Finance Council, the Archdiocesan Pastoral Council (a mix of about a hundred people, sisters, brothers, deacons, laypersons, priests and others), the Council of Auxiliary Bishops, the Legal Advisory Committee, and a variety of other such groups. Sometimes such consultation can be frustrating, in that it may take me next to forever to get things done. But it pays off. Such conferees temper my temper, slow me down and try to assure that things are done properly.[8]

There is a reality factor, nonetheless, in my decision-making process which outweighs everything else: official Church teaching, particularly that which involves basic moral principles. I don't have the moral luxury of giving first place to expediency, or to what may seem to make the greatest number of people happy, or to merely avoiding controversy.[9] Here's where the question of purposes and goals and the primacy of certain values come back into play.

Many of our goals and value orientations are not only *different* from the goals of the State and of secular society, they are in intrinsic, unavoidable conflict. In such cases, no amount of consultation, no desire to avoid controversy, changes anything. As Archbishop of New York I have a major responsibility to teach what my Church teaches, and to assure to the degree possible that its world view is reflected in the conduct of institutions that bear the name "Catholic."

As far as I know, the Mayor doesn't have any "City teaching" to worry about, so he has a freedom I don't have in regard to the crucial

8. In 1988, after four years of preparation, we held an Archdiocesan Synod, an assembly of some 250 representative laypersons, religious sisters and brothers, priests, bishops, young people and others, to propose new policies for the Archdiocese, after an extensive consultation in which we mailed lengthy questionnaires to more than 2 million people, asking them to express their needs, desires and recommendations. We even took to the streets and consulted homeless people face to face, as we did with residents in nursing homes. This was by far the most extensive consultation ever attempted in the Archdiocese.
9. The Church in New York is a "cell" of a living organism, the Church Universal. In moral and doctrinal matters, it does not teach or act independently of the living body of which it is a member.

"reality factor" that binds me in decision-making. He does, however, have a personal ideology and his own personal value system. And he must confront a different kind of reality factor that I am completely free of: the political reality of elections. He is restricted in other ways, as well, in which I'm not. He gives the impression at times of being bound hand and foot by a frightening web of regulations. Whether those regulations have increased since the scandals that shook the City in 1986 and 1987, or whether City employees are simply being more careful, is hard to say, but a veritable paralysis seems at times to take hold.

I *have* learned this much about Church-State problems in New York, however: Whether the conflicts involve jurisdiction or differences of purposes and values, virtually every problem is exacerbated and its resolution made more difficult when there is a lack "civility" on either side. Lack of civility complicates life for all of us, and makes it difficult and depressing to engage honorably in public service as representative of either Church or State.

Civility is a lot more than simple courtesy, although this is certainly part of what we need. Civility requires as a minimum that we tell the truth and that we treat others justly and respectfully. At its best, civility includes a good bit of charity in our interpretations of the actions of others. When civility is lacking, on the part of those involved in the discussion at hand (as well as on the part of observers, casual or otherwise), a great deal of energy and time is spent reestablishing lines of communication and a sense of trust. Without civility, there is little possibility for an ongoing working relationship.

Yet, ironically, efforts to maintain civility in what might be perceived as almost naturally adversarial relationships can generate problems of their own, by way of what we might call a "halo" effect (or even a "negative halo effect"). For example, there is a public perception that if you are seen at dinner together, or are photographed shaking hands, you approve of each other's activities or positions. The same is true if one fails to denounce the other publicly for behavior that annoys various sectors of the electorate. The perception is that you either approve of the behavior yourself, or that you remain silent out of friendship.

Another factor is at work as well. During an "election year" (which in our political system is *every* year), a churchman is expected never to praise or denounce by name the behavior of any elected official or candidate. That can lead to many a Catch-22 situation. If the church-man seems to support either by praise or by silence a public official's questionable behavior, he can be accused of misusing his Church posi-tion on behalf of a friend and to the detriment of another candidate. If he denounces the elected official's behavior, he is accused of "im-posing" his morality on others, and again misusing his Church office. (One of our country's widely read columnists warned, for example, that my own statements about the positions of various Catholics in public life threatened the tax-exempt status of churches! A major newspaper editorial warned that I was threatening the acceptability of Catholics in public office, hard won, they said, by John F. Kennedy.)

If it is difficult for a churchman to be friendly with an elected of-ficial, it can be at least as difficult for an elected official to be friendly with a churchman. For example, if an elected official supports or re-fuses to denounce a controverted position held by his friend the churchman, the elected official is instantly accused of political motives, such as to win votes among the churchman's congregants. Some people seem to forget that the churchman's congregants may *themselves* disagree with their churchman's position, so that the elec-ted official may be risking their wrath whichever way he goes! Thus are the vagaries of the halo effect, an effect so often resulting from efforts to maintain the civility so important to Church-State conflict resolutions.

The problems introduced by the halo effect may indeed explain why churchmen and statesmen often seem to keep their distance from one another, or even, in some cases, engage in outright incivility. What-ever the causes, incivility—ill-will—has had a long, dishonorable his-tory in New York, although it has often yielded its share of laughs to those who haven't taken it too personally.

The feud between Mr. James Gordon Bennett, editor of the old *New York Herald* and Archbishop John Hughes, first Archbishop of New York, may not have seemed funny in 1841, but despite the echo of King Henry II, it's consoling to read more than 125 years later.

Archbishop Hughes had just given, to the cheers of the early Irish, a rousing talk that virtually everyone but himself saw as out-and-out political, aimed against some candidates for public office and in favor of other candidates. Mr. Bennett fumed magnificently, warning that had this happened anywhere but in New York, "this foolish prelate, the abbot of unreason" would be in grave danger. Calling Archbishop

Hughes the "Bishop of Blarneyopolis," he warned the Irish that the Archbishop's mind "must be blinded to all facts—to all truths—but the dogmas and drivellings of the Catholic Church in the last stages of decrepitude. . . . Send the priests back to saying Masses for the dead," he advised them, "forgiving sins, marrying at five dollars a head and drinking good wine at generous tables." [10]

And James Gordon Bennett was a Catholic!

10. Richard Shaw, *Dagger John: The Unquiet Life and Times of Archbishop John Hughes of New York* (New York: Paulist Press, 1977), pp. 167–168

I I

THE MAYOR
COMPASSION
and
COMMON SENSE
IN GOVERNMENT

THE CARDINAL
NATURAL MORAL LAW
and the
HUMAN PERSON

THE MAYOR

I have often said that the clergy see as their prime obligation the saving of souls while I, as Mayor of the most ethnically diverse and politically progressive city in the greatest country the world has ever known, see as my prime obligation the saving of lives. I told this to a reporter once, and I remember that the Cardinal became angry, because he believes that he also is in the business of saving lives. I don't dispute him for one minute. But if he had to choose between saving the soul and saving a life, as a prelate his priority would be the soul. Mine is saving the life because I don't know enough about the soul.

Certainly the values of government, and the goals that we have in the City of New York, more often than not correspond with religious values. Our mutual presumptions are rooted in the Judeo-Christian ethic. The difference is that our values, and the public policies that evolve from them, must encompass the beliefs and expectations of many different and sometimes divergent denominations; on some issues, like birth control and abortion, our policies may contravene the theology, the dogma of a particular church. But these practices, despite the absolute and unstinting opposition in certain circles, are perceived as generally acceptable by millions of people, many of whom are religious. Contrast this to the imposition of Prohibition in the twenties: the illegalization of alcohol was ratified by Congress, not by the people; it proved to be a disaster, and it was repealed.

The Cardinal refers to "the highest standards that our American ideals aspire to." Our government does embody these ideals. Government must of course deal with the basic needs of people: adequate nutrition for every person; affordable housing for every person; and the opportunity to enter the job market and enhance your skills so as to increase the value of those skills when you pick up your paycheck at the end of the week. Justice, however, must top this list.

I embrace as a fundamental tenet of government—and one that is certainly compatible with the teachings of any church—that the basic imperative for a just city is to provide equal justice before the law to everyone, regardless of race or creed or political temperament, and to provide equitable treatment as it relates to services. There is a difference here: With respect to equality under the law, there can be no equivocation; with respect to equitable treatment, this is dependent upon your station in life. Those who are able to fend for themselves to a greater extent should receive less by way of services; those who are at the bottom of the economic ladder have to receive the maximum that we can provide within fiscal limitations and common sense.

The reality is that government must indeed function within fiscal as well as common-sense limitations. Government can never do enough, in construction and renewal and human services—and obviously not all that advocates demand that we do. Advocates (who along with the media and elected officials are the conscience of our system) will clamor for far more than any city can provide in just about any area of social concern. They are not concerned about budgetary constraints. Mayors and governors and presidents, by necessity, must be.

One advocate whom I always point to because I have much affection for her is Trude Lash, a leading partisan who has argued passionately on behalf of children. She directed a study five years ago for the Foundation for Child Development that concluded that the City had betrayed the needs of poor children in light of severe federal budget cuts. As ammunition for its argument, the report cited increased revenues for the Department of Cultural Affairs at a time of significant federal cutbacks in programs for kids. "We're not doing well by our children," she said. "We are doing less well than we have been doing. We are particularly neglecting the children who need our help most, namely, the poor children." Added the manager of the study: "It is striking that the City continued to decrease the share of City tax-levy money to the Human Resources Administration during a period when youth unemployment was officially reported at 30 percent for all teenagers and approximately 50 percent for black teenagers while it continued to increase the share of City tax-levy revenues to the Department of Cultural Affairs."

Now this sounds fine out of context, but it's ridiculous, a statistical connivance. We are in fact spending billions of dollars on children and their families in our various educational and social-service programs—even with what has been a sharp drop in federal aid. Still, education gets fully 25 percent of our budget, and human resources another 25 percent. Our educational system serves students who are more than 72 percent minorities, and the clientele served by the Human Resources Administration is overwhelmingly minority.

In 1983, when this report was released, we had been spending all of $63.5 million in support of our cultural institutions. In fiscal 1984, we upped this figure by less than $2 million. This is a relative pittance, and certainly not nearly as much as advocates for culture and the arts would have us allocate. But this city could not be the cultural capital of the world, or the international capital that it is, without supporting the arts. And our children certainly benefit from the cultural enrichment that the city offers.

As Mayor, you have to weigh and you have to balance. When you have to engage in budgetary dispositions and, on occasions when you are cutting the budget, one of the essential services has to be support of cultural institutions. The Mayor's mind-set cannot be the same as the advocate's mind-set, unless you consider him an advocate for all the needs of the city. To argue otherwise is simplistic.

On the other side of the ledger, when we were forced to reduce spending for many City services in order to balance the budget, we exempted education because everybody agreed that the education of our kids was so inadequate that we could not reduce the dollars even though the money was not being spent to its maximum effect. And to reduce our outlay for education would have given the administrators an excuse to say, "Well, it isn't our fault that the students aren't learning because 'they' have taken away our dollars." So we decided to exclude education from budget reductions.

We did lessen our support for libraries—it was by a very small amount—and people were yelling and screaming. Of course, they were yelling and screaming about everything, but they weren't the ones who had to make the hard choices. I remember a small picket line in front of City Hall of mothers and their children. There was a little seven-year-old kid carrying a sign that read, MAYOR, PLEASE DON'T CLOSE MY LIBRARY. Of course we weren't closing the library; we might have been shortening the hours that it would be open. But if we don't cut here, where do we cut? Subway service? Fire protection? Highway maintenance? We're still reeling from the effects of cutbacks in bridge and road maintenance during the fiscal crisis of the mid-seventies.

As part of the social contract, government is charged with responding to the needs of the people. Most of our efforts—police protection, garbage collection, parks, recreation, the obvious responsibilities of government—represent ongoing responses to continuing needs. Often, circumstances demand ingenuity and innovation. Sometimes we have to attempt strategies that stir controversy. Let's take the AIDS situation as an illustration. We're urging the use of condoms as one aspect of "safer sex," and we're urging the use of clean needles—and setting up, as an experiment, a pilot project for a very limited number of addicts, only two hundred of them—to help control the spread of this virulent and devastating disease. We can't tell people: "Just Say No." New York City is not fantasyland.

The goal of the study is to discern if, by providing clean "works" and counseling, we can reduce the needle sharing that is responsible, in great measure, for the spread of the AIDS virus. What the study isn't is carte blanche for drug addicts throughout the city to indulge their "joneses" at society's expense. The so-called clean-needle approach, which is only one element in a range of ongoing and expanding activities, is endorsed by an overwhelming majority of eminent public-health authorities, including Surgeon General C. Everett Koop and the city's commissioner of health, Stephen Joseph, the National Academy of Sciences and the World Health Organization. Because they see all too clearly the epic health crisis looming before us.

We decided to initiate this pilot program only after considerable thought and debate. Which is how we make decisions at City Hall. Now, I probably am the most stiff-necked public official in the United States in terms of my approach to government, which is consistent with my approach to issues as a legislator. If I take a position, and if I think I have the expertise to support it, even if it is challenged and attacked, I will stand like a rock unless you convince me that I'm wrong. (Some people, some of my advisers, say I stand too long and that I ought to "cave" more than I do. But if I believe that I am right I hold my ground.)

In areas in which I don't have any particular expertise or knowledge, I adopt a position based on common sense and the information provided by those who do have special knowledge; in these instances I am much more persuadable.

In matters on which I have no opinion—and there are lots of such matters, although I think people find that hard to believe—I am willing to listen and learn and, as a result of a consensus, adopt a position. But in adopting a position involving what I perceive to be morality in a very strict sense—and while you cannot govern if every issue takes on a profound moral context, there might be a handful of such issues—you couldn't persuade me, you couldn't change my mind; you can throw me out of office but you won't get me to change my position on matters of morality. Let me offer a couple of examples:

When I was a congressman, some people—they were animal protectionists—came to me and said, "We don't believe in kosher slaughtering." This practice, which requires the cutting of the aortic artery of the animal, originated in biblical times and to what we as Jews perceive to be a covenant with God. Now, these people would prefer instead that you stun the beast and render it unconscious by hitting it on the head with a mallet before you cut its throat. This would be more "humane," they reason. However, this would violate Jewish law. It didn't register with the animal protectionists that kosher slaughtering is humane because it is instant death for the animal. The real pain and suffering is the result of the shackling and hoisting as required by civil law to prevent the animal from falling into its own offal, a situation that can be avoided with the use of the Weinberg pen, which keeps the animal upright. I always wondered why, in their fervor to protect animals, they didn't lobby for the mandated use of this pen, notwithstanding its cost.

But I was told by a number of these animal activists that if I didn't support a federal bill to outlaw kosher slaughtering, they would wage a campaign to defeat me. I said, "Go out and start waging the campaign, 'cause you're not gonna move me on that." That's a tenet of my religion (even though I'm not kosher and I don't have the will to give up the foods that I like which are not edible under kosher laws governing the diets of Jews—and Muslims, I might add).

I also believed in 1971 when I was serving in Congress—I represented the 17th District in Manhattan for nine years, beginning in 1969—that amnesty ought to be granted to the so-called draft dodgers who had fled to Canada rather than submit to the draft and possibly get sent to Vietnam. I even went to Canada to speak with several of these men, who did what they did out of a serious conviction that the war was morally wrong. I was pilloried for that. People told me that I would lose my reelection bid. They told me I'd better recant my position. And I said, no, that was a matter of high morality for me and if my constituents didn't agree with me, if they couldn't accept my position, then they could elect somebody else.

I won a resounding victory.

One thing I am is a very good listener. Some say I'm an even better talker, but I do listen. To all points of view. I employ the Socratic method. I want to understand the shades of gray that will influence my decisions. Most people who have participated in meetings in my office will tell you that I'm a pretty good questioner and that I will get to the heart of a matter more quickly than most. This I think comes from my training as a lawyer.

Where possible I try to arrive at a consensus. But consensus, sometimes, can be elusive, and at times the split, the divisions among the people in my office—budget, operations, deputy mayors, commissioners—are enormous. Yet unlike some mayors, who believe that if you sit on a problem long enough it will go away, I don't believe in procrastinating. Maybe sometimes I should, because sometimes a problem does fade—in reality and in the public consciousness. I believe, however, that people elected me to make decisions within my authority. And so, if I've heard all the arguments, and I don't think there is any more material of relevance that affects an issue at hand, even if my advisers cannot come to a consensus I will signal the fact that I have arrived at my conclusions by clapping my hands and saying, "Let me tell you what we're gonna do." And then I say, "This is now the policy."

Now, what has to guide my decisions is their potential to affect the future of the City. As Mayor I have to do my best to keep the City healthy fiscally and economically, to prevent New York from becoming unattractive to taxpayers and employers and middle-class people who pay the taxes and create the jobs. And at the same time to balance these considerations with the obligation to take precious dollars and allocate them not on a per capita basis but rather on the basis of need, which can skew your budget—as it should be skewed—in favor of the poor.

Look at our capital budget. Of necessity we have to fill the void caused, in great measure, by the abdication of the federal government in the funding of construction of housing for the poor and the working poor. (And given the cost of most things these days, many middle-class New Yorkers consider themselves members of the legion of the working poor.) Advocates are always criticizing us, blaming us for a situation not exactly of our making.

But in the City of New York we in fact have the largest program of housing construction and rehabilitation since—and I put this joshingly—the Pharaohs built the pyramids in ancient Egypt: We are building 252,000 housing units, which will house something like 900,000 people when this ten-year program is completed. And it's on schedule. We will be spending over $5 billion, and this money will build apartments for people, 87 percent of whom are either on welfare or are working poor or have what we call "moderate" incomes. Some 60 percent of the money we spend and the housing we create will go to families whose annual incomes range from nothing to $19,000. Twenty-seven percent will help families whose incomes range between $19,000 and $32,000. Only 13 percent of the apartments will go to "middle-class" families, families whose annual incomes, no matter how many people in a particular family work, exceed $32,000—which is not a great deal of money. I have mixed feelings about this. While it's not fair to, in effect, discriminate against middle-income people by giving them so few subsidies and opportunities for affordable housing, it is, in the final analysis, a matter of justice. This may not be fair, but it is just.

The Cardinal also believes in justice. He and I obviously view many of the same issues differently. Not because of differences in our religions; I think that, fundamentally, our two religions share the same values and ideals and are so closely associated that you couldn't distinguish between us on this basis. But I believe that we may come at things differently in part because the way a cardinal "governs" an archdiocese is different than the way a mayor governs a city. A cardinal is appointed, and for life. A mayor is elected for a four-year term.

I have to run for reelection and I have to defend my record before the public. The Cardinal has to keep faith with his Archdiocese, his clergy, his pope and God. I think that the Cardinal has a profoundly greater challenge than I do when it comes to accounting for our respective records. But there is no question in my mind that these different kinds of accountability lead to distinctly different styles of management and governing.

Our outlooks are different in other important respects, too. The Cardinal, it seems to me, holds that religious tenets and convictions have a primary influence in shaping an individual's life, including, I believe, his own. I believe that faith and conviction are indeed powerful influences; but I believe that character and personality are, in greater measure, genetic. While I don't exclude, certainly, the impact of education and environment on the development of character and personality, on ability and ambition and outlook on life, much if not most of whatever I am today has at its root the chromosomes, the genes of my mother and father.

Now, my parents were very ordinary people, each gifted, as almost every human being is, in a special way. Although my father was a very sweet man who was liked by everybody, he was not the equal of my mother in native intelligence. My mother was the brains; she was an incredibly able woman. She had little in the way of formal education when she came here from Poland when she was fourteen. But she learned to speak English without an accent, to write English by hiring a tutor though she was poverty-stricken at the time. Because she wanted to be an American in the fullest sense, as she saw it. My father, on the other hand, never lost his European-Jewish accent. He never learned to write English except he could write his name. He did, however, learn to read English. I like to think that I have my father's personality and my mother's intellect.

As a young Jew growing up in the thirties, I was very conscious of anti-Semitism. I didn't experience it personally very much, although as a kid I was once beaten up because I was Jewish. But the formative experience for my generation was World War II and the fight against Hitler. Of course, we only really found out the dimensions of his depravity after the concentration camps were liberated. Although I was not among the liberating forces when I served in Europe in World War II, I did see these evil places. Twice. In 1961 I visited Dachau. While my memories of that hellhole are no longer fresh, I have never forgotten how difficult the Germans made it to get there. It was hidden; the sign on the road was so small that if you weren't careful you would have missed the turn in the road. I believed then, and I believe now, that this was intentional.

When I decided to go to Poland in 1987, it was primarily to see

Auschwitz. Every year I participate in the ceremony to commemorate the Warsaw Ghetto uprising. This is always a very moving, very emotional observance for me, and I am always asked to speak and very grateful to be asked. I talk with the "survivors," as they're called. Every year they're older, particularly the women who light the candles to commemorate the six million dead, and someday soon they will all be gone. The world should never forget the horrors of the Holocaust.

So I wanted to see Auschwitz. It was extraordinary.

Auschwitz was not only a concentration camp, where people were imprisoned, worked to death, beaten, tortured, gassed to death. It was also part of a larger complex that included Birkenau—an extermination camp—thirty times larger than the original Auschwitz. There was a difference between the two, a difference in means if not ends: In Auschwitz people were permitted to work before being gassed; in Birkenau the sole purpose was to put the prisoners to death as quickly as possible. They killed as many as 700 people at one time in one of the gas chambers and then they hauled the bodies into the ovens to be burned. At the height of this horror 24,000 people a day were killed in Birkenau. Think of it—24,000 human beings wiped out/eliminated/exterminated in 24 hours.

This complex was ultimately responsible for the deaths of four million people. Over three million of these were Jews. The rest were Poles, Gypsies, Russian prisoners of war. Most of these were Christians. But the non-Jews were permitted to work, albeit under absolutely inhumane conditions. For them the sole goal was not extermination; for Jews, who were brought to Auschwitz/Birkenau by boxcar from twenty-four countries, it was. Because they were Jews. Christian children weren't killed; Jewish children were. Because Hitler was bent on the extermination of the Jews. Because Hitler and his minions believed that simply by carrying Jewish blood in your veins you were less than a human being. Christians could save themselves; they might "atone" for whatever "crime" they had "committed" against the Reich. But not Jews.

My tour of Auschwitz/Birkenau will remain a vivid memory for the rest of my life. I remember that it was snowing, and a lot of snow had fallen already when we entered Auschwitz. Over the gate the sign still remains: ARBEIT MACHT FREI (WORK WILL FREE YOU). The barracks, originally one story high, had been built in 1914 to house 340 Austrian soldiers. As a concentration camp each barracks held over 1,700 prisoners. The Nazis had added a second story to each building. Little more than shells, these barracks were unheated. Then and now. Even though I was wearing a heavy coat, I was very cold. The prisoners, it was explained, were compelled to sleep three to a bed with neither mattress nor blanket. Each bed was a triple-decker, so there were nine prisoners sleeping on the wooden frame. There were no toilets in the building. The inmates were allowed to use the central toilet facilities once a day for no longer than ten seconds.

We were shown a forty-year-old film made by the Soviet Union. The film is narrated in several different languages and shows the liberation of the camp. Strikingly, what it does not indicate is that most of the inmates were Jews. Now, every life is precious and all those who lost their lives in these death camps must be remembered, must be mourned. But the sheer horror of the genocide perpetrated against the Jews is lost when the overwhelming number of victims are not identified as such, particularly because it was their very Jewishness, which they could not shed even if they wanted to, that caused their terrible deaths.

There was one exhibit in one of the barracks that did memorialize the killing of Jews. There were hundreds of suitcases inscribed with the names of their owners. There was a sampling of the hair of women who had been shorn, hair cut from the head that had turned gray with the passage of time. The most piteous sight was an assemblage of thousands of little shoes belonging to the children who had been killed at Auschwitz. It was hard to comprehend. It must never be lost to memory.

At one point we were taken to a wall. It was about fifteen feet wide. We were told that prisoners who engaged in some infraction of the rules were brought to that wall and shot: a bullet in the brain at the Wall of Death. And I remember having thought at that moment about what Jews do when they go to the Western Wall in Jerusalem, and about how Jews touch the Torah, the Five Books of Moses, as it is carried through the synagogue. I felt a compulsion to touch the wall with my hand, as though with a kiss after touching my lips. I did that to establish communion, some symbolic contact, with those Jews and Christians who had perished there.

The morning following my visit to the camps, a middle-aged man came over to the table where I was having breakfast and said, "Shalom, Mayor Koch." I returned his greeting. He introduced himself as Mel Mermelstein, and said he was from California. He asked me what brought me to Poland.

I recounted my visit to Auschwitz and described it as one of the most emotional experiences I'd ever had. When I asked if he intended to go there, this is what he said:

"I have been to Auschwitz fourteen times. I was a prisoner there and I come back as often as I can to pray at the crematorium. My family was brought to Auschwitz from the Carpathian Mountains in Hungary, in a boxcar. When we unloaded at Auschwitz, they separated the women from the men. I could see a Nazi officer, whom I later learned was Dr. Mengele, pointing to my mother and directing her and my younger sister toward one line and my older sister toward another. I later found out that had my older sister gone to the line she was directed toward, this would have allowed her to live at least for a short period of time while working at Auschwitz. However, my mother and my younger sister, they were not fit, according to Dr. Mengele, for working. They were being put into the group marked for immediate extermination. And my older sister, crying because of the separation, broke away and ran to my mother. The three of them were taken to Birkenau, where they were gassed and cremated.

"My father, my brother and I were placed in Auschwitz. At one point my father said that at least one of us must stay alive, and in order to do that we had to separate. He said that whoever survived must tell the world what happened so that it will not be forgotten. I have done that. I survived. My father and brother did not.

"I was part of a special detail which hauled the bodies from the gas chambers and took them to the crematoria. When the war was almost at its end and the Russians were close to Auschwitz, the Nazis took two thousand of us and marched us on the roads to Dachau. There, in the final stages of the war, I contracted typhus, just before the liberation by the American army. The Nazis actually deserted the camp, and for six days before the U.S. Army arrived we were alone. When the Americans came, they placed barrels of food in the camp. Because many of the prisoners were so weak and not accustomed to eating anything other than watery soup, as soon as they ate the good and substantial food they became ill. Many died. I go back every year now, in memory of my parents, my sisters, and my brother."

As Mr. Mermelstein told his story, my eyes filled with tears.

Later on during that trip, I met with Cardinal Macharski of

Kracow. We discussed Auschwitz. He said that it was the greatest hell on earth ever created by man, even more horrible, in his opinion, than Hiroshima. I asked him about the protests by many groups over the location of a convent of cloistered Carmelite nuns on the outskirts of Auschwitz. I agreed with those who felt that placing a Roman Catholic convent just outside the barbed wire where more than three million Jews were killed intruded upon the horror committed overwhelmingly against Jews. I told the cardinal that there should be a place of ecumenical worship or a synagogue at Auschwitz as well (even though in Poland, where the largest community of Jews—three and a half million—lived before the war, the number of Jews has shrunk to perhaps ten thousand, and they're all old).

When I returned to New York, I received a call from Cardinal O'Connor, who had received a telegram from his counterpart in Kracow. Cardinal Macharski said that he intended to pursue plans for the construction of a synagogue in Auschwitz. This was partly in deference to requests made by survivors' organizations to close the convent. Later, I was informed that the cardinal had decided to move the convent to a less sensitive site.

It is these realities of our times that have shaped me, that continue to hold sway over me. I am not, as Cardinal O'Connor undoubtedly is, very philosophically oriented. I don't pretend to have read the seminal works of philosophers and thinkers of any period. I'm much more present-oriented, and I don't say this with any degree of pride. I should have read more but I haven't. I have few heroes and no idols. In surveying the politicians and statesmen who have dominated the political scene over the past half-century, there are some whom I admire: I love the bounce and the feistiness of Harry Truman. I love the intellect of Adlai Stevenson. I love the compassion and sense of justice for his fellow human beings of Hubert Humphrey.

And La Guardia, who is more myth than fact. (What people today don't remember is that the reason he didn't run for a fourth term was that he was not well liked during his third term.) He became a mythic figure in what you might call the revisionism of history. And that's fine. Because while he had lots of frailties, one great facet of his personality and his administration was that he loved New York. He was devoted to making his job one in which he could make the lives of his fellow New Yorkers better.

He set the standard; I've tried to follow in his footsteps, and I believe history will judge that I have.

I think that historians will say that I did three things as Mayor. I brought fiscal stability and responsibility and balanced budgets back to the City. Which is absolutely essential. I began the reconstruction of the infrastructure of the City. And I gave a bounce and a jauntiness and a sense of pride back to New Yorkers who had lost a sense of themselves because they were so distressed, even ashamed, by having been brought to the edge of bankruptcy by some of my predecessors. That's what I think I'll be remembered for.

THE CARDINAL

"As a public health official, I don't have the luxury to be a moralist." Thus does *Time* magazine quote an important New York physician and public-health official to the effect that it was his responsibility to speak *only* as a physician, not as a moralist.

What does the doctor really mean? By the very fact that he admits to a responsibility for people, he is speaking of a moral value. He is saying, for example, that if as a physician, he believes that distributing "clean needles" will help prevent the spread of AIDS, and therefore help reduce the number of deaths, it is his moral responsibility to so recommend. He is thereby making a *moral* judgment, based on his conviction that saving lives is a higher moral value than preserving some "abstract" moral principle.

I disagree with the clean-needle theory on both moral and pragmatic grounds, but that's not my point at the moment. My point is that the physician in question is acting as a moralist at the very moment that he is arguing that, as a physician, he hasn't the luxury of being a moralist.

This is a common phenomenon in our society. Public officials, perhaps more than most people, are fond of saying they have no right to impose their moral beliefs on others. That's equivalent to saying their obligation is to make only value-free judgments. That's nonsense. They would have to remain mute about all public-policy issues. To make a value-free judgment is to make no judgment at all. There simply is no such thing as a value-free judgment about public policy, and no self-respecting public-policy maker refrains from making judgments. That's his job. Whatever values he expresses, his judgments are value judgments.

This is another reason why I believe it so important to pursue what I have discussed in the first chapter: the fact that Church-State conflicts almost inevitably arise not only over questions of jurisdiction but over questions of *values*, of purposes, of goals. These differ in many crucial instances for Church and State; hence, for the official representatives of each. Moreover, neither makes what could accurately be called "value-free" judgments on public-policy issues.

Mayor Koch and I agree on a number of issues, share some important values. I hope it is not egotistical for me to say that this is good for New York, not because I want to overestimate my personal importance, but because the Archbishop of New York represents a large number of people. In my judgment (and to use the political jargon of the day) the Mayor is often more conservative about many "traditional" values than he is liberal. Further, he approaches many values with simple common sense. So, for example, one need not argue with him that drug abuse is bad for everybody, or that, with all our faults, the United States is a great country. On some issues his is a very basic, old-fashioned, "my mother used to say" morality.

On a number of other critical issues, however, we are at opposite ends of the world. In my more objective moments, I see the Mayor as a public-office holder for whom public office has its own set of values, its own set of moral imperatives, which I can understand, but with which I frequently cannot agree. I offer one revealing conversation, without violating any confidences. (I believe the Mayor and I and our associates speak freely over a dinner table on the unspoken assumption that the discussion is private. I have the Mayor's consent to discuss one item of the many we have talked about. I choose this one because it is so illustrative of our divergent positions.)

"What would you think," the Mayor asked at dinner, "if I issue condoms to prisoners in jail, on the grounds that we know some engage in homosexual practices that could transmit AIDS?" (I appreciate it when the Mayor asks not what I will *say* publicly, but what I *think*. That gives me the impression that he is honestly seeking my opinion, rather than trying to test political fallout.)

"I think it's about as bad an idea as you could have," I replied, then followed up with my reasoning. "You already know my thinking about the condom question, so obviously that's not what you're asking me about. Apart from both moral and pragmatic questions about the *use* of condoms, then, let me talk about the broader public-policy issue."

"Fine, I'm listening." (I read once in an unflattering book about the

Mayor that he never really listens except when he's talking about himself. On the contrary, I find him a serious listener to serious argument.)

"What you are suggesting is preposterous, and another example of the 'quick fix' that marks so much official problem-solving in this City. Something's broken, fix it, without any regard for why it broke, how real the fix is, or, worst of all, what the effect is going to be on the whole social system. What is being done to counsel prisoners? Why are prisoners vulnerable to attack by other prisoners? What is really being done about the whole prison mess, the unconscionable crowding, the 'broken' criminal-justice system that nobody seems to know how to fix?" I was only warming up.

"Tell me most of all what you are saying to New York. You are saying that with all your power, prestige and authority as Mayor of one of *the* major cities of the world, one of the very few mayors internationally known, you can't prevent criminal action even in your own jail cells, with prisoners under lock and key. If that's true, how can anybody feel safe on the streets, in the subways, in their own homes? You are saying: 'I, Mayor Edward Koch, hereby abdicate. I have lost control. I can no longer assume responsibility or be held responsible.'" There was more to come and he was still listening intently.

"Let me tell you, Mr. Mayor, what I believe to be one of your gravest responsibilities and highest privileges as Mayor of this great City. You have a grave obligation to maintain the highest standards that our American ideals aspire to. You have a grave obligation to help people actualize their fullest potential as human persons. You have a critical responsibility for saying to the world: 'Here are the standards. Here are the laws. Here are our human values. We will never lower our standards, prostitute our laws, demean our society.' I do not share the popular opinion that politics is inherently shabby and that the politician must be corrupt. Aristotle spelled it out centuries ago, that politics can and should be a noble art: the second noblest art after religion, said Saint Thomas Aquinas. We speak of a united people in a free society as the body politic. You are elected to help that body function at the highest, not the lowest level. You are not elected to do what a bad plumber can do, patch our ills with quick fixes. You have an imperative, a mandate from the people, to exercise the highest form of moral leadership—not religious leadership, not sectarian leadership—but very explicitly *moral* leadership. Your mandate from the people does not lend itself well to handing out condoms in prison."

The Mayor's reply was plaintive: "But I *must* stop the transmission of this terrible disease that's killing people."

"Of course, you must," I answered, "or help and inspire and coordinate the efforts of others to do so. But remember that there is a Natural Moral Law at work in society that warns us of the proverbial absolute about free lunches. There are none, as you learn very quickly in politics."

"Meaning what?" the Mayor asked.

"If I didn't have an early Mass in the morning I could tell you tonight what I mean. It's too long a story for quick telling. One version of it goes back in recorded history at least to Sophocles' *Antigone*, gets one of its very best expressions in Cicero, but bursts forth with radically new meaning and in full splendor in the Founding Fathers and in the Declaration of Independence, profoundly advanced and enriched by force of the Judeo-Christian tradition.

"Very briefly, one aspect of Natural Moral Law can be crudely likened to, although it is really quite different from, the natural physical law. If I turn this cup of coffee upside down, gravity doesn't excuse me. Down goes the coffee, sloshing all over your rug. It obeys the *law* of gravity. It's a physical law that runs through and governs all of nature on this planet. Even the Mayor of New York can't legislate against it. I repeat that the notion of Natural Moral Law differs significantly from that of natural physical law, but is equally inexorable. Violate it and somebody pays the consequences.

"One of the reasons why you and I disagree on a number of critical issues is that we come at things from different sets of values, or moral philosophies. Our country has been shaped by a variety of moral philosophies: Pragmatism, Utilitarianism, Social Darwinism, Natural Moral Law, and others.[1] As your question about condoms in jail suggests, you tend to look at things largely from the perspective of one or all of the first three of these moral philosophies. On the contrary, all

1. Natural Moral Law is presented in some detail in this chapter. In subsequent chapters I shall discuss more succinctly some of the other value orientations that have strongly influenced American political life, in my judgment primarily to our detriment. However else I justify this excursion into moral philosophies, it cannot be questioned that their impact on Church-State relations at every point of our history, and certainly today, really *demands* close scrutiny by all citizens. For those interested, it will at least explain why I go at issues as I do, and why I believe the Mayor goes at the same issues as he does.

my training inclines me to view things from the viewpoint of Natural Moral Law as interpreted and applied by the Scriptures, traditional Catholic theologians and, for our day, the Second Vatican Council.[2] That doesn't mean that either of us isn't influenced by a variety of moral perspectives, leaning at times toward one rather than the other. But in general, I operate from a base of moral absolutes and you don't."

The above undoubtedly sounds pompous and contrived. It may also appear to have been constructed for the purpose of this book, and never to have actually taken place. But strange or not, that's the kind of thing we do discuss and in that kind of language. Were there a record, it would show that the above is almost verbatim.

How else would you talk to a Mayor who is quite inclined to greet you with such a question as: "Tell me about this latest document from the Vatican on medical technology and *in vitro* fertilization that I've been reading about in the newspapers." So at it I go, often in highly philosophical language, and inevitably find that such questions provide excellent springboards to discuss housing, homelessness, racial problems, the horrors of our transportation system and a variety of other practical problems. I argue basically that all such questions are meaningful only if we admit to the sacredness and worth and dignity of every human person. If you're transporting or housing cattle, you use one set of rules; if human persons, another.

I try to approach every major public-policy issue with the Mayor, issues on which we agree and those on which we disagree, by insisting that no such issue is value-free, and that there is no such thing as a value-free decision or policy relating to such issues. The only question is *whose* values, or *which* values, are to prevail, *Who Gets What, When, How?* Within this context, in my view, the essential question to be asked about *any* public policy is the question asked of our entire socioeconomic system by the Catholic Bishops of the United States in the Pastoral Letter on the economy: "What does it do *to* people? What does it do *for* people?" In other words, how does a particular public-

2. Both Catholic theologians and the Second Vatican Council lean heavily, for example, on St. Paul's Letter to the Romans: ". . . the demands of the law are written in their hearts. Their conscience bears witness together with that law, and their thoughts will accuse or defend them." (2:15). Later in this chapter I discuss the meaning of Natural Moral Law in the Catholic tradition, but I did not attempt any extensive discussion in the dinner conversation with the Mayor. Enough was enough.

policy decision account for, preserve, or enhance our commitment to the worth and dignity of the human person?[3]

Honesty compels me to say that while I have always been taught and believed that every human person is made in the image and likeness of God, I didn't always have the sense of urgency about the worth and dignity of the human person that drives me today. I have not always insisted so strongly as I do today that the ultimate test of any value orientation, or moral philosophy, or political system is its understanding and treatment of the human person. It's all in the traditional Catholic theology in which my entire life has been steeped, yet the imperative urgency of it did not fully emerge for me consciously and personally only through that teaching. What had been always deep within me virtually exploded into my consciousness one day at Dachau.

I therefore want to talk briefly here about my first visit to Dachau, not because of what it did to my life, but because of what it did to my political thinking. Except for the Dachau experience, it is most unlikely that I would be writing this or any book with this or any mayor. I had never been a "political activist," had rarely ever expressed anything that could be construed as a political opinion. Usually, as a civic duty, I voted, but not always, and never had more than a chance relationship with any political party. (That hasn't changed. In New York I am registered as an Independent, despite a *Washington Post* columnist who has accused me, with sinister implications, of being a Republican!) I thought little about public policy, and less about involving myself in trying to shape it. I was, after all, a chaplain with the United States Navy and Marine Corps, bouncing around the world (by the time of the Dachau visit, for twenty-three years). While I had taken studies in political theory, it was for some work in which I was engaged while in uniform, and certainly not because of any interest in "practical" politics.

Dachau changed much of my thinking and my *feeling*. On the practical level, it made me a *confronter* of every situation within my own sphere of responsibility that has serious implications for the human person. There is no special nobility in being appalled by homelessness, by political exploitation, by racism, by violence, by contempt for the human person, after you have visited Dachau. There you learn, if you

3. *Economic Justice For All: Catholic Social Teaching and the U.S. Economy* (Washington: National Conference of Catholic Bishops/United States Catholic Conference, 1986)

had not learned before, that every human person is sacred and every human problem, to the extent possible, calls for us to be our "brother's keeper," when our "brother" cannot help himself. This is why, all these years after that first visit, I find myself jumping into New York's problems with both feet (or perhaps too frequently, head-first), because they are *people* problems, and every human person is sacred.

Dachau affected me on more than the emotional level. It forced me to articulate for myself a political philosophy that would have something to say to a world that too often treats human persons as cattle.

One goes to Dachau by way of Munich, a big, bustling city. A few miles outside the city one comes upon a rather pleasant little town with lovely flowers growing on either side of the street. Almost suddenly there's a prosaic-looking field surrounded by a very ordinary-looking cyclone fence. One enters the gate and looks out at what could be a big playing field, uninterrupted except by a couple of wooden barracks. One is surprised. This is Dachau.

The two wooden barracks that are standing are but two of the many that had been there and were torn down. One enters a barracks built to hold about 40 people and learns that 140 people were packed into it at any given time, people literally crushing one another. They didn't stay there very long. They were taken off to the big shower rooms, much like the shower rooms attached to any gymnasium except that the "shower" nozzles in the ceiling could pour out lethal gas.

Next one goes to the semicircular red-brick ovens, the crematoriums. That's where it all hit me. I put my hand on the floor of an oven and felt, in retrospect, the intermingled ashes of Jews and Christians, of laypersons, rabbis, ministers, priests, men, women, and children. My heart became a ball of lead and dropped into the pit of my stomach as I asked myself: "Good God, could human beings actually have done this to human beings?"

I've spent much of my life in various parts of the world, engaged in a broad variety of experiences, but never had there been anything quite like Dachau, never anything quite so chilling. Certainly never anything that affected my life and my thinking more profoundly.

Later, I went into the large museum which consists primarily of a display of blown-up pictures. Some are huge, showing heaped-up mounds of bones and the emaciated figures of those who were still alive but hardly even human-looking at the time the Allies arrived to liberate them. Among the memorabilia is a blown-up cutout of a letter written initially in German script by the commandant of Dachau, a medical doctor. Writing personally to Adolf Hitler, he says in essence: "My dear Führer: I am enthralled by my responsibilities here. I am given enormous opportunities to engage in almost inconceivable medical experiments and I know that we are going to achieve the means of purifying the human race." He goes on to describe in glowing terminology the opportunities given him there. Then he concludes in a brief paragraph: "But my dear Führer, much as I love my work, I hope that you can arrange to have me transferred to another camp of this sort where I can do the same thing, but where the weather will be a little bit more amenable, because you see, it's very damp and cold here."

I'm not sure why, but that letter more than anything else chilled me. The incredible callousness, the unbelievable insensitivity of a medical doctor—certified to save life, now so completely and so cruelly indifferent—glorying in "the experimental work" he was performing on human bodies and minds. Engaging in the grimmest torture, yet experiencing a kind of ennui even while doing that, and suggesting that because of the climatic discomforts he should be transferred.

I left Dachau after my first visit moved and shaken. Later I became very familiar with the works of Elie Wiesel, now my good friend. Elie Wiesel had been taken to Auschwitz and then Buchenwald as a young boy and saw his mother and sisters stuffed into a furnace. He then tried to survive with his father (his father finally died) until the day that the liberators would come. In the final words of his book *Night*, in which he describes that experience, he says he looked for the first time into a mirror after all that period in the concentration camps. "From the depths of the mirror, a corpse gazed back at me. The look in his eyes, as they stared into mine, has never left me."[4]

I don't want to demean the depth of *his* feeling by comparing it to my own, but my experience in Dachau has never left me. I've been back, and each time it's the same. During the years since, I've tried to detach myself from the emotional impact, and to analyze Dachau's lesson rationally. Each successive analysis convinces me even more deeply than its predecessor of two fundamental truths, two overwhelming values: one, the sacredness, the worth, the dignity of every

4. Elie Wiesel, *Night* (New York: Bantam Books, 1982), p. 109.

human person; two, the objectivity and immutability of Natural Moral Law. It has become, I suspect, a psychological impossibility for me to evaluate a public-policy issue or any facet of our political system without viewing it through the prism of the Dachau experience and the truths and values that experience revealed. It is with this value orientation that I look at what happens each day in New York and in our nation at large. It is on the basis of the two truths that have spelled themselves out so clearly for me in the wake of my Dachau visits that, for better or for worse, I examine the vision and the reality of our political system, particularly at this time of my life, in New York.

First, the sacredness, the worth, the dignity of the human person. I am convinced that absolutely nothing is so crucial to any rational political system as awareness of and reverence for the wonders of the human person, the human person that Catholicism and many other religions believe is fashioned individually and uniquely by the hand of Almighty God. Forgetfulness or denial of this reality results inevitably in the grossest distortion and perversion of the fundamental purpose of authentic political life. Such distortion leaves us helpless when confronted with the complex human problems that we meet every day, those problems that give us a continuing sense of national uneasiness.

We seem to know that we are doing so many things right as a nation, but we seem to know too, or we *feel*, a vague uneasiness and, at times, an acute anxiety that we are doing some things terribly wrong. Many New Yorkers feel this deep within themselves as they work their way daily in a city they love.

We know there is something wrong, as we pass the bag ladies, the bag men in the streets, about gentrification that flushes lonely, elderly people out of homes and apartments with absolutely nowhere to go. We know there is something wrong when drugs control and destroy our neighborhoods, when we can't build prisons fast enough to meet the demand. We know there is something wrong when the worst pornography is defended as freedom of speech, when child abuse reaches horrifying proportions, when people are disenfranchised or exploited because of where they were born, or their sex, or the color of their skin. We know there is something wrong in the sexual exploitation and violence that various agencies deal with every day in virtually every city, and with the hopelessness of burned-out buildings all over the country and certainly here in New York. We know, we *have* to know, there is something wrong when more than one and a half million children in their mothers' wombs, waiting to be born, are destroyed in our nation each year before they see the light of day.

And all of this knowledge pains us. The pain comes from knowing that we are doing some things terribly wrong, and from either not wanting to right them, or not seeming to know how to right them, or not trying to find the way to right them through our political system. The pain comes from knowing that our political system has been too frequently perverted.

No matter what political scheme, what social programs are elaborated to enhance life in the city or to elevate the so-called "quality of life," unless they are prompted by the fact that the city, the nation, *exists for persons*, not persons for the city or the nation, then every effort is frustrated at the very outset. It therefore becomes imperative that both conceptually and practically we shout from the housetops our practical commitment to a belief in the intrinsic worth of every human person as the very *raison d'être* of our entire political system.

Otherwise, we simply can't win. We have no real motive for winning, and we hardly even *try* to control or eliminate the corruption, the cynicism that marks so much of our political and economic life. We must demand that the human person be protected in our complex political system. We must ask how we can preserve or rebuild those structures so critical to the perdurance of a sense of dignity and worth for every person. The political system exists for the person and not the person for the political system.

The second fundamental truth that I have come to appreciate so much through Dachau is the objectivity and immutability of Natural Moral Law.[5] My understanding of Natural Moral Law didn't begin there, but it came into focus there. Everything I had believed about it was verified and came alive there. I reflected on what the international community had to go through to judge the Nazi atrocities at the conclusion of the war. Very quickly during the Nuremberg trials it became clear that the atrocities were legally *permissible* under the laws of the Third Reich. In fact, they were not merely permissible, they were encouraged and mandated. As a result, those responsible for the

---

5. Below, I risk being an unconscionable bore and pedant by outlining that philosophy, a political philosophy rooted in Natural Moral Law. Short of the theological, or the purely religious, I cannot find in any other political philosophy, and certainly not in any other of those that have shaped America, a consistent safeguard against ultimate dehumanization of human beings, or a consistent policy for enhancing the dignity of human beings. I ask indulgence, therefore, for the somewhat academic discussion of Natural Moral Law concluding this chapter.

worst atrocities, even those who *directed* such atrocities, disclaimed responsibility on the basis of orders of superiors, written orders, written mandates—indeed, the law of the land. Confronted with this reality, those from outside Germany who had to establish a tribunal to judge the guilt or innocence of accused parties found themselves unable to speak reasonably of violations of laws of the land or international law. Consequently, they had to resort to Natural Moral Law—the law that completely transcends the law of any land, a law that cannot legitimately be violated by any civil law because it is above all civil law.

Cicero summarized the Greek philosophers' and Roman lawyers' particular understanding of Natural Moral Law before Christ was born.

> There is in fact a true law, namely right reason, which is in accordance with nature, applies to all men and is unchangeable and eternal. By its commands this law summons men to the performance of their duties, by its prohibitions it restrains them from doing wrong. . . . It will not lay down one rule in Rome and another in Athens. . . . But there will be one law eternal and unchangeable, binding at all times upon all peoples. There will be, as it were, one common master and ruler of men, namely God, who is the author of this law, its interpreter and its sponsor. The man who will not obey it will abandon his better self.

Some seventeen centuries later in his "Second Treatise of Civil Government," John Locke was to say something startlingly similar.

> Thus the law of nature stands as an eternal rule to all men, legislators as well as others. The rules that they make for other men's actions must, as well as their own, be conformable to the law of nature, i.e., to the will of God, of which that is a declaration, and the fundamental law of nature being the preservation of mankind, no human sanction can be good or valid against it.

The Founding Fathers inherited this long tradition, if perchance through the mediation of philosophers like John Locke. Their familiarity with Natural Moral Law tradition was explicated with elegance and precision in many of their writings. We need but cite a few, almost at random, such as George Mason, American revolutionary.

> Now all acts of legislature apparently contrary to natural right and justice are, in our laws, and must be in the nature of things, con-

sidered as void. The laws of nature are the laws of God: whose authority can be superseded by no power on earth— All human constitutions which contradict his laws, we are in conscience bound to disobey. Such has been the adjudication of our courts of justice.

With Justice James Wilson, appointed to the Supreme Court by George Washington himself, and one of the six who signed both the Declaration of Independence and the Constitution, we see more clearly some of the impact of Christianity on Natural Moral Law thinking.

Our Creator has a supreme right to prescribe a law for conduct, and we are under the most perfect obligations to obey that law. . . . The law of nature is immutable; not by the effect of an arbitrary disposition, but because it has its foundation in nature, constitution and mutual relations of man and things. . . . In compassion to the imperfection of our internal powers our all-gracious Creator, Preserver and Ruler has been pleased to discover and enforce his law by a revelation given to us immediately and directly from himself. This revelation is contained in Holy Scriptures. . . . On some important subjects . . . our knowledge is greatly improved, refined and exalted by that which is revealed. . . . What an enrapturing view of the moral government of the universe! Over all, goodness infinite reigns, guided by unerring wisdom and supported by Almighty power. . . . What is the efficient cause of moral obligation of the eminent distinction between right and wrong? . . . the will of God. This is the Supreme Law.

What a distance from Justice Wilson to Justice Holmes!

Such positions taken early by the Founding Fathers (and one can quote one after the other, including Thomas Jefferson and George Washington himself) are critical to our understanding of what our political system was intended to be. Clearly the Founding Fathers rooted their vision of their country and its laws in a Natural Moral Law which impregnates all of nature and demands that a political system recognize that a divine order has already been implanted in the hearts of human beings and of all creatures. [6]

6. The Jeffersonian phrase in the Declaration of Independence is a fine example of the political expression given to Natural Moral Law by the Founding Fathers: "When, in the Course of human events, it becomes necessary for one people to dissolve the political bands which have connected them with another, and to assume among the powers of the earth, the separate and equal station to which the Laws of Nature and of Nature's God entitle them, a decent respect to the opinions of mankind requires that they should declare the causes which impel them to the separation."

Catholic Natural Moral Law tradition calls upon many of the same sources as those basic to the understanding held by the Founding Fathers, and uses much of the same language. But the Church focuses on another and even more profound dimension. The Church teaches that we are but pilgrims in this life, destined for another. We reach that destiny in part by truly being what God intended us to be. We are human beings, not dogs or cats. We have *human* nature, not simply animal nature. If we refuse to act in accord with our human nature, we "self-destruct." The Second Vatican Council put it well:

> Deep within his conscience man discovers a law which he has not laid upon himself but which he must obey. . . . For man has in his heart a law inscribed by God. *His dignity lies in observing this law* and by it he will be judged. (GS 16) [Emphasis added]

I have observed above that Natural Moral Law is quite different from natural physical law, although analogous in some ways. Natural physical law controls us whether we like it or not. If I jump off a building without a parachute or wings, I will crash to the ground. If the building is high enough, I will almost certainly be killed on impact. It's again the law of gravity. If I use a parachute, natural physical laws of aerodynamics come to my rescue.

I can *choose*, however, to observe or to ignore the Natural Moral Law. Nothing obvious will necessarily happen either way. Since the law is a guide to my being what I am intended by God to be, however, to violate the law is in some way to affect adversely my very being. If I choose to bark like a dog or run around on all fours, I do something to my human "dignity," as the Vatican Council puts it. I am not behaving as a human being.

There's a natural physical (biological) law which says that if I shoot drugs into my body, I'm going to change it for the worse. If I do it enough, or the drugs are powerful enough, I destroy my body, and almost certainly my mind. I have violated laws physically inscribed in my biological nature. My body won't be fooled.

It is *morally* wrong to destroy my body by shooting it with drugs, whether I use clean or dirty needles. Who says so? The Natural Moral Law says so, the law that makes very clear that my body is basically good, even if weak, sick, crippled, imperfect or whatever. My body was not intended for the purpose of shooting it full of drugs. It is "inhuman" to do so.

Judeo-Christian law teaches that murder is always wrong. Had the Ten Commandments never been revealed, it would still be clear that murder is a violation of Natural Moral Law. Theoretically, we don't even need civil law or criminal law to tell us murder is wrong. Let murders run rampant and a society would fall into chaos.

I am personally convinced that when we try to prevent AIDS by in any way supporting or encouraging something grossly unnatural (a grave violation of natural biological law), we risk similar chaos. To argue that giving people "clean" needles helps prevent AIDS yet does not support or encourage drug abuse is nonsense. Basically, we are saying that as a society we have accepted drug abuse by default. As I see it, we are committing ourselves to a violation of both physical and moral law—violating the very nature of both the individual human person and society itself. To believe we can do this with impunity suggests a naïveness about both forms of law, the natural physical (or biological) and the Natural Moral. That naïveness can be terribly destructive of our society.

Whatever violates Natural Moral Law ultimately violates the human person and his or her pursuit of happiness, and inhibits the opportunity that is given to be fully human. How could any public official, therefore, really think it a luxury to be a moralist? Or how could he hope to contribute to the happiness of those he serves without in fact being a moralist? Indeed, I can't imagine a distinguished public health official saying that he doesn't care whether or not a course of action is morally sound as long as it's medically sound. What I'm certain he does, on the contrary, is convince himself that if it's medically sound, it's morally sound; that is, if medically it will save lives, it is the morally right thing to do, regardless of the means used. So he really does take the "moral" into account. It's simply that he gets mixed up in the way he does it—mixed up and ever so pragmatic—but really very "moral" after all.

Mayor Koch's proposal about condoms to prisoners is quite like the doctor's approach to clean needles, in its appeal to what he thinks of as compassion and common sense. Once allowance is made for political expediency, I believe that Mayor Koch really does feel that compassion and common sense require and justify his attitude about trying to prevent AIDS both with clean needles and condoms, about abortion, and about many other issues.

But "common sense" must offer some reliable evidence for its position. I have yet to see any reliable evidence that either condoms or clean needles will do what the Mayor seems to believe they will do in controlling AIDS.

Compassion is another matter altogether. Shakespeare speaks of the "charity which drives out charity." The orthopedic surgeon is not compassionate who refuses to fix a broken leg because the fixing will hurt. The therapist doesn't encourage an alcoholic to continue drinking because it will be painful to stop. A drug counselor doesn't recommend continuing on heroin because withdrawal is agonizing.

Etymologically, *compassion* means "to suffer with," not simply "to feel sorry for." It can be easy to feel sorry for people. Funeral parlors resound with "I'm sorry for your trouble." To suffer with a bereaved, really to be torn apart or empty or desolate, is not nearly so common. Many of us, however generous we have been in paying our call, or even attending a funeral, go home pretty much untroubled. The day's events readily overtake us.

Feeling sorry about a situation can readily lead to a quick fix. True compassion forces you to look at all the circumstances. What will be the aftermath of my "helping"? I feel sorry for a man trembling for want of a drink. Do I give him a drink even if it may kill him? Whom am I really feeling sorry for, the drunk or myself? Whom am I getting off the hook by giving him the drink, him or myself?

Compassion requires intense personal involvement. I can give a hungry street person money "for a sandwich," knowing it might be used for drugs, or I can go with him to a restaurant and buy him a meal. We are told that the famous Good Samaritan "had compassion" on the man who had been beaten, robbed and left for dead. The Samaritan picked him up, treated his wounds, took him back to an inn he had passed, asked the innkeeper to take care of him and promised he would return to pay for the man's room and board. Had the Good Samaritan simply felt sorry for the victim of crime, he would probably have kept going, shaking his head about the terrible things that happen to people.

Because we feel sorry for the poor, we may argue that a poor woman's abortion should be funded. If we are truly compassionate, we want to know why she is poor, why she seeks an abortion, how we can offer her an alternative. If she has the abortion, we will suffer its effects with her. We don't make her the victim of our "common sense"—that it will cost society so much if she delivers her baby. We don't make her the victim of feeling sorry for *ourselves,* and not really for her at all.

I believe that almost as an unconscious defense against the reality that human lives are involved—and human deaths—we can become extraordinarily abstract in our approach to abortion and other critical issues. It's not deliberate or malicious. It doesn't mean we're insincere. But in a world, in a city, in which we have so very many crushing problems, so many seemingly without solutions—crack, AIDS, violence, unwanted or undesirable pregnancies—we leap at "quick fixes." We weary, all of us, confronted with the overwhelming on a daily basis. In time, we try to preserve our sanity by distancing ourselves from the reality. Compassion tends to become an abstraction. It's what the heroic Dr. Rieux began to experience in Camus's *The Plague,* and it's understandable. But it fixes nothing.

Visiting and treating one dying plague victim after another,

> Rieux had nothing to look forward to but a long sequence of such scenes, renewed again and again. Yes, plague, like abstraction, was monotonous; perhaps only one factor changed, and that was Rieux himself. . . . All he was conscious of was a bleak indifference steadily gaining on him. . . . Rieux had learned that he need no longer steel himself against pity. One grows out of pity when it's useless. And in this feeling that his heart had slowly closed in on itself, the doctor found a solace, his only solace, for the almost unendurable burden of his days.[7]

The Natural Moral Law dinner was one of my longer dinners with the Mayor.

---

7. Albert Camus, *The Plague* (New York: Vintage Books, 1972), pp. 85–86.

THE MAYOR
EXECUTIVE
ORDER 50

THE CARDINAL
EXECUTIVE
ORDER 50
and
CHILD CARE

THE MAYOR

The struggle for justice in the City of New York has a long and proud history. The most recent group seeking justice, heretofore denied, has been the homosexual population. My own feeling is that justice denied to any group of our citizens requires us to say that justice is thereby denied to all of our citizens. For some reason, homophobia has been a constant in our society from time immemorial. In my judgment it is hard to justify such prejudice. On the other hand, it's also difficult to argue with religious beliefs, even though I might not agree with them. For example, while I personally deplored the Mormon belief that blacks could not enter heaven, I did not feel that I could denounce the Mormon religion. (The Mormon point of view on this subject was subsequently changed.) Neither do I denounce the Jewish Orthodox faith for believing that women cannot play a larger role in my religion as rabbis and cantors or even sit next to men in the synagogue. I just don't condone such beliefs. But I remain a member of the Conservative wing of the Jewish faith, and when I attend services it is at an Orthodox synagogue that observes the practices I deplore. Similarly, when the Catholic Church considers homosexual behavior to be totally unacceptable and a major sin, and declines to allow homosexual groups to have their own services, who am I to tell the Catholic Church that it has to change? That is for Catholics to do, not me, even though I personally deplore this particular position. Some believers—Catholic, Protestant, Jewish—say that "we hate the sin and love the sinner." I think it's fair to say that many of those committing the alleged sin are not so much interested in being loved as in being respected. In this case, love is not as important as respect and equality.

Clearly, government has an important role in bringing about the necessary changes. When I came into office, I immediately issued an executive order stating that City agencies may not discriminate against any person on the grounds of sexual orientation or affectional preference "in any manner of hiring or employment, housing, credit, contracting, provision of services, or any other matter whatsoever." The order was issued within the first thirty days of my administration, so it was one of my first official acts as Mayor. However, it protected people only from public discrimination. It took me another eight years in office to win, through enactment of the Gay Rights Law in 1986, the struggle to provide the same kind of protection against discrimination in the private sector. Imagine all the unnecessary suffering that took place in that period that might have been alleviated. The ultimate change in the law did reduce, though not eliminate, the discrimination. Much of it still exists, but it's now against the law. Since it is against the law, those who are discriminated against have a right to take legal action by going to the New York City Commission on Human Rights, which has the power to award compensation to those who have been subjected to discrimination and provide other remedies like reinstatement in a job with back pay.

It took a long time for the City Council to enact the Gay Rights Law, something made possible only because of a change in council leadership. While we were working to pass the legislation, I sought to impose by executive order restrictions on government contractors which would have eliminated some of the discriminatory practices in the private sector and bring it more in line with the public sector. I wanted to impose on those seeking to do business with the City of New York a requirement to agree, upon accepting city funds, not to discriminate.

On April 25, 1980, I issued Executive Order 50, which says that city contractors must be equal-opportunity employers. They may not discriminate on the basis of sexual orientation or any of the other grounds that have been covered by civil rights laws—race, religion, sex, national origin, marital status, age and disability.

In my opinion, the executive order did not require an employer to tolerate social behavior or types of dress that would be inappropriate on the job. It did not require any contractors to recruit people on the basis of their sexual orientation, and it certainly did not require a quota or goal of any kind. How could it? Since a person's sexual orientation should be, and under my executive order is, a totally private matter, no employer has the right to ask questions about anyone's sex life.

On May 28, 1980, I issued a directive to all City agencies setting forth procedures for implementing the order. I also transmitted to the various City agencies contract language prohibiting discrimination that was to be used by all of them in doing business with City contractors. That language was immediately included in all new contracts. Everything went along smoothly until 1984.

It was then, with the coming of John Cardinal O'Connor, that the Church for the first time since the issuance of the executive order took the position that it could not enter into these contracts. The Roman Catholic Church, through Catholic Charities, and in agreement with the City, entered into a lawsuit against the City so that the court could decide the executive order's legitimacy. Similar lawsuits were filed by the Salvation Army and Agudath Israel, an Orthodox Jewish social-service organization.

But it was the Salvation Army that first decided it could not continue to accept City contracts if they required a prohibition against discrimination based on sexual orientation. The aggregate of their contracts as I recall it was $4 million, and they are superb providers of services. I certainly did not want to lose their services to children and the homeless, and sought to convince them not to withdraw. But they were adamant. Then came similar threats by other religious providers to end services to the City if they were required to submit to this executive order. They took the position that the executive order was illegal and that they would challenge it in court, which from my point of view was totally responsible and the right place for the legal issues to be resolved.

The challenge by the Church was predicated partly on its view that under the First Amendment, the executive order was an unconstitutional infringement on religious freedom.

Another theory on which the religious groups based their challenge, and on which they ultimately won, was that, as Mayor, I could not issue an executive order concerning sexual orientation because there was no applicable federal, state or local legislation supporting it. In fact, just two weeks before the religious organizations started their lawsuits, the state's highest court decided a case that supported this theory.

The State Court of Appeals had struck down another executive order, one I had issued creating a set-aside program for small businesses to ensure that they would be awarded a percentage of the City's construction work. The purpose of the order was to encourage bidding by more minority construction firms, and firms headed by women, without imposing racial, ethnic or gender quotas. The Court of Appeals said that regardless of how desirable the purpose of my order was, it was invalid on the grounds that it exceeded the power of the mayor because there was no legislation authorizing me to create such a program.

Even before the religious organizations brought their lawsuits, we knew that the court decision invalidating the set-aside program raised a question about the City's continued ability to enforce the provision of E.O. 50 concerning sexual orientation, since at that time there was no federal, state or local legislation prohibiting discrimination on that ground. There was a lot at stake. The City's ability to protect the workers of all City contractors, not only the religiously affiliated organizations, was in jeopardy. The E.O. 50 program covered thousands of contracts, worth close to $3 billion annually. The Catholic Church organizations' share of this amount was about $70 million. I had to see what could be done to make sure that all of E.O. 50 could continue to be enforced.

At that time, the chance of getting the City Council to adopt legislation concerning sexual orientation was less than slim. The legislative battle for enactment of a gay rights law had gone on for years. We continued to fight the battle, and eventually we won. But I needed a more immediate way to address the problem. Since the Board of Estimate has considerable power over City contracts under the City Charter, my legal advisers and I determined that it would be useful to have the Board of Estimate adopt a resolution that could serve as legal authority separate from the executive order, and would allow the City to continue to ensure that employees of City contractors would not have to face discrimination on the basis of sexual orientation if that aspect of E.O. 50 was held to be invalid. The Board adopted a resolution on June 28, 1984, that ratified E.O. 50 and specified that City contracts should continue to prohibit discrimination by City contractors.

On September 5, 1984, State Supreme Court Judge Alvin Klein ruled that the sexual-orientation provision of the executive order was invalid because there was no legislation prohibiting that kind of discrimination. He also ruled that the resolution adopted by the Board of Estimate ratifying E.O. 50 was "of no consequence" because the Board of Estimate is not a legislative body.

I was dismayed by the court ruling, and so were the other members of the Board of Estimate. The Board met on September 12, 1984, and we talked about what to do next. Corporation Counsel Frederick A. O. Schwarz, Jr., was asked whether the Board could decline to approve a contract unless the contractor agreed not to discriminate against homosexuals. He advised us at the meeting, and in a written memorandum later, that, yes, it could be done. He reasoned that under the City Charter, the Board of Estimate could insist that particular terms be included in a contract. Did the State Supreme Court's decision about the executive order mean that the Board of Estimate could not exercise this power with respect to a term concerning sexual orientation? The memorandum acknowledged that the decision could be interpreted that way, but concluded that the issue really remained open, and that the better view was that the Board of Estimate could insist on including such a clause in contracts that came before it for approval. In fact, the State Supreme Court later upheld this view.

When I received the legal memorandum, I wrote immediately to the Board of Estimate urging the members to require that each contract contain a provision prohibiting discrimination based on sexual orientation.

The Board of Estimate adopted such a resolution on October 25, 1984. It applied to sixty-one proposed social-service contracts, including extensions of contracts with religious organizations. Within days, the religious organizations were in court with a new lawsuit seeking a temporary restraining order, which was granted on October 31, 1984. However, after hearing arguments in the case, State Supreme Court Judge David Saxe issued a decision on November 15, 1984, that denied a preliminary injunction and vacated the temporary restraining order. He ruled not only that the Board of Estimate had the authority to require the nondiscrimination clause, but also that the Board of Estimate had a duty under the federal and state constitutions to ensure that government funds not be provided to those who practice invidious discrimination, including discrimination based on sexual orientation.

This was the first judicial vindication of our position that the City could act to protect the rights of homosexual employees of its contractors. We were elated. The religious organizations appealed.

In May 1985, the Appellate Division reversed Judge Klein's ruling and held that the sexual-orientation provision of the executive order and the resolution adopted by the board of Estimate back in June 1984 were valid. However, this new victory was short-lived. On June 28, 1985, the Court of Appeals issued its ruling that the sexual-orientation provision of the executive order was invalid because there was no legislative authority for it. It was a great disappointment to me, and I believe it caused a great deal of pain for many New Yorkers. But it actually could have been worse. At least the court left open the question about the government's ability to enforce such an order against religious organizations.

After the decision came down, I asked the corporation counsel for advice about whether to appeal it to the U.S. Supreme Court. He consulted with civil rights organizations, all of which agreed that an appeal would not be wise, and could even result in greater harm by giving the Supreme Court the occasion to determine what protection the Constitution affords to individuals from discrimination on the basis of sexual orientation. It is important to pick the right case as the test case when asking the Supreme Court to determine such a highly significant issue, and for various reasons the executive-order case did not seem to be a strong test case. The better test case seemed to be the one concerning the resolution adopted by the Board of Estimate in October 1984, which was still pending, and in which the City had so far prevailed. Unfortunately, you can't take a case you're winning to the Supreme Court.

According to the Court of Appeals, what was needed to validate the sexual-orientation provision of E.O. 50 was legislation. We had been pressing the City Council for years to enact a gay rights law, and we redoubled our efforts to obtain this legislation. This time, because there were several new factors in our favor, we achieved a breakthrough.

Council Majority Leader Tom Cuite, an implacable opponent of gay rights legislation, had resigned. The new Vice-Chair and Majority Leader of the Council, Peter Vallone, while personally opposed to a gay rights law for religious reasons, said that this was a matter of conscience and he would not prevent the bill from being brought up for a vote in the General Welfare Committee.

The Chair of the Council's General Welfare Committee was Sam Horwitz from Brooklyn, a very compassionate and able man who had not been publicly identified with support for this bill. He told me that he did, in fact, support it and believed that in a quiet way he could put together a majority on his committee. He said it was important that there be no amendments to the bill because once the amendment procedure began, he wouldn't be able to control the final version of the bill adopted by the Council. So we agreed that we would do whatever we could to prevent amendments once the bill was on the floor for a vote by the full council.

Many questions were raised at the Council committee hearing about the effects of the proposed bill. Would it promote homosexual behavior? No. The bill stated explicitly that it would not endorse or give special privileges to a particular group or community, or promote any particular behavior or "life-style." Would the law require employers to meet quotas concerning employment on the basis of sexual orientation? No again. Quotas would violate the privacy of the very people the law was meant to protect; you can't enforce quotas without asking pertinent information about an employee's sex life, and such questioning was clearly prohibited. Would the law require employers to tolerate inappropriate behavior at the workplace? Definitely not. The law stated clearly that employers have the right to insist that employees meet bona fide qualifications for the job. That includes proper dress and behavior in the office or at the work site.

Other questions were raised at the committee hearing. If the new law expressly prohibited quotas, did it instead call for hiring goals and timetables? Would it require schools to teach about homosexuality in the classroom? Corporation Counsel Schwarz and I testified that the law would not require these things. Our testimony was backed by a legal opinion the Corporation Counsel issued to the committee before its vote. It explained that the same bar to quotas in the bill—the prohibition against employers asking questions about a worker's sex life—would also prevent goals and timetables for hiring. As to the law's effect on schools, the opinion made clear that nothing in the bill or the City's Human Rights Law authorizes the City's Human Rights Commission to require teaching on any subject, or permits it to interfere with school instruction in any way.

Our arguments were persuasive. The committee voted in support of the bill and reported it to the full council. We weren't done running the gauntlet, however. Even though we believed that a majority of the council members would support the Gay Rights Bill, there was a movement afoot that placed it in jeopardy. I was advised that a number of council members whose votes were essential for its passage were concerned that the bill would have an adverse impact on small homeowners who lived in multifamily homes. There is a provision in the City's Human Rights Law that exempts owners of two-family houses who actually live in their house from the prohibition against refusing to rent to tenants on the basis of race, religion, sex, national origin, marital status, age or handicap. This provision essentially means that if you own the two-family house in which you live, you don't have to rent the other part of it to anybody you don't want to share a roof with. Some council members felt that in the case of sexual orientation, the two-family home exemption should be extended to cover three- and four-family homes as well.

It appeared to me that there might be a sufficient number of votes to defeat the Gay Rights Bill if the issue of exemptions for multifamily homes was not addressed. The Council's vote was scheduled for March 20. It seemed that there would be enough votes in the Council on that date to adopt an amendment forcing through the multifamily-house provision. Under the law, when the Council adopts new legislation it can do so by a simple majority vote. But the law also provides that if the Council amends or changes a bill on the same day it votes on it, a two-thirds majority is required for the bill to become law. We did not think there would be enough votes for a two-thirds majority. If the housing amendments were adopted by the Council, we would have to ask that the vote be postponed until it could be determined by a simple majority. By law the postponement would have to be for at least seven days. But if that happened we might well lose the momentum that had been building for the bill and was crucial to its passage.

I had to do something to make sure that we wouldn't lose the votes of the members who were concerned about the housing issue. I offered a compromise. If they would vote for the bill in its present form, I would not oppose the enactment of another law later on amending the Gay Rights Law to provide an extended housing exemption. I agreed to allow this to happen as long as the exemption went no further than one comparable to the exemption provided in the federal Fair Housing Act, which covers owners who live in multifamily homes of up to four families. I made it clear that I would not support such an amendment, but neither would I use my veto power to block it. The compromise was accepted, and the law enacted on March 20, by a vote of 21 to 14. I signed it on April 2. The room was packed. When I put my pen to the paper and actually signed the bill into law, you could feel the elation in the room. Judging from the jubilant celebration that broke out, it was apparent that for many people, this was their version of the Emancipation Proclamation.

We weren't finished yet, however. Since the council was next going to consider the housing-exemption amendment, I thought it would be a good idea to offer other amendments that would clarify for any lingering doubters the questions as to whether the law had hiring goals and timetables or dictated that courses on homosexuality be taught in the schools. On May 6, the Council adopted a bill amending the Gay Rights Law to include these provisions. It also extended the housing exemption, but not in accordance with the federal Fair Housing Act. The exemption adopted by the Council was much broader, covering apartments occupied by family members of a building's owner, plus three additional apartments in the building. This meant that a five-family building would be totally exempt if it was occupied by the owner in one apartment and a member of the owner's family in another apartment, with the remaining apartments occupied by non-relatives. Depending on the number of apartments occupied by the owner's family members in a given building, owners of much larger apartment buildings might be able to discriminate at will. I couldn't go for that. I had agreed to hold my veto in check for a housing amendment, but not this one and certainly not for this result.

The law requires that I hold a public hearing within twenty days of the adoption of new legislation by the Council. On May 23 I held such a hearing. Not a single member of the public came forward to ask that I sign the housing amendment into law. But a great number came forward to plead that I veto it. The Corporation Counsel and the General Counsel for the Human Rights Commission had already advised me that the housing amendment was a violation of the agreement I had reached with members of the City Council. On June 4, backed by this sound legal advice and strong, well-informed public opinion, I vetoed the amendment and set forth my reasons in a formal veto message to the Council.

Because the housing amendment was tied to the two amendments I had proposed, I was vetoing them as well. But as I explained in the veto message, the questions about hiring goals and teaching about homosexuality in the schools which they sought to clarify had been answered at the council hearing, and in the Corporation Counsel's formal opinion, so that the amendments were not needed. While the amendments I had proposed would have promoted greater public understanding of the law, it was not essential that they be enacted. I explained that if the Council adopted another bill, which provided a housing exemption no larger than the exemption I had promised not to veto, I would feel morally bound to live up to that promise. But I expressed the hope that the Council would not adopt a housing amendment at all. I said it wouldn't be right to distinguish among classes of people protected by the Human Rights Law by offering a different level of protection against discrimination on the basis of sexual orientation. Any such differentiation in the law would surely be challenged, and the litigation would prolong the divisive controversy over the Gay Rights Law.

The Council did not override my veto, and it never adopted another amendment to the Gay Rights Law.

After the gay rights legislation had been in effect for a year, *The New York Times* did an article in which it examined its impact. They quoted the statement I made at the time I signed the bill: "The sky is not going to fall. There isn't going to be any dramatic change in the life of this city." *The Times* concluded that what I predicted had, in fact, occurred. However, tremendous benefits came from this legislation. Gay men and lesbian women finally believed they had a right to be treated with respect and without discrimination, and those who engaged in illegal discrimination could be punished. Regrettably, an increasing number of complaints before the Human Rights Commission today are those of gay men and lesbian women complaining of physical violence perpetrated against them. However, when those same complaints existed earlier, there was no civil forum in which to voice them. Today there is a place to complain and, if you establish the validity of your complaint, to receive compensation for your damages. I am proud of the fact that I had a major role in establishing that principle.

The enactment of the Gay Rights Law gave me the necessary authority to again require that City contractors not discriminate on the basis of sexual orientation. On June 20, 1986, I issued another executive order, number 94, amending Executive Order 50 to reflect the

Gay Rights Law. Executive Order 94 contains special language about religious organizations, which is taken directly from the Gay Rights Law. Basically, it says that the law does not bar religious organizations from selecting employees in a manner calculated to promote their religious principles. Since the State Court of Appeals has said that my authority to issue executive orders must be based on policy embodied in legislation, and the Gay Rights Law contains this policy about religious organizations, the special provision was included in the executive order so that it would be consistent with the law.

Some religious organizations take the view that this special provision exempts them from the entire law. The City does not agree. We take the position that there might be constitutional limits on how far the exemption can be applied under the executive order.

If we insisted on perfectly resolving this issue there probably would never be another contract signed between the City and a religious organization. We agreed therefore to leave the interpretation to such a time as there was a specific complaint about the lack of compliance with the executive order by a religious organization.

The underlying issue between Church and State as to whether or not the Church is subject to this order—we believe it is and they believe it is not—has not yet been resolved. But we hope the ongoing dialogue and cooperation between Church and City will lead to a clear and workable resolution. Even without one at this point, we have managed to accommodate one another. Church and State found a way in New York City to work together and respect each other.

Every year there is a Gay Pride parade on Fifth Avenue. About 100,000 people come from all over the nation to march in the largest parade of its kind. There is great goodwill from the spectators who line the sidewalks. How do I know? Because I march in that parade as I march in every other Fifth Avenue parade (except the Fourth of July and Labor Day, when I am out of town, at the beach). There are about twenty of them, representing various racial, ethnic and religious groups. Those who join the Gay Pride parade are just one more of the groups living in the city that I have a responsibility for, and for whom I show respect by marching. The parade starts at Central Park, goes down Fifth Avenue, turns west at Washington Square Park and continues over to Christopher Street in the West Village where it passes the site of the Stonewall bar, a special place for the gay community. It was at the Stonewall in 1968 that gays battled with police who sought to arrest them in a crackdown on gay bars. I join the parade at Forty-second Street every year, and I am often asked why. The answer is because of the continuing hostility gays have toward the Archdiocese and the Cardinal's position on gay rights. There is always a demonstration—sometimes civil and sometimes not so civil, including mockery of the Church—in front of St. Patrick's Cathedral at Forty-ninth Street. I do not want to be perceived by anyone as part of such demonstrations or in any way condoning them by being in the parade when it passes in front of St. Patrick's. So I pick up the march at Forty-second Street. It's another accommodation between Church and State.

The relationship between Church and State came under even greater strain in the case of *Wilder* v. *Bernstein*.

The Wilder Case was initiated by the American Civil Liberties Union in 1973—long before I became Mayor. About ten years later, after a decade of complex legal motions, judicial rulings and attempts at negotiation between the parties, the Wilder Case had reached a critical juncture. The case had to be either tried or settled. The stakes were high. The resolution of the Wilder Case threatened the long-standing contractual relationship between the City and the Catholic Church under which the Church provided essential foster-care services. Resolution of *Wilder* also placed strains on my new friendship with the man named to replace Cardinal Cooke in the midst of the *Wilder* controversy, Archbishop John O'Connor.

At the center of the *Wilder* story is the ACLU lawsuit. The American Civil Liberties Union filed the *Wilder* brief on behalf of black children who were neither Catholic nor Jewish, alleging that New York City's foster-care system was unconstitutional because it violated the religious freedom of these children, violated the First Amendment's guarantee of separation of Church and State, and denied these children equal access to foster-care services because of their race and their religion.

Although the legal issues involved in the Wilder Case may sound arcane, what was ultimately at issue was the survival of the foster-care system of New York City—a system that had a unique history of complex relationships between the City and religious organizations.

The City of New York provides direct services to only a small percentage of the children in foster care. In June 1988 there were slightly more than 20,000 children in foster care. The City, through Special Services for Children, a City agency, operates a direct-care program for only 1,500 of them. The rest are cared for through City contracts with private child-care agencies, most of which have religious affiliations.

Because of the unique history of immigrant populations in New York City, the religious organizations most involved in providing foster-care services were Jewish or Catholic, and understandably, they provided services principally to their own orphaned and abandoned children. Protestant organizations were less active in the area of foster care, in large part because there was less of a need within that community.

Over the last thirty years, the nature of the foster-care population has changed dramatically. The children who are now in the foster-care system are older. They more frequently exhibit behavioral problems. The foster-care population has also changed from being overwhelmingly white to being overwhelmingly minority, mostly black. Due to the increase in the numbers of black children in foster care, Protestants have now become the dominant group. Responding to this change in the population, the clientele of the private agencies has necessarily changed. Now, Jewish and Catholic agencies are accepting increasing numbers of black and Protestant children.

Against this historical backdrop, the *Wilder* suit raised a difficult question. Should the religious affiliation of the private agency and the religious background of the child play any role in the placement of the child in foster care? Or should the system operate blind to any religious considerations and evaluate solely the physical, psychological and emotional needs of the child? What should be the role of religion in a child's upbringing, and what role should the City play in providing for a religious environment?

In the course of the discussions in the Wilder Case, the City and the American Civil Liberties Union agreed that the Orthodox Jewish children should not be treated on first-come, first-served basis, distributed among all private agencies, but rather should be serviced exclusively by an Orthodox Jewish organization. The rationale was that their religious beliefs were especially rigorous, permeating every aspect of their daily activities. They posed a unique situation, much like the Amish children who had been treated differently by the Supreme Court in earlier cases. Furthermore, their numbers were very small (slightly over one hundred). So they were excluded from the discussion regarding the extent to which the religion of a foster child should be considered in making an assignment to a foster-care agency.

Should we be blind to a child's religious background when providing for foster care? My own feeling, from the very beginning of our deliberations on the Wilder Case, was that we could not lightly dismiss the religious dimension of the services being provided nor the religious needs of the children. As a result of my intuitive belief in the value of the religious dimension in the provision of foster-care services, I was sympathetic to the Church's resistance to the notion of first-come, first-served assignments.

I believe that one should respect the religious claims, beliefs and doctrines of other people. You can't trample on someone else's religion. Religion is something you are born into. When you become an adult, you have a right to change your religion. And no one should force anyone else to practice a religion, except perhaps for the very youngest. So, in my thinking about religion, I start with the conviction that religious beliefs constitute the ultimate personal attribute, defining one's relationship to one's self, family, community and God. Government should not lightly say that such a deeply personal attribute is irrelevant to deciding what is the appropriate environment for children who need foster care when they cannot be with their natural families.

My views on religion go beyond merely saying that all of us—particularly those of us who, as public officials, act on behalf of the government—must be respectful of the religious beliefs of others. I have a positive belief that a religious upbringing—whether it is Orthodox or, as was the case for me, simply an acknowledgment of religious and cultural traditions with (regrettably) only occasional visits to synagogue—is helpful in setting a child on the right course in life.

Allow me to turn to the school system to elaborate upon this point. I believe heart and soul that the religious values imparted at parochial schools have made those schools better—at least in perception, and, I think, in fact—than our public schools, where values are not as central to the school's teachings. Obviously, all teachers, by virtue of the content of the classroom instruction, are imparting values to their students, but in public schools they don't teach values directly, whereas in the parochial schools they teach them directly as spiritual values that are derived directly from religious beliefs.

Thus my own upbringing, my respect for the inviolability of religious beliefs, and my observations about the benefits of religious instruction made me sympathetic to the position of the Catholic Church in the *Wilder* controversy. I did not believe, as some argued, that the City would be better off if *none* of the foster-care services were provided by religious institutions. Quite the contrary—I believed that the children received better services because so many of them received those services at agencies infused with a religious dimension.

So, to be true to my personal convictions, I sought to retain a foster-care system in New York City in which religious institutions played a major role.

If this was my objective, one might ask, then why did the City enter into settlement negotiations with the ACLU? Why did we not go to trial and defend our system against their attack? The lawyers for the City who advised me during this period of time argued strongly that it was in the City's interest that we enter into negotiations with the other parties. In that way we would be able to retain control of the foster-care system rather than run the risk of losing in court and having the system administered by a federal judge.

In my opinion, the risk of losing was too great. If we suffered an adverse federal ruling, our entire foster-care system would have had to be provided directly by the City. The Catholic, Protestant and Jewish welfare agencies would no longer administer social-service programs under contract. We would have stood nearly a century of philanthropic tradition on its head. Aside from the tremendous disruption such a ruling would have produced, we would also have lost something that both I and the Cardinal valued—the role of religious institutions in providing services to children.

When the *Wilder* controversy came to a head, the Corporation Counsel was Fritz Schwarz. He had been involved in extensive negotiations with the American Civil Liberties Union and had produced, after long negotiations with the ACLU, a proposed settlement. Throughout the negotiations, we had consulted with the private religious agencies involved in the foster-care system.

When I discussed the Wilder Case with Fritz, it became clear to me that his major concern—and the fundamental concept underlying the proposed settlement—was that the foster-care system should make a logical match between a child and the right service provider. As outlined in the proposed settlement, children entering the foster-care system would be assigned to the various agencies that receive local funds primarily on the basis of the service needs of the individual child. This seemed to make eminent sense to me. Contrary to some characterizations of the proposed system, by plaintiffs other than the Catholic Church, it would not operate strictly on a first-come, first-served basis—that sort of purely random assignment would be too impersonal and would not account for the particular needs of each child and the differing quality and range of services provided by the agencies.

I also liked the fact that the proposed settlement did not totally ignore the religious dimension of the foster-care system and the religious needs of some children. According to the complex terms of the proposed agreement, if a child was to be assigned to a congregate-care setting, the child's parent could specify that the child should be assigned to an agency with a particular religious affiliation, and that request would be honored unless there was another child with greater need for the bed. And in the case of the foster boarding homes, the religious background of the child could legitimately be considered, but not as the exclusive factor. Thus, although the child's religious background could play a role in making the match between child and agency, it would never be the sole, automatic determinant.

The position of the Civil Liberties Union was that if Catholic agencies were allowed to prefer Catholic children and Jewish agencies were allowed to prefer Jewish children—in other words, if a child's religion was used to place the child in foster care rather than the totality of the child's needs—the black Protestant children would be accepted only by Protestant agencies, which, in the view of the ACLU, provided the lowest-quality services among private agencies.

The Catholic and Jewish organizations involved in the Wilder Case disputed the assertions of the ACLU and strongly objected to the proposed remedy of first come, first served according principally to need, not religion. The Archdiocese pointed to statistics to show that they did not discriminate on the basis of race, ethnicity or religion—in fact, they said they would provide services to children whether they were Protestant or Catholic (they received only a handful of Jewish children).

As the controversy unfolded, the allegations of racial discrimination receded into the background and other volatile issues involving Church-State relations took center stage. In addition to the role of religion in placing a foster child, the Wilder Case involved two other sensitive questions: Should religious social-service organizations under contract with the City be required to provide access to family-planning information—including information about birth control and abortion, both of which are anathema under Catholic doctrine? And should those agencies also be required to downplay their religious character by limiting the display of religious symbols?

Understandably, the Archdiocese cared strongly about the fact that the Civil Liberties Union was insisting that as part of the settlement agreement, the presence of religious symbols—including the ultimate symbol of Christian religious belief, the crucifix—should be limited in the congregate-care settings run by the Catholic Church. Not surprisingly, the Church was deeply distressed with this proposal by the ACLU.

Like their Catholic counterparts, all of the Jewish organizations were incensed that under the proposed settlement, they would not be permitted to prefer a Jewish child coming through the system over a Catholic or Protestant child who, in most cases, would be black or Hispanic. (Remember that the proposed stipulation excluded the ultra-religious Jewish organizations that took care of Orthodox Jewish children, a relatively small number.) The *raison d'être* of the Jewish organizations for entering the welfare field was twofold—to take care of Jewish kids (which was not unreasonable), and to offer charity by providing social services, paid for in great part by taxes but, in addition, involving the expenditure of large sums of money out of the organization's own budget. Why, they argued, should they provide any services at all, since they no longer would be able to have a minimum, let alone maximum, number of Jewish kids in their system? It didn't make sense!

As I mentioned above, for a number of reasons I was sympathetic to these arguments. I told Fritz I thought that Catholic organizations ought to have *some* right to select Catholics over Protestants and Jews, and Jewish organizations should have *some* right to prefer Jewish children over others. On numerous occasions, the Jewish and Catholic groups came in and remonstrated with me, sometimes in the presence of the Corporation Counsel and sometimes not, and said they would withdraw from providing their services if they were pressed to accept this agreement. I did not doubt the depth and sincerity of their position and took seriously their statement that they would consider no longer providing services under contract with the City.

We were clearly at an impasse. Because I was convinced that the City should not go to trial and risk a federal-court ruling that we could not enter into contracts with religious organizations (why increase the risk of losing the services of the Catholic and Jewish agencies?), I believed we should abide by the settlement, thereby preserving a role for religious foster-care agencies. At the same time, the Catholic and Jewish organizations wanted to test the validity of their legal position.

So I asked Fritz Schwarz why we couldn't suggest that the Archdiocese and the Jewish groups be given an opportunity, with our encouragement, to present their argument at a full hearing before the district court? If they were then still not satisfied, they would be free to take an appeal from the final order of the court when we entered into the stipulation, and while we would be required to defend the order, we would not in any way seek to impede their making their full arguments and getting the appeal expeditiously heard. At first both the Archdiocese and the Jewish groups wanted us either not to agree to the stipulation or to take the appeal. But we had already decided that we would not reject the stipulation and go to trial. So we urged the Cardinal and his lawyers not simply to withdraw as they had threatened to, but to pursue their options before the federal court, including taking an appeal, which they did. We made the same suggestion to the Jewish groups and they joined with the Archdiocese in the appeal. The appeal was heard by the United States Court of Appeals for the Second Circuit on June 24, 1987.

They lost the appeal—or so it seemed. When I got the call from Peter Zimroth—who knows that my position in this matter is very sympathetic to the position of the Church and the Jewish organizations—he said, "Ed, I've got both good news and bad news. Which do you want to hear first?" I said, "Tell me the good news." He said, "We won a big case." Then I said, "Tell me the bad news." "We won the Wilder Case." It was rather cute—he was recognizing my feelings on the matter. What's so interesting about our adversarial judicial system in cases like this is you don't necessarily have clear losers or winners: As I understand it, the Cardinal's lawyers told him they'd won at the same time the Corporation Counsel was reporting to me.

Both sides viewed the court of appeals decision as a victory. The question now became: Could the City and the Archdiocese agree upon contractual language that would meet the requirements of the federal law and the requirements of religious doctrine?

Stan Brezenoff, the First Deputy Mayor, and Monsignor William Toohy, the Cardinal's representative, worked out contract language that was acceptable to both sides. It made no mention of the family-planning services to be provided. It made no mention of the Wilder Case by name. It simply said:

"It is expressly understood and agreed that the services provided [under the contract] shall conform, comply with, and be provided in accordance with the applicable provisions of federal, state and local laws, rules and regulations, as well as those court determinations, including without limitation, decisions, orders, judgments, etc., generally or specifically applicable to the operation of the 'child welfare' or 'foster care' system and any of the parties to the Agreement."

In more straightforward layman's language, we simply said that all laws, rules and regulations would have to be carried out under the contract. No mention of *Wilder*. No mention of birth control. No mention of religious symbols. Simply an agreement to abide by all laws—which now include the *Wilder* decision, which, as a federal decision, is the law of the land.

We did, however, include a stipulation in the contract that has come to be known as the "conscience clause." We agreed that the City could not "demand or require the [Catholic Church] to the performance or implementation of any service, activity, policy practice or procedure which may be contrary to the [Church's] religious beliefs or moral convictions." With this clause the Church reasserted the inviolability of its religious beliefs and practices—something that the City never intended to threaten.

So the Wilder Case draws to a close. The case does not stand for the proposition of first come, first served. It stands for the proposition that foster children with needs should be assigned on the basis of their needs, not solely on the basis of their religion. Putting this proposition into concrete terms, it means that if three children need foster-care placement and one is white and Catholic, another is white and Jewish, and the third is black and Protestant, and the third child is most in need, that child will be given preference over the other two. In other words, the black Protestant child would be placed in a Catholic or Jewish agency ahead of a Catholic or Jewish child who was less in need.

The Wilder Case also means that federal law will be carried out that requires access to family-planning and abortion services. We will not require that religious institutions directly provide these services in violation of their religious doctrine, or that individuals do so in violation of their religious beliefs. Instead, the City of New York, through its own personnel, will provide family-planning information and abortion services away from the property of the religious foster homes. But, under our agreement, the religious institutions may not decline to make the children available when the City requests them for that purpose. Obviously the Church can apply to the court for relief if we make demands they believe to be in violation of their rights or which violate the court's ruling.

I think the outcome of the Wilder Case is a fair resolution of a set of particularly thorny issues that go to the heart of the relationship between the Catholic Church, and its Cardinal, and the City of New York and its Mayor.

But we all have our obligations of office. The Cardinal has his. I have mine. My primary obligation is to carry out the law. In the Wilder Case, I think I was able to see that the law was carried out while still preserving a role for religious institutions in meeting the needs of our City. The Cardinal found a way to continue to serve the children of the City and keep his religious values. It may be that all we have done is postpone an impasse to another day. But each additional day of service is one more good day for a child so served.

THE CARDINAL

Historian Barbara Tuchman argues that "the pursuit by government of policies contrary to their own interests" is a "phenomenon noticeable throughout history regardless of place or period." She argues well. In her study *The March of Folly: From Troy to Vietnam,*[1] she calls the Trojan Horse "the prototype of all tales of human conflict," and begins her study with the story of the famous Wooden Horse built outside the gates of Troy by the Greeks. Most everyone knows the story. The Trojans, persuaded against all reason and instinct, accept into their city the Horse which they believe is a gift from the Greeks. They are overcome when the Greek soldiers hiding inside the Wooden Horse open the gates of Troy to their compatriots lurking in ships hidden nearby. Slaughter, rape, pillage follow. Troy falls, the Trojan War ends with the Greeks victorious.

Mrs. Tuchman brilliantly reveals the "Trojan Horse" in historical episodes in the folly that has rejected reason and has driven government after government to open its gates to its own destruction. She does not exempt Church government by those Renaissance popes whose "folly lay not so much in being irrational as in being totally estranged from [their] appointed task."

Mrs. Tuchman will not be distressed if I do not necessarily agree with every one of her conclusions. (I might even be tougher on some popes than she is.). Nevertheless, I take her and her basic theme very seriously indeed: The folly of irrationality has far too frequently marked civil government, and the folly of estrangement from its ap-

1. Barbara W. Tuchman, *The March of Folly: From Troy to Vietnam* (New York: Knopf, 1984)

pointed task has too often marked Church government. This is, in my view, a tragically accurate analysis. It is the folly of both irrationality and estrangement that can drive us to abandon our respective jurisdictional responsibilities and values, delineated in the first chapter, and to open our respective gates to a Trojan Horse that conceals within itself the power to destroy us. I use as illustrative the unattractive stories of Executive Order 50 and the fifteen-year child-care battle, *Wilder* v. *Bernstein.* I begin with Executive Order 50.

The details are tedious, but they have never been fully published, and much of the confusion about this pivotal case is attributable to ignorance of the issues. Further, the case was important because it promised to affect for a long time to come the nature of my relationship as Archbishop of New York with the Mayor of New York, and with a number of people in and outside the City, in and outside the Archdiocese. But the primary reason I shall discuss this case in some detail is that it is an excellent example of the conflict that arises between Church and State over questions of jurisdiction and values. Executive Order 50 is part of New York's history now, a classic illustration of the way in which the City can upset the Church-State balance by attempting to exercise excessive jurisdiction.

I came to town close to midnight on an auspicious date, the seventeenth of March, the Feast of Saint Patrick. The year was 1984. The annual parade had gone without a hitch. The Friendly Sons of Saint Patrick had wrapped up their annual dinner. I was to be formally installed as the eighth Archbishop of New York on the nineteenth, Feast of Saint Joseph, my choice. I had never heard of Executive Order 50.

Executive Order 50, signed on April 25, 1980, by Mayor Koch, antedated my arrival by almost four years. Among other things, the order prohibited those contracting with the City from engaging in employment discrimination on the basis of "sexual orientation or affectional preference." The Bureau of Labor Services (BLS) was created to enforce the order.

As far as the institutional memory of the Archdiocese has been able to tell me, the order didn't seem to generate a great deal of practical anxiety, because, one gets the impression, nobody thought it would be implemented. It was apparently interpreted as political lip service.

Evidently the Bureau of Labor Services interpreted it differently. The BLS issued twenty-eight pages of detailed regulations on January 21, 1982, to implement Executive Order 50.

It sounds simple. The Mayor issued an order saying that those organizations who receive money from the City to perform services (for example, child care) may not discriminate on the basis of "sexual orientation or affectional preference." What mischief that phrase was to provoke. A little background will be helpful.

The responsibility for the care of children rests upon the State when parents are unable or unwilling to meet their obligations as guardians. The State, standing in the place of parents, must address all needs of the child, including health, educational and religious requirements. The City contracts with private child-care agencies, such as those associated with the Archdiocese of New York, and then reimburses a portion of the costs borne by these agencies, as provided by New York law. The majority of these agencies (some 90 percent) are owned and operated by religious organizations, some going back to the early nineteenth century. Fifteen child-care agencies are run by or are affiliated with the Archdiocese of New York.

The Mayor's executive order was not merely a restatement of existing antidiscrimination law (prohibiting discrimination on the basis of race, creed, handicap or sex, etc.). It attempted to add a "protected category" not recognized by any state or federal law. The new protected category ("sexual orientation or affectional preference") had never been legislatively approved, despite the introduction of gay rights bills to the City Council. Furthermore, the implementing regulations of E.O. 50 required "affirmative action," which meant Church-sponsored agencies would be required to actively *recruit* persons of homosexual and bisexual inclination. The practical effect of the regulations was that any organization contracting with the City would have to agree to having a fixed percentage of homosexuals and bisexuals in its employ, the quota being established by the BLS.[2]

In the fall of 1983, the BLS demanded that Church-sponsored social-service agencies (Jewish, Protestant, Catholic) comply with the executive order or lose the funding that came with City contracts for child care (involving many millions of dollars).

Some of our child-care agencies had contracts with the City that were up for renewal. On advice of counsel, these agencies signed the contracts containing E.O. 50 language but did two things: (1) They struck out the words "sexual orientation" and "affectional preference" whenever they appeared in the contract and (2) they added a dis-

---

2. The City seems to deny repeatedly that "recruiting" was a requirement. It need only read its own BLS regulations.

claimer that acknowledged the application of and continued compliance with all city, state and federal human rights laws, but excluded the new "protected category" E.O. 50 attempted to create.

The Salvation Army requested a religious exemption on the grounds that it did not discriminate, but because of religious convictions could not pledge to ignore homosexuality in all its hirings. The request was denied and the Mayor publicly announced that in 1984 Salvation Army contracts would not be renewed. The episode received extensive press coverage and the Mayor publicly stated that in 1984 he could not understand the Army's position since Catholic Charities had signed the contracts. (The Mayor did not publicize that Catholic Charities had signed contracts only after substantially altering them with disclaimers as noted above.)

All this had happened before I arrived in the Archdiocese. When I became involved, following the death of my predecessor, Cardinal Cooke, some of the press took me to task on grounds that Cardinal Cooke hadn't objected to the order. Why should I? The answer was clear to anyone who had been tracking the case. Cardinal Cooke had become far too ill to be pursuing such cases personally well *before* the BLS began enforcement of the executive order. As the case began heating up, he was actually incommunicado, hanging to life by a thread of will. He died on October 6, 1983, before the BLS "take it or leave it" demand was activated. The media critics not only hadn't done their homework, they didn't know Cardinal Cooke. The cardinal was a very gentle man, but no lion ever protected his domain against invaders more fiercely than he protected his beloved Church.

In any event, as memory serves me, I was in office for all of one week when I was confronted with having to make a momentous decision concerning a matter about which I knew literally nothing. My then vicar general, Bishop Joseph T. O'Keefe (now bishop of Syracuse, New York), an astute and experienced counselor, knew the Archdiocese as the back of his hand. He and the director of Catholic Charities, the agency immediately responsible for child care, informed me that the BLS was serious about E.O. 50 (all a mystery to me), and that the ax would fall on our child-care institutions in June. City funding of child care under Catholic auspices in the Archdiocese[3]

3. This would initially affect only those agencies in and under the jurisdiction of New York City. As noted previously, the Archdiocese extends well beyond the borders of the City.

would cease unless child-care agencies agreed to sign contracts that included the provision of E.O. 50, without any alterations of language or disclaimers of any sort.

A lot of money was involved. Around $140 *million* every year. Some 70 of these millions came from the City, another 50 million from federal and state governments, and 20 million from private contributions. Receipt of federal and state funds depended on eligibility for City funds. We were, therefore, put in the peculiar situation that monies coming from the federal and state governments, which did *not* require of us what E.O. 50 required, would apparently be withheld from us by the City if we did not meet the City's executive order. It was a real "gotcha."

I was still too new to know how our own system worked. How many children were we talking about? In how many institutions or other settings? How many youngsters were disabled and what specialized care was needed? What were the daily costs and the daily reimbursement rates? (I ultimately discovered that our costs inevitably exceeded reimbursement rates. Far from operating child-care agencies for profit, we had to go to private funding to pay deficits. So despite federal, state and city reimbursements, the system actually cost the agencies and the Archdiocese a good bit of money—at least $20 million a year.)

I had to make a decision before having all the facts I would like to have had. Later, I was to have many meetings with the administrators of the child-care agencies, their lawyers, members of their boards, and others. But an answer had to be given immediately to the question: "Will you or won't you sign new contracts that accord with the BLS requirements?" That was a very lonely moment. I had been given to understand that the Diocese of Brooklyn, under the experienced leadership of Bishop Francis Mugavero, felt that it could "live with" the provisions of E.O. 50. That was a sobering thought. Who was I, newly arrived, to move in a different direction?

At the same time, the Salvation Army and Agudath Israel (an Orthodox Jewish charitable agency) strongly protested the E.O. 50 requirements, and intended not to sign new contracts. Would I seem to be deserting my "own," the Church in Brooklyn, in favor of a joint position with these two agencies?

Then there was the embarrassment of it all. Could my refusal of some $120 million be perceived as anything but flamboyance? A grandstand play? Outright blackmail? Far more important, would our agencies and our child-caring potential be destroyed?

These were questions I couldn't readily answer. One thing was certain: It would be the Archbishop who would be blamed for "throwing youngsters into the street." Other allegations would follow: that I hated homosexuals, that I was an autocrat, that I did not understand the New York scene. These allegations did in fact appear regularly in print. The Archdiocese of New York had always been blamed for Gay Rights legislation's being tied up in committee, never reaching the floor of the City Council for a vote. There were those who argued that the Mayor had mandated E.O. 50 because he had failed to effect passage of this bill. In fact, during the E.O. 50 case, there was a new effort to pass a Gay Rights Bill. This confused the deliberations concerning E.O. 50 all the more, and intensified charges that I was discriminating against homosexuals. Actually, E.O. 50 and the Gay Rights Bill were distinct and separate. Unfortunately, they were inevitably lumped together.

The second of these charges, that my own obduracy would result in throwing children out into the streets, hurt as much as the charge of discrimination, and was equally untrue. In this regard, I believe I took much of the criticism that was really due the City. The City knew very well that if we were forced to close our agencies, they would be left with the impossible task of caring for the large number of needy youngsters in New York City. In fact, the Mayor publicly stated that he did not know what the City would do if we closed our doors. Still the City insisted that we accept their new jurisdictional mandate which, as I have mentioned, had nothing to do with the care of children and nothing to do with discrimination. This was a perfect example of irrationality on the part of government and I am convinced that it was the City's obduracy that could force us out of child care to its own detriment.

My instinct was and is that the purpose, the values of the Church, as I understood them, had to take priority. I had to do what many would consider irrational, callous and heartless. Others might consider religious priorities of little account, but concern about a Trojan Horse inside the Cathedral Gates was paramount. Homosexuality as such as not in fact the issue. It was the perceived issue—perceived by the press, the public and those who believed I personally hated and feared homosexuals. What I really *did* fear was State intrusion into a critical area of Church jurisdiction. For me it was a Church-State jurisdictional question from the outset.

From a Church perspective the issue is simple. For more than a century the Church had assisted the City of New York in caring for children. Children were properly fed, housed, clothed and otherwise taken care of. For well over a hundred years, the City had been pleased with the Church's child-care system. If anything, the Church's system had *improved* during that time. Staffs were better trained and educated, advanced methods of child care had been developed, continuing improvement could be anticipated. Yet throughout the entire period, the Church had carried out its child-care activities according to its own value system. This aspect of the system had not changed.

Suddenly, however, the system was being declared inadequate unless it would incorporate Executive Order 50. We were not dealing with a piece of legislation openly reviewed and debated before enactment. What might the City require next? What other Church value would be violated or ignored by executive decree? Would the City's jurisdiction in child care, primarily dealing with health, education and safety regulations, be extended to jurisdiction over religious beliefs and moral convictions? The requirement to hire homosexuals was clearly not being introduced on the grounds that the Church was not properly taking care of children. The requirement had nothing to do with the care of children. It had everything to do with trying to force the Church to accept what the City considered a value, a recently conceived value at that. Who, then, would say how *religious* agencies would be administered, the Church or the City?

If we were to acquiesce in this City intervention, why would we be doing so? Because it would be in the best interest of the children? Not at all. Had we accepted, would it have been so that we wouldn't lose over $100 million a year? Our rationalization, of course, would have been that we were so concerned about the children, and so wanted them to be under Church auspices, that the lesser of two evils (accept the City's requirement or "throw the children out" and close down our institutions) would be to yield to the City, sign the contracts and let the devil take the hindmost.

It must be said here that we never intended, as some charged, to "throw the children out." They would have been cared for until the City developed the resources to take over their care, however long that took. Care and service that we provided during this phase-out period would have been provided without a contract but on a purchase-of-service arrangement and *without compromising our values.*

My position rested on the Trojan Horse principle: If we accepted this "gift" from the City (the reimbursement), we would be opening ourselves to the jurisdictional control of the City, surrendering our Catholic identity. This is why I publicly stated, on a number of occasions, that we would not sell our souls for any price.

What plagued me most, however, as I honestly tried to maintain a position that I believed was required by a proper respect for the Church's jurisdiction and a fear of the Trojan Horse, was the constant charge of discrimination. If truth is the first casualty of war, it is even more vulnerable to charges of discrimination. It was to take months before even some of my own people recognized that I was motivated by my obligation to uphold Church teaching; I was not interested in discriminating against homosexuals or anyone else.

From the outset, I tried to make it clear that we were not knowingly excluding anyone from employment because of homosexual *orientation.* [4] I repeatedly stated that we would be willing to consider for employment even an individual who had actively engaged in homosexual behavior in the past, and who might, through human weakness, do so again in the future. As long as such an individual was sincerely trying to be chaste, we would willingly consider employment. The "rules" would be the same for those who, unmarried, have engaged in or might in the future engage in, what we would consider to be illicit heterosexual relations. We are profoundly aware of human weakness, and it may well be that we already employ people who have slipped homosexually or heterosexually. We engage in no witch hunts. All of which is quite different from *recruiting* the homosexually oriented or being told by the City we must employ them. That, I believe, is "excessive entanglement" in Church affairs on the part of the State. I was adamant. We would not, we could not, yield our right to employ individuals ready, willing and able to support the *Church's* values in providing child care.

Suddenly, contract-signing time was upon us. Archdiocesan

4. In a later chapter I discuss Church teaching on homosexuality and the distinction between homosexual orientation and practice.

120

legal advisers gave me to understand that the Mayor had no authority to issue E.O. 50 in so far as it made sexual orientation a new "protected category." With such advice in mind, Archdiocesan representatives met with City representatives throughout the spring of 1984, and with representatives of the Salvation Army and Agudath Israel. From time to time, the Mayor and I would join in these meetings. My own objective was to try to resolve the conflict with civility. In this regard, I had hoped that the newly developing personal relationship between the Mayor and myself would be helpful, particularly if we were to come up with a solution in the best interest of all the people. The Mayor appeared to be amiable. I thought he understood my dilemma, and I was certain that he knew categorically that discrimination was not part of my agenda. He gave me the impression that he respected my "jurisdictional" argument, my insistence that the Church had to maintain its unique values and jurisdiction or it wouldn't be the Church. At the same time, I tried to understand the Mayor's political dilemma, as well as his commitment to the executive order.

While few acrimonious words were spoken, there was no levity about either of our positions. The Archdiocese and the other church-sponsored agencies insisted that the First Amendment right of free exercise absolutely entitled us to a "religious exemption" where there is conflict between employment practices and religious principles. We pointed out that such a "religious exemption" is guaranteed by the New York State Executive Law.[5]

When no agreement could be reached, the Mayor and I issued a joint statement on June 20, 1984, that the issues of law raised by E.O. 50 would be presented to the court for resolution. The newspapers said that I had taken the Mayor to court. Factually, we had mutually agreed to ask the court to resolve the dilemma.

The months to follow found Church and City at opposite ends of a seesaw, trying to achieve a balance. A series of legal and extralegal maneuvers began assuming a life of their own. Church administrators and their staffs underwent considerable stress. Was a century of outstanding and self-sacrificing service to the children of

5. For example, the New York Administrative Code provides that "any organization operated for charitable or education purposes, which is operated . . . by or in connection with a religious organization . . . [shall not be barred from] limiting employment . . . as is calculated by such organization to promote the religious principles for which it is established or maintained." (New York City Administrative Code, Section B1-7.0(9)

the City headed for oblivion? How was an orderly transfer of the children to be made, if we had to close some or all of our institutions? What of our employees' job security and retirement plans? Could they sign contracts if they attached disclaimers of refusal to carry out the provisions of E.O. 50? Could we get extensions while court action was pending?

The Mayor then took a step that surprised me very much and made me feel I had been naïve about both the "civility" of the negotiations in which we had been engaged and the City's desire to accommodate the Church agencies' obligation to safeguard Church teaching and practice. He asked the City's Board of Estimate (on which he has two votes) to adopt Resolution 520, declaring that all City contracts approved by the board must provide for nondiscrimination with reference to "sexual orientation or affectional preference." The board did so on June 28, 1984, and it looked for a time that even if the court found that the Mayor did not have the authority to issue E.O. 50, the order would still be part of the contracts! It was a neat political gambit, but I must confess my severe disappointment that the Mayor had done this. It taught me a painful lesson. I made a deliberate decision not to let the Mayor's action rupture the friendship we had been developing, and I definitely did not want it replaced by incivility harmful to the common good, but I honestly felt betrayed.

We did win in court; on September 5, 1984, Judge Alvin F. Klein of the State Supreme Court held that the challenged portion of E.O. 50 was an impermissible usurpation of legislative power by the Mayor and permanently enjoined the City and the Mayor from enforcing it. The City appealed the decision and, by doing so, was able to obtain an automatic "stay" of Judge Klein's decision, thus remaining free to enforce E.O. 50 while the case was on appeal.

Moves provoke countermoves. Late in October we sought a declaration in State Supreme Court that the contract clauses relating to sexual orientation and affectional preference authorized by the Board of Estimate were void and unenforceable, since sexual orientation and affectional preference was not a protected category under the Human Rights Law. On November 15, 1984, the judge held that the Board of Estimate did have authority to require contractors with the City not to discriminate on the basis of "sexual orientation or affectional preference."

May I take a break here to invite commiseration even from my enemies, not about the justice or nobility of my cause, since some might question both, but about my own state of mind after a mere nine months in New York? I had never been involved in a lawsuit in my life, much less taken on a city! If what I have written above sounds confusing even after I have had three years to sort it out and confer with a dozen lawyers on how to express it, think of how I felt in the middle of it, not even knowing then that the State Supreme Court is not the *highest* court in New York. (I still haven't figured that one out.)

So this was the big time, I thought, in the big town. Maybe I should become a truck driver. Back to the case.

In May 1985 we received the bad news that the Appellate Division of State Supreme Court upheld the Mayor's authority to issue E.O. 50. We saw little choice but to appeal to the Court of Appeals, the highest court in the state of New York. We did so, and our effort was rewarded on June 28, 1985. The court held that the challenged portion of E.O. 50 was void and unenforceable because the Mayor's action was an unlawful usurpation of the legislative power of the City Council. The permanent injunction against enforcement of the challenged portion of E.O. 50 was reinstated.

I was pleased by that decision. The City decided not to appeal to the Supreme Court of the United States, which I believe would have upheld our position. I was grateful that Executive Order 50 was finally a dead issue, but I felt no sense of victory and no desire to dance in the streets. The struggle had been costly in too many ways, and too many people never understood why we were waging it. These people found it easy to believe that we were driven by hatred for homosexuals and were guilty of grave discrimination. Moreover, my trust in the Mayor's fairness and openness had been tested, and I was not sure what I should believe.

The issues in the E.O. 50 case were complex, and the fact that the Bishop of Brooklyn and I took different approaches added to the confusion. I can certainly understand the confusion on the part of the press and their question: "If it's acceptable to Bishop Mugavero, why isn't it acceptable to you?" That's a fair question. Its answer would require an analysis of circumstances that would take too much space. The structure and composition of child-care activities in the Diocese of Brooklyn, for example, differ quite significantly from those in the Archdiocese of New York. Other differences could be found in other areas as well. Suffice it to say, Bishop Mugavero and I are committed to the same Church doctrine. If at times we take differing approaches on how best to preserve that doctrine, such is to be expected of men of different temperaments, and in differing sets of circumstances, even though we are both headquartered in the same city.

One or another City agency harassed us pretty shabbily while various appeals were pending. Such harassment verified for me the Trojan Horse nature of the case. If City agencies would do this while their authority was still in question, what would they do if really in the driver's seat, uncontested? We had some startling examples. For one, I had planned for months a spiritual rally of high schoolers, some 40,000 of them, in Yankee Stadium. Programs had been designed and re-hearsed, buses rented, staffs and faculties prepared. We were guaranteed the use of Yankee Stadium for four hours at a cost to us of $30,000.

Only days before the scheduled date, with everything set to go, I was informed that we couldn't use Yankee Stadium. Why not? Be-cause we had refused to include the provision of Executive Order 50 in the contract. My protest to the Mayor brought relief. We were given a waiver for a period of approximately four hours!

The harassment did not end there. Prompted by the Mayor's appeal to churches, and, even more, by the bitter cold of the winter of 1984–1985, I asked every pastor and everyone else who had space in a parish hall, a school auditorium or wherever, to open that space, how-ever small, for the homeless. The response was gratifying. At the end of the winter, participating parishes who used their facilities for the homeless received twenty-three pages of regulations attached to the fuel-reimbursement forms. These included sections requiring com-pliance with E.O. 50. We were appalled to be told that no reimburse-ment could be given because we would not sign forms that included the provisions of Executive Order 50. Another protest to the Mayor brought the reimbursement.[6]

In my view, that kind of thing is "kid stuff" on the part of City agencies, reflective of considerable bad will and a determination to control, to make us knuckle under. That's sad, but it highlights well, I believe, my reason for concern over *jurisdiction*.

6. Father Ritter, founder of Covenant House and the lesser-known Under-21, was not exempt from harassment. For the first time in all of his years of taking thousands of youngsters in off the street, he was accused of discriminating on the basis of religion because the Mission Statement of Covenant House read: ". . . our efforts together in the covenant community are a visible sign that effects the presence of God, working through the Holy Spirit among ourselves and our kids."

On June 6, 1985, in the midst of the Executive Order 50 battle, the *New York Post* ran an editorial on the matter. In addition to addressing what I considered the correct issue ("[D]oes Executive Order 50 pose a threat to the right of church-run agencies to operate in accordance with their religious principles?"), the *Post* noted an important and frightening possibility: "The City's interpretation is that the agencies are using public funds to promote religious ends. This distinction is too sharp. If rigidly enforced, it would indeed secularize the agencies. *They might be required, for instance, to offer abortion counselling in violation of Catholic moral principles.*" [Emphasis added] Enter *Wilder* v. *Bernstein.*

This distressingly *possible* arrogation by the City over Church jurisdiction was more than possible; it was happening. *Wilder* could require the Church to make available abortion counseling, against Church principles, if it was to retain child-care contracts with the City. It was another Trojan Horse. The connection made by the *Post* between E.O. 50 and *Wilder* was one I had wanted to make but had been advised against making by archdiocesan legal advisers. With due respect to our lawyers, I believe I should have done it anyway.

We have repeatedly mentioned the Wilder Case because of its very special importance. Now we must present it in some detail—and the battle that has accompanied it. The Wilder Case, too, began long before my arrival in New York, and at this writing, some fifteen years after its commencement, the matter has not yet been completely resolved.

I take up the Wilder Case in 1986. (For thirteen years before that, various challenges to the constitutionality of New York's approach to child care had been dismissed.) The American Civil Liberties Union (ACLU), the originators of the 1973 action, sued the City of New York and various privately operated child-care agencies, alleging that religiously operated agencies were discriminating against black Protestant children. The City had appropriately withstood the ACLU allegations for over ten years when suddenly, in October of 1986, the City capitulated and signed a settlement agreement with the ACLU, for no discernible reason.

If I felt betrayed during the E.O. 50 case, I felt far more so with *Wilder* when, after all those years and without any warning, the City signed the settlement. That we learned of this only after the fact made one question whether the rules of civility were really taken seriously. I am not sure that my relationship with the Mayor and with the City has ever been quite the same. The Mayor had called the ACLU's charges "ridiculous," yet signed the settlement anyway. I felt caught in the web of political game playing. To this date I have received no explanation of why the City suddenly gave in to the pressures of the ACLU.

Three terms of that settlement are important to any understanding of what is at stake for religious bodies in this controversy.

The first is the provision that "religious matching" would no longer be used as a determining factor for child placement. The New York State Constitution allows children to be placed according to their religious background. Under the new settlement, the City would place children on a first-come, first-served basis with the hope that the "expression of a religious preference shall not give a child greater access to the best available program over other children for whom such programs are also appropriate." The settlement allowed parents to designate a religious preference, but that preference would be secondary to the first-come, first-served scheme.

It should be noted here that the ACLU *at all times* acknowledged the superior quality of Catholic and Jewish agencies. It is for this very reason—the outstanding quality of our child-care institutions—that the ACLU was making claims of discrimination. Simply stated, the argument alleges that non-Catholic children are not placed in the best institutions, which are Catholic and Jewish. We were being penalized for one hundred years of quality child care! Furthermore, *at no time* during the entire Wilder Case has the ACLU ever demonstrated (or proved) any discrimination on the part of Catholic agencies. Indeed, during the course of the legal battle, the ACLU was forced to drop the charges of discrimination against the religiously operated child-care agencies.[7] (It will be seen in the later chapter on the press that despite this fact, as much as a year later, a major newspaper was still editorializing that this was a case involving discrimination against minorities. The editorialists hadn't done their homework, and many hundreds of thousands of people were misinformed. There is a truly Alice in Wonderland quality about this entire case.)

---

7. For the record, here are some of our child-care statistics for 1987–1988: We served over 6,000 children, of whom over 60 percent were classified as Protestant, other or no known religion. Approximately 70 percent of the total child-care population in our agencies are black or Hispanic.

The second settlement provision relevant to our discussion here is much more troublesome. It concerns family-planning services. The settlement provides: "SSC [Special Services for Children] shall ensure that all children have meaningful access to the full range of family planning information, services and counseling to be provided either by the agency or by a suitable outside source or both. . . . The tenets of any religion with regard to family planning will not be conveyed to a child other than in the course of providing religious counseling." It was made clear that the "full range of family planning information" included abortion and contraception. While we would not have to provide abortion and contraceptive counseling on our premises, we would, however, have to provide meaningful *access* to such for all children. What we wouldn't have to do directly, we would have to do indirectly.

A letter to the director of Catholic Charities, dated January 26, 1987, from Monsignor William Smith, moral theologian at St. Joseph's Seminary, specified the religious issue involved. "[T]he problem of referral is a moral problem which Catholic theology calls 'cooperation.' Given the fact that Catholic agencies have long since stated their non-cooperation in abortion services [and] artificial contraceptive services, when the Court orders religious agencies to refrain from conveying religious tenets, apart from 'strict religious counseling' in effect, the Court tells the Catholic agency both what it has to do, and what it can *not* say or witness."

Monsignor Smith continues: "Not only the rights of children are involved. The rights of the agencies must also be considered. [8] The stipulation drives an intended or unintended wedge between the Catholic agency's ethical commitments and its delivery of helping services. That wedge requires the agency to separate its values and commitments from its delivery of services."

The third term of the settlement which must be discussed is the one concerning religious symbols. The settlement reads: "Religious symbols that are present in the child's room shall be permitted so long as they have been requested by the child. Agencies shall not display excessive religious symbols." What is an excessive religious symbol? A crucifix? A Star of David? A Roman collar on a priest? A veil on a sister? A picture of the pope or the cardinal in the lobby? Anything the court, the ACLU or any other agency may define it as being? Will

8. "Institutional conscience" is discussed on page 208.

we be permitted to have prayers before and after meals? Will we be allowed to teach that sex before marriage is wrong? Will we be allowed to teach that *anything* is wrong?

On June 24, 1987, Catholic and Jewish agencies argued before the United States Court of Appeals for the Second Circuit, requesting that the court set aside a lower court's approval of the settlement on the grounds that the remedy fashioned by the settlement was unwarranted because there was not a single factual showing of discrimination. The court upheld the settlement. However, the court did "acknowledge that some of the provisions pose a risk of excessive entanglement."[9] Using as an example the provision regarding "excessive religious symbols," the court stated that even if the provision is construed narrowly, in the course of enforcing the provision there may be some impermissible entanglement. "Nevertheless," said the court, "we do not believe the provision is inherently vulnerable, and we believe it prudent to await whatever implementation of the provision may occur, if any."[10] I do not believe that our agencies should be placed in this "wait-and-see" position. Nor should the children.

Both the City and the Archdiocese immediately began to negotiate contract language that would allow the Archdiocese to continue in child care without our committing ourselves to positions opposed to Catholic teaching and practice. We would not sign *any* contracts if our values and moral principles were to be ignored, or if the government should attempt to infringe on what is properly Church jurisdiction. New contract language that would allow the Church to continue operating in a manner consistent with its moral teachings was, in fact, worked out in August of 1988. I am hopeful that it will withstand future challenges, and that we will be able to continue our long tradition of quality child care in New York.

What do these very real, very complex stories teach us about Church-State relations and about the Trojan Horse? First, they demonstrate in real-world terms the questions always at stake in Church-State conflict, questions of jurisdiction and of purpose, of values and goals. I reemphasize that these are the quintessential questions of both civil and ecclesiastical government, and certainly of their relations with each other. Second, they underscore the danger of

9. *Wilder* v. *Bernstein*, 848 F.2nd 1338 (2nd Cir. 1988), p. 1349
10. Ibid., p. 1349

the Trojan Horse, which often comes in the form of many millions of dollars.

The Church must be free to administer its own affairs and carry out its own purposes, rooted in its own values. I have strong feelings about this.

No sensible citizen objects to legitimate governmental regulations. However, charitable activities have become so hamstrung by government, on the one hand, and so financially tied to the government, on the other, that we may wake up one day in the United States and discover that private charity is simply unable to operate any longer except on government terms. To most fair-minded people such oppressive dominance is not good for civil society, where volunteerism has always been treasured. Certainly it threatens the good works of religious bodies, which supposedly are free, as free as the press or the entrepeneur.

It is not until we come to the question of purpose and values, however, that my concern becomes a real fear. It is one thing for the government to determine that a nursing home must have a physiotherapy facility in order to qualify for government reimbursement. It is quite another thing for the government to say that the "plug" must be pulled on certain types of patients after a certain period of time; that is, that they must be deprived of, let us say, intravenously administered food and drink after thirty days in a coma. What if government should decide that Catholic hospitals must meet "do not resuscitate" standards that the Church considers immoral? Would a hospital be deprived of reimbursement for sustaining a patient's life? Or even worse: Would a hospital be deprived of its license? What of a requirement to perform tubal ligations? Or abortions? All such and more are very real possibilities for the future. And what is possible as a government requirement when government reimbursement is involved is equally possible when *no* government reimbursement is involved. Things like the above help me to envision a day when every Catholic hospital and nursing home could be forced to close unless willing to violate our Catholic teachings.

This is why I took what some observers saw as an arrogant, intransigent and heartless stand in regard to Executive Order 50. No longer was the City simply imposing normal health and welfare requirements for the care of children; it was imposing a *value* requirement that *could* impede one of the very *purposes* of our conducting child-care institu-

129

tions. This, to me, would be a qualitative change in City requirements and would establish a radically different balance between City and Church. This balance was further upset when the City *agreed* to require what the Church considers immoral activity on the part of child-care agencies.

In both the Executive Order 50 and the Wilder Case, it is obvious that the Mayor and I were acting out of different sets of values. The Mayor insisted publicly that he very much wanted the Church to continue in child care, not only because the City did not have the capability to assume additional numbers of children, but because he believes the Church does a better job than the City. For whatever reason, however, the Mayor was insistent that what he saw as the paramount values of indiscriminate hiring and particular forms of family-planning counseling override what the Church saw as the value of safeguarding its own teachings and practices and of preserving its own jurisdiction in such matters.

I believe that Church and State will be in continuing conflict for years to come, although I hope that both will work harmoniously together for years to come as well.

I sincerely fear government intervention. I was even hesitant about agreeing with the Mayor to go to court over E.O. 50—not that I feared losing, but that I am wary of seeming to encourage even the courts to intrude excessively into the rightful domain of the Church. As a germane aside, I should observe that I have strongly mixed feelings about most "school cases" involving federal or state aid to private education. That an appropriate and legitimate formula could and should be designed, were all parties of goodwill, I have no doubt. But without the near-perfect formula, all government aid to Catholic education must be viewed very warily, much more warily, indeed, than the Trojans viewed the Wooden Horse bequeathed them by the wily Athenians.

All government funding that helps the Church meet the needs of society is both welcome and deserved. When used to control, to modify values, to divert the Church from its appointed purpose, it must be feared and feared mightily. There is no room for a Trojan Horse in the City of God.

IV

THE MAYOR
THE PRESS

THE CARDINAL
THE PRESS

THE MAYOR

The press plays a crucial role as a watchdog over public officials. When the press is on the mark it can turn public policy in the right direction. But sometimes in the haste to meet deadlines and portray events as colorfully as possible, the press goes astray. Complex issues become oversimplified. Debate over public policy is reduced to headlines and slogans. And the line between hard-nosed reporting and unfair advocacy gets blurred.

That, I suppose, is why most politicians live in fear of the press. They're afraid to defend themselves, their ideas and their policies against unfair criticism in the media. I am not. If I find a reporter's story particularly unfair, I bring it up the very next day at a press conference. I do this only in particularly unfair cases because if I responded to just plain old unfairness I'd be doing it all day long.

My advisers constantly tell me not to criticize the press. Occasionally I take their advice. Usually I don't. My reasoning is simple. I am not a punching bag. If someone hits me, I hit back, and reporters don't like being hit back. Sometimes it makes them even more critical in subsequent articles. So to some extent my advisers are right. I create my own problems with the press. But that's me.

When you consider how many public statements I make or how many times I am asked for my opinion in the course of a day, I rarely put my foot in my mouth. On a given day, I may hold as many as a dozen press interviews, some scheduled and some off the cuff. Any reporter can ask me any question on any subject, and I will try to answer to the best of my ability. Sometimes I make mistakes and when I do, "It's a beaut," to quote Fiorello La Guardia. But generally my answers to reporters are substantive and descriptive. To put it another way, reporters generally find such answers are helpful to their stories.

Looking back over my years as Mayor, I once made a statement that reporters have never stopped trying to disprove. I said, "Every day, seven days a week, three hundred sixty-five days a year for eleven years, I have been mentioned in at least one story in the newspapers, on the radio or on television."

Part of public service is being able to get attention for your ideas and programs. I've always done pretty well in this regard, beginning with my years on the New York City Council in the mid-1960s. For example, I once introduced legislation to bring North and South Vietnamese children injured in the war to New York for treatment in city hospitals. It was an idea that stirred a lot of interest. Even the supporters of Ho Chi Minh loved it.

Nowadays, I don't have to seek coverage. The reporters come to me, assuming—correctly—that I will comment on any question they need answered. There are about two dozen reporters based in City Hall, and their livelihoods depend on producing stories. When a "slow news day" comes around, we have a regular ritual in City Hall. The reporters ask to speak to me and are generally told to wait in the rotunda near a large radiator that has come to be known as the "steam table." I stand next to the steam table and take on all comers, answering whatever questions come up.

Some reporters don't bother to read the enormous amount of written policy material that the press office puts out. Much of this material contains the hard news—both good and bad—of city government. Since a few reporters don't bother to examine this material on their own, I sometimes highlight it for them. To be candid, this is also a good way to get across the accomplishments or plans of the government and gives me a chance to emphasize some of my successes. But it also means I have to accept responsibility for any problems. On balance, I think open access works well, and it's the best means I have for communicating with the people of New York City.

During my first term, this accessibility was extremely helpful. It allowed me to get my point of view across even though some of the media were making adverse comments. People tell me they recognize my voice immediately. Maybe it's too high-pitched, too fast-paced and too New York in inflection, but it's very distinctively mine. Television and radio are best for communication since they allow me to address the public directly.

Each member of the media has different needs. Radio reporters are generally more interested in color, in sound bites, than in analyzing events or the news. However, many of them do a terrific job on sub-stance as well. They also tend to be less hostile than print reporters. Sound is their stock in trade and they handle it with respect and honesty for what's actually been said. Print reporters tend to edit statements. Radio journalists do far less editing. TV reporters do some editing, but at least the parts they leave in are accurate.

During my nine years in Congress I had wonderful training in han-dling the press. In the House of Representatives, members are permit-ted to make statements from the floor on any issue they want under the one-minute rule. I think I made more of these statements than any other member except Larry McDonald, the Georgia congressman who was killed on the Korean Airlines flight the Soviets shot down. I was on the political left. He was on the right. We balanced each other in the number of statements we made in *The Congressional Record.*

Under the one-minute rule, a House member can stand up at 12:00 noon every day and speak about any subject he or she wishes. But your remarks can take only a minute. The challenge is to get your message across in two hundred words or less. If you have done this as often as I have—which was every day when Congress was in session—it sharp-ens your wits. That training helped me focus my thoughts into a quick sound bite for radio or television.

One of the things that makes being Mayor so fascinating is the wide range of interests the job entails. Obviously, City issues come first, and I am very proud of what I have accomplished in terms of restoring and safeguarding the City's fiscal integrity and delivering expanded services.

The Mayor of New York also has to be a leader in dealing with Congress and the State Legislature. I've been outspoken on many is-sues in Washington and Albany, trying to get the best deal possible for my City and—as an occasional spokesman for the U.S. Conference of Mayors—for all cities. Sometimes my arguments carry the day, some-times not. But it is through the press that I lead the charge, whether the subject is the war on drugs or reform of the educational system.

Out-of-town reporters who cover me when I arrive in their cities don't seem to be accustomed to a politician who speaks so freely, is so accessible and is willing to answer all questions. As a result, the local press is usually present in large numbers. During my trip to Amster-dam in 1988, Dutch reporters couldn't believe how available I was to the press. They referred to my visit as a "permanent press conference" and didn't hesitate to join their colleagues from New York in taking advantage of these opportunities.

Reporters ask why I often get involved in foreign issues. The answer is that New York is the capital of the world. Our industries have an international impact. Foreign corporations are a large and valued part of our local economy and we constantly welcome dignitaries from every corner of the globe. The United Nations is headquartered here. New York is also home to 175 different ethnic, racial and religious groups and each one of them expects support from their Mayor on issues that concern them. Everyone knows how proud I am of my Jewish faith and my support for Israel. But I'm also deeply involved in fighting apartheid in South Africa, denouncing military dictatorship in Haiti, defending Solidarity in Poland, standing up for the rights of Greeks in Cyprus, soliciting aid for the Jamaican victims of Hurricane Gilbert and welcoming large new communities of Koreans, Dominicans and Asian Indians to the city. Unfortunately, the press coverage of my involvement in foreign affairs is highly selective and sometimes conveys the impression that my interests are limited. They certainly are not.

I have always had an interest in national and foreign-affairs issues. In Congress, I was a leader in the fight to end our involvement in Vietnam and pioneered efforts to end aid to Latin American dictatorships. As Mayor, it was only natural that I would maintain that interest.

I've always been anti-Soviet because I perceive a resemblance between the Soviets and the Nazis, a resemblance dramatically obvious in the huge numbers of people they murdered in the name of ideology. I am aghast at the cynical way people distinguish between the cruelty of the Soviet Union under Stalin and that of Nazi Germany. The only major difference is the basis upon which people were murdered. The Nazis killed on the basis of race and religion. The Soviets killed on the basis of political belief and social class. Even if the Jews had been pro-Nazi, it would have made no difference to Hitler. They had to die because they were Jews. The same fate awaited Gypsies, many Slavs, or any of the other so-called subhuman races scorned by the Nazis.

Of course, the Nazis also killed people on the basis of their beliefs, such as Communists, Social Democrats or Christians who believed in brotherhood and defended Jews. But basically, the Nazis acted out of a total dedication to the principle of racism. The Communists also killed out of race-hatred in some instances. But their primary rationale for mass killing was ideological. I've always felt compelled to speak out about those who condemn one form of totalitarianism but approve of another. I attack all forms of tyranny. No one would criticize me for condemning the Nazis, but my attacks on the Soviet Union make some people uncomfortable.

This same prejudice shows up in other areas as well. Look at Chile and Cuba. Here in the United States, many people say the Chilean regime is more brutal than the Cuban regime. Unfortunately, this point of view is especially prevalent among my fellow Democrats. But which regime has brutalized more of its citizens? I believe that it's Castro's. But somehow he is not held responsible the way Pinochet has been. Yet who has given the people an opportunity to determine their political fate at the ballot box? Pinochet, not Castro. Can anyone name a Communist country where the people have been able to vote out the leadership? I don't know of one.

That's not true of countries on the right. I can think of Spain, Portugal, Argentina and Chile, assuming Pinochet carries out his commitment to step aside as a result of the vote against him. Jeane Kirkpatrick was loudly criticized for her opinion that there is a difference between authoritarian regimes on the right and totalitarian regimes on the left. I believe time has proven her analysis correct.

I have never understood why the press is not supposed to ask public officials about their political background if that background includes Communist activities. For example, one New York legislator was an active member of the Communist party and sat on the executive board of a local Communist organization. Reporters are fearful of asking about this legislator's record. They've bought the line that it's McCarthyism and Red-baiting to ask a Red if he or she was in fact a Red. Yet reporters would never be reluctant to raise the issue of a public official's former membership in the John Birch Society or the Nazi party. That would be fair game.

Beyond the question of a reporter's political agenda—right, left or center—is the question of a reporter's sensitivity. Reporters are much more sensitive than I am and I am very sensitive. Most reporters are acutely distressed at even the mildest criticism of their stories.

I remember when a particular journalist was first assigned to City Hall. This reporter filed a story that showed absolutely no understanding of the basic issues of the City's finances. He wrote that the City had overcome its financial crisis in 1975 and that nothing I was doing had any bearing on the City's financial future. It was an indefensible statement. The City was on its knees when I came into office in 1978. Felix Rohatyn, head of the Municipal Assistance Corporation, warned that we had better "fasten our seat belts" because the City was in worse fiscal shape than at the height of the 1975 crisis.

The reporter didn't know any of that, yet his article was circulated nationally and created a false impression about the City's financial condition. I wrote a letter attacking his piece, but sent it only to the New York paper that ran the story, rather than to the national wire service he wrote it for. One of the reporter's friends urged me not to make him look bad in front of his bosses.

The same thing happened with a *New York Times* reporter who later co-authored a sharply critical book called *I, Koch*. The *Times* reporter wrote an article that contained several mistakes about the City's financial condition and I refuted him in print. He could not accept the fact that he had erred. As far as many reporters are concerned, the only people who make mistakes are public officials.

I don't accept that view. When a reporter gets something wrong or, even worse, misrepresents the facts, I insist on setting the record straight. My response can take several forms. I write six columns a week for newspapers in the City and consider them an important forum for my views. Often, I will use my flagship column in the Sunday *Staten Island Advance* to correct a reporter's mistakes or to respond to a columnist's attack.

I also write letters, either to the editor of the paper that published the mistaken report or directly to the columnist or reporter in question. People tell me that columnists love to be attacked by me in print. It makes them feel important to be singled out for attention. Frankly, I don't believe it, but even if it's true I insist on responding to my critics.

First, I correct factual errors. Otherwise reporters, columnists and editorial writers will accept whatever has appeared in print as factual, even when it's not. This is especially true in my case because by now journalists know how much I read and figure if I haven't responded to something, its probably because I have no quarrel with it, not because I haven't seen it. Of course, it's impossible for me to read everything that's written about City government or correct every error.

I also believe my letters and my columns will be part of the historical record of this administration. They provide an opportunity for me to explain in detail the choices I made or the policies my administration pursued. I think historians and researchers will find this material valuable.

Overall, I believe, the press does a pretty good job, even though reporters resent the fact that I sometimes go over their heads and break news in my columns and letters and in live appearances on television and the radio.

I think it would be a good idea to have some sort of forum for those who feel they have been wronged by inaccuracies in the press. Obviously, such a forum would have to respect the constitutional protections the press is entitled to and that our society needs to preserve free expression.

Brooklyn congressman Charles Schumer has proposed legislation that I support. The Schumer bill would allow an individual to sue a publication in order to establish the truth or falsity of an allegation, without the possibility of collecting damages. The result would simply be a determination of whether or not the facts presented by the publication were correct. Such a system exists in other democracies—France comes to mind—where courts do rule on the accuracy of reporting without awarding substantial financial damages. I'm not interested in chilling a free press. But there should be some recourse for those who have been the subject of inaccurate reporting. It might be a good idea for newspapers to establish some kind of independent arbitrator in such cases and leave the courts out of it. But newspapers don't want to do that either. They will accept nothing that would upset their right to misrepresent the facts and get away with it.

Since a forum for correcting errors does not exist, I take reporters on directly. Without question, this cost me dearly during the corruption crisis. Even though only a handful of people in my administration were indicted, the press saw an opportunity to attack. Columnist Jimmy Breslin went on television shortly after Queens Borough President Donald Manes committed suicide and said I would be out of office or removed within six months. Though his prediction proved to be as accurate as most of his other insights, it made me mad, particularly coming from Breslin.

After all, three people who figured in the corruption scandal were close friends of his: Michael Dowd, Shelly Chevlowe and Melvin Lebetkin. He didn't write about their corruption because he didn't know about it, even though he was personal friends with them. And yet here he was saying *I* should have known about the corruption of people I'd never met.

Then there is Jack Newfield, a politician masquerading as a journalist. Newfield spent some twenty years writing for *The Village Voice* before joining the more respectable *Daily News*. Regardless of who employs him, he has always treated reporting as something to be manipulated in the service of political goals. His most infamous attempt at political power brokering occurred during Bella Abzug's congressional campaign in 1970. There was a great deal of controversy over whether or not Bella was against the United States selling jets to Israel. Bella said that she was at a certain private political meeting but that she realized the folly of any such statement and vehemently denied ever making it. Newfield claimed he was at the same meeting and heard Bella say she was against jets for Israel, but publicly lied about it on her behalf so that she would win the primary. Newfield later confessed that he had lied, in an open letter to *The Village Voice*. This may be old news to some, but I believe that it remains representative of the kind of journalist Newfield is and makes it highly unlikely that he has changed his behavior since joining the *Daily News*.

Apparently Newfield also sees himself as a power broker first and a journalist second. Last year he tried to exert his influence over the mayoral campaign early and publicly by writing an article proposing several candidates to run against me. It wasn't your standard bit of journalistic prognostication either, but essentially his idea of a campaign strategy to defeat me. Indeed, it is common knowledge that Newfield has privately been the political adviser of at least one of my potential opponents.

Newfield also exercises influence by feeding stories or rumors to a small group of reporters who meekly adopt his slant on a story, while he trashes reporters who don't follow the Newfield line. The saving grace of all this is that many people in politics, and journalism as well, know that in pursuit of his political goals he has lied before in print and undoubtedly will lie again.

Jack Newfield notwithstanding, sometimes I hear people say I had a long honeymoon with the press. I think it was simply a case of the press not having anything substantive to use against me. The revelations about Donald Manes's corruption gave them an opportunity to display their anger, which had been there all along.

It should come as no surprise that reporters are more than mere recorders of the passing scene. They are human beings and have all the human emotions, strengths and weaknesses, including a tendency to either like or dislike the person they are covering, which can influence them to write either a "puff piece" or a "hatchet job." And, like all people, reporters sometimes oversimplify issues, although it's not always their fault. They have to produce stories against tight deadlines and space is limited. Their editors also have opinions about what constitutes a good story and about what kind of coverage should be given to a particular issue or individual.

For all these reasons, reporters are under constant pressure. The result can be oversimplified stories. One of the most common ways to simplify a story is to target a public official for one kind of coverage or another. If the official is currently in favor, then the coverage will tend to put things in a favorable light. If the official is under a cloud for one reason or another, the coverage will tend to portray things in a cloudy light. Sometimes this leads to errors that can be either trivial or damaging.

For example, I flew down to Puerto Rico for the inauguration of Governor Rafael Hernández-Colón. During the flight, I got up to use the bathroom. One reporter, in search of a story, wrote that I was "working the aisles" (i.e., engaging in political campaigning) during the flight. It made the trip to Puerto Rico seem like a political maneuver, always a welcome story in an election year. The reporter could have asked me *why* I walked up the aisle. I only left my seat once in the entire trip. But KOCH GOES TO BATHROOM would not have made a good story. Or maybe it would.

To cite a more serious example of distorted reporting, the *Daily News* wrote that I presided "over a corruption scandal that has produced convictions of nearly 200 city employees." The intent of the writers was to convey the impression that corruption is rampant in my administration. In fact, they got the number two hundred by lumping together scores of civil-service employees such as building and restaurant inspectors—who are not appointed by me and whose misconduct was almost always uncovered by the city's own anticorruption arm, the Department of Investigation—with independently elected officials. By adding them all to the six public officials appointed by me who were

convicted of wrongdoing, they achieved an inflated figure of two hundred, thus creating the desired impression of systemic corruption without acknowledging systemic and successful efforts to uncover it. That's
one of the ways an unscrupulous reporter can shape a story into a
political weapon.

As chief executive of the City, I take responsibility when things go
wrong. I've taken a lot of heat for not having known about the corruption of public officials. In this regard, I recall something said by Jim
Smith, a journalist who once ran against me for mayor. Smith had
asked me at a City Club meeting about a Board of Estimate contract
that had been awarded to Stanley Friedman, which Smith didn't think
was appropriate. I told him that if he knew of any corrupt activities—
and he made no such allegations to me—he should run, not walk to
the district attorney with the evidence. Regrettably, the law allowed—and still allows—a county leader to do business with the
City. I don't like this practice and I have urged the State Legislature
to make it illegal, but it has refused to do so.

Two years later, Jack Newfield, who rarely misses an opportunity to
attack me, also appeared before the City Club and praised Smith for
confronting me on the question of Stanley Friedman's contract with
the city. To his credit, Jim Smith stood up and said to Newfield,
"Why didn't you do something about it? Everybody read about this in
the press. Where were the reporters? They didn't do anything. You
didn't do anything." And Newfield, who is shrewd, simply said,
"Guilty."

Some of the reporters and columnists who've been around for a long
time get jaded or maybe even bored with what they do. Instead of
going into an issue in depth, it's easier for them to divide the world
into good guys and bad guys. There are no shades of gray, no need to
be reflective. If you're on the outside, you're a good guy. If you're on
the inside, you're a bad guy.

I started in politics as an outsider, an insurgent. Some of the first
favorable coverage of my career came from Murray Kempton, then a
columnist for the New York Post, and Sydney Schanberg, then of The
New York Times. I was on the outside looking in. Now the reverse
is true. Since I'm the establishment and not the underdog, I'm
the enemy. Today, Kempton and Schanberg are among my harshest
critics.

It's the job of the press to be critical. It's not the job of the press to be unfair. On occasion I wonder if editors make deliberate decisions to slant the news in one direction or another. Sometimes I will participate in a "good news" event and the next day there is a story in the paper without any mention of my presence. There are times when a newspaper will focus on a negative story about my administration, leaving out facts that could soften the point of the story or show things in a more positive light. When I ask City Hall reporters why certain facts were omitted from a piece, they often say the city desk or a particular editor made the final decision to eliminate information from their favorable story. Now, I'm not sure who actually took it out, but editors are ultimately responsible because they control which information appears in a story and which does not.

My relationships with certain newspapers have changed dramatically since the first time I ran for mayor. I could not have won election in 1977 without the support of the *New York Post* and the *Daily News*. I often agree with the *Post*'s editorial point of view. For a New York paper, the *Post* is conservative. In the rest of the country, it would be considered liberal. I find the *Post* moderate.

I used to agree with *Daily News* editorials far more than I do today. Their editorials are often out of touch with real life in the city. I write them letters in an effort to correct the record, but they publish only excerpts. It's hard to set the record straight in four or five sentences.

I consider *Newsday* to be much more liberal than its readership. To their credit, they sometimes publish full-length letters or op-ed columns.

The New York Times is still the best paper in the world. More often than not, I agree with its editorials.

El Diario is a good newspaper, but the editor appears to think that I'm responsible for all the evils of the world. *Noticias del Mundo* is a superb paper, though some people discredit it because it is owned by the Reverend Moon.

The *Staten Island Advance* provides excellent coverage of city news and thoughtful editorials. We sometimes disagree on community issues, but overall it is a superb paper.

New York City also has a number of weekly papers, most of which are moderate in their views and responsible in their coverage of the news. A few, such as the *Amsterdam News* and *The Village Voice*, are more radical. To put it mildly, we are usually on different sides of the issues.

There have been a handful of first-rate reporters during my tenure at City Hall. These are not reporters who wrote valentines to me, but reporters who were fair, even when they were critical. I am not offended by criticism of me or my administration when it is supported by the facts or when it is reasonable. Clyde Haberman, Lee Dembart, Joyce Purnick, Rick Levine, Alan Finder—all from the *Times*—were all tough when they thought they should be, but also tried to be objective.

Bill Murphy, the bureau chief of *Newsday*, is very bright. He is one of the few reporters who pays attention to the written material distributed by the press office and reads the complex budget and management reports. He's fair, but occasionally he turns on the venom.

David Seifman of the *New York Post*, Jack Shanahan of the Associated Press, and Dan Andrews of United Press International are tough but fair.

Newspapers have one function that's not often mentioned. They set the agenda for the electronic media. When the newspapers go on strike, most of the television reporters don't know what to report or where to turn for guidance. Of course, television news also has some very talented reporters and editors. They're fair and work hard to tell the whole story. Among them are Josh Mankiewicz and Jim Jensen of Channel 2, David Diaz, Tony Guida and Ralph Penza of Channel 4, Jim Ryan, Bill McCreary and John Roland of Channel 5, Doug Johnson of Channel 7, Denise Richardson of Channel 9 and Eric Shawn of Channel 11.

Among the television reporters, Gabe Pressman is probably the most contentious. The public thinks highly of him because he's been around for so long, but, in my view, he's not always fair.

Andy Logan, a writer for *The New Yorker*, does a monthly column on City Hall. She asks venomous yet intelligent questions.

In eleven years of columns she's never written a single one indicating that I ever did anything good. Considering that when I came into office, the City had a $1 billion operating deficit, no capital budget, no credit rating and an unemployment rate three points higher than the national average, and that today we've had eight years of balanced budgets with a surplus, a capital-spending plan of more than $5 billion, a bond rating of "A" and unemployment below the national average, I must have done *something* positive on occasion. But you'd never know it from reading Andy Logan.

Her relentless criticism used to distress me until one day, while I was waiting for a plane in Chicago, a woman came over to me and said enthusiastically, "Mayor, I really admire you. I just read Andy Logan's latest piece in *The New Yorker* and it was marvelous! Keep up the good work!"

Now I smile when I read Andy Logan's columns.

THE CARDINAL

A funny thing happened to me on the way to New York in March of 1984. A *New York Times* editorialist ambushed me, sandbagged me, strung me up by my heels, and made it generally clear to the world that it would be Scranton's loss and New York's gain if I stayed in Scranton!

It was an interesting experience. However, the matter didn't end there.

That very day a *Times* reporter called me. He said he was interested in my reaction. Although hampered by the niceties of clerical language, I managed to convey my feeling that the *Times* might have been mildly excessive, but that I couldn't really evaluate it till I got out of my body cast.

Two days later occurred what I'm told was an event extraordinarily rare in the annals of journalism: *The New York Times* apologized! Well, maybe they didn't exactly *apologize*, but they did sort of imply that they would were it not undignified to do so. Those things happen.

It was all really the best thing that could have happened to me, short of a séance with Madame Defarge. Speculation had been running high over the choice of Cardinal Cooke's successor in New York. Not even Jimmy the Greek had ever heard of me, yet here I was, en route to Broadway. Much as I hated to leave the great people of my native soil, I was all puffed up with myself to be catapulted into such prominence, Yankee Doodle Dandy himself. The *Times* restored my sense of balance, brought me back to earth, sobered me most admirably.

That brings me to my point. The point is not the issue on which

The New York Times attacked me—that in a Gabe Pressman interview I compared aspects of abortion with aspects of the Holocaust. I talk about abortion in another chapter. My point here is that the *Times* taught me more in one editorial about the triangular relationship of Church, State and Press than I had learned in some sixty years of being able to read and write. For that, I am grateful.

No book on Church and State or Religion and Politics in this media center of the world would be even marginally complete without a reflection on the role of the press. The reflection would miss the mark altogether, however, if it were simply another diatribe, or a compilation of media foibles. Few people, including reporters and editors themselves, need me to tell them what's wrong with the press, or what's right with it. Anybody who reads more than one newspaper or magazine has a pretty good idea.

Here I am interested in the press as the "third dimension" of Church-State relations, one regularly underestimated or ignored. The impact of the press on both Church and State, and on their relationships with each other, needs much further exploration. This is particularly true in a day in which both Church and State quite openly try to use the media to their respective advantages, while the media use both for whatever news value they may yield.

The two *Times* editorials cited are classic in revealing the "third dimension" in Church-State relations. Here is what they respectively said. The first, March 13, 1984, excised five sentences from an hourlong interview by Gabe Pressman of NBC-TV.

HITLER AND ABORTION

The next leader of New York's Catholic Church, Bishop John J. O'Connor, has telegraphed ahead some theological and political views with highly offensive implications:

"I always compare the killing of 4,000 babies a day in the United States, unborn babies, with the Holocaust. . . . Now Hitler tried to solve the problem, the Jewish question. So kill them, shove them into ovens, burn them. Well, we claim that unborn babies are a problem, so kill them. To me it really is precisely the same."

Implication No. 1: that Hitler had a problem called the "Jewish question," and that only his remedy was evil.

Implication No. 2: that the thousands of women who make the personal, usually painful choice of an abortion are practicing Nazi genocide, organized, calculating and malevolent mass murder of millions.

Implication No. 3: that public figures who personally oppose abortion but resist imposing their theology on others are hypocrites and, indeed, sponsors of Hitlerian murder.

Much turns, of course, on the Bishop's doctrinal conviction that a fetus is in fact a baby and that to impede birth at any time after conception is murder. For citizens without his certitude, the question of when life begins remains.

How Bishop O'Connor answers that question theologically is his affair. But if he means to instruct the community at large, a change of tone would be welcome.

End of Editorial Number One.

It was on the same date that the *Times* reporter called, and on March 15, the *Times* printed its version of mollification.

OF ANALOGY AND ABORTION

It's good to have Bishop John J. O'Connor's explanation greatly narrowing the sense in which he would compare abortion in America with the Nazis' slaughter of Jews. He expresses outrage that this page read his initial remarks as implying that Hitler had a "Jewish" problem needing solution and that women choosing an abortion were guilty of a crime comparable to the Holocaust. That is a welcome clarification.

The next Archbishop of New York's Roman Catholic Church intends to preach against abortion as he always has, retaining the analogy. He asks that his meaning be understood in this way.

"The abortion mentality that has swept the country, that has simply declared the unborn to be nonhuman—that is what I compare to the Holocaust. . . . I very sincerely believe that an abortion mentality, structured and legalized in this country, does not differ in essence from that mentality that legalized putting Jews to death in Nazi Germany."

That sincere conviction is clear without inflammatory analogy. The Bishop believes, as do many others, that an unborn fetus is human and that preventing birth any time after conception is therefore murder. He thus concludes that treating abortion as legal is to legalize murder.

Neither American nor German history justifies the leap from that proposition to the view that Americans reason like Nazis and have "simply declared the unborn to be nonhuman." But analogies aside, the Bishop does now focus on the central question: When does life begin?

Incertitude about that offends some theologies, but the doubt is well within the bounds of humane contemporary thought. Accommodating such differing views is not easy—and the political task is surely easier if each side will respect the humanity and piety of the other. It is in that spirit we welcome Bishop O'Connor to New York, a gloriously contentious, tolerant and democratic community.

So much for both editorials, for the moment, except to compare them with what was actually said in the portion of the Gabe Pressman interview from which *The New York Times* editorial extracted its five lines.

PRESSMAN: On January 31st you said that stopping abortion and defending human life would permeate "everything I do, my number-one priority, the life of the unborn." How? How do you intend to fight against abortion in New York?

BISHOP O'CONNOR: Well, first let me clarify. Certainly I focus on the unborn because they're the most helpless. Almost everyone else seems to have some advocate. Now, I'm terribly concerned about the homeless, about the hungry, about the naked. . . .

PRESSMAN: The constituencies that are most helpless.

BISHOP O'CONNOR: The most helpless constituencies. I think that that's a major responsibility of mine. And as one goes down the scale, if you will, of helplessness, to the absolutely most vulnerable, one finds the infant in the womb. And it's imperative, therefore, that this is where we start. I see all life as a continuum.

You know, I try not to indict anyone. I certainly do not condemn, by any stretch of the imagination, nor does the Church, the poor, young confused girl who, not knowing which way to turn, has an abortion, or the family that supports her in doing so. I think it's a tragedy. I think objectively it is gravely sinful. A human life has been taken. But I don't condemn the individual who acts out of confusion and desperation.

But I have absolutely no tolerance, I must confess, for those politicians, political figures or political campaigners, who deliberately, now, *deliberately and intentionally*, not because of their own personal convictions, but *deliberately and intentionally* exploit the political potential of this issue, try to sit on the fence with this business of "I personally am opposed to abortion but, after all, we must have a choice." You show me the politician who is prepared to say, "I personally am opposed to bombing cities with nuclear weapons, but we have to have a free choice." "I personally am opposed to killing Blacks or Jewish people or Methodists or Lutherans or Catholics, but we have to have a choice." That's—you know, that's—to me, that's a sheer absurdity.

And therefore, either you have to admit that you're talking about a real, live human being in the womb or not. If it's not a real live human being, that's a totally different story. If it's a real, live human being, at what point do you say it's all right to kill a human being?

The law right now permits you to take the life of a baby, to kill a baby nine months old, one second before it's born. Now, why then can't you kill an elderly blind person? Why can't you kill someone with cancer? Why can't you kill the street people who are, quotes, "robbing us of our social resources"?

PRESSMAN: So you're saying, really, that the abortion issue involves a kind of latent Nazism?

BISHOP O'CONNOR: Well, I always compare it, and some of my Jewish friends support me in this—for instance, I had six Orthodox rabbis come to see me recently, who are very, very strong in the pro-life movement. I always compare the killing of four thousand babies a day in the United States, unborn babies, to the Holocaust. The most impactful moment, I guess, in my life in—well, that's hard to say; lots of things impact on you. But a tremendously important moment in my life was when I stood in a concentration camp in Dachau and put my hand in the semi-circular red-brick ovens and felt on the floor of the oven the intermingled ashes of Jew and Christian, rabbi, minister, priest, lay person, in memory. And I thought, good Lord, human beings actually did this to human beings.

Now, Hitler tried to solve a problem, the Jewish problem. So kill them, shove them into ovens, burn them. Well, we claim that unborn babies are a problem, so kill them. To me, it really is precisely the same. And, while I try to be sensitive, sympathetic, understanding to those who don't accept this position, I really don't understand why they don't accept it.

PRESSMAN: Does it make you angry?

BISHOP O'CONNOR: It doesn't make me angry, but it sure—it sure turns me inside out. Nothing hits me as that does. Nothing tears me up as that does. And, you know, it gives me a sense of frustration and futility. That's because I don't have enough faith. It's still God's world and, you know, we have to—we have to leave a lot of it to God. But I sure will do my best to . . .

PRESSMAN: You don't have enough faith and you're going to be the leader of all these Catholics in New York?

BISHOP O'CONNOR: No, I don't—I don't have enough faith. None of us have enough faith. Certainly I. I'm . . .

PRESSMAN: Are you still working on it?

BISHOP O'CONNOR: Still working on it.

PRESSMAN: At age 64.

BISHOP O'CONNOR: Oh, boy. At age 64. If I— If I live to be 164, I don't think I'll make it. No, not by a long shot. But that's the—maybe that's why I've been appointed to this, this peculiar position. Maybe people seeing how weak I am will have some hope themselves and be encouraged.

Enough of the interview, presented here verbatim.[1] Is there a significant difference between what I said in *context*, both in tone and in content, from what the *Times* portrays me as saying and the manner of my saying it? I personally believe there's all the difference in the world, but that, of course, is *my* opinion.

There's the rub. Presumably the editorialist believed that he was reflecting my words and my tone quite accurately and quite fairly. Yet he or she omitted so much that I thought explained the section quoted: for example, my expressed concern for women who have abortions, my recognition of their anxiety and confusion, my refusal to condemn them. Did the editorialist miss my intention to make clear that if we become contemptuous of the worth and dignity and sacredness of *any* human life, then we risk what happened in Nazi Germany? Did the editorialist not *hear* what I said about my experience at Dachau? Did what I meant by describing my feelings on that occasion simply not come through clearly?

---

1. Provided by *News 4orum*, NBC, courtesy of Gabe Pressman

I could ask any number of such questions. I can't answer *any* of them. Even as I read the transcript more than four years after the televised interview, I must confess I still can't answer such questions.

What is my point in recounting any of this?

An archbishop and a mayor are much alike in their respective obligations to *communicate* with their congregants or constituents. People have a right to knowledge, information, truth, in both religious and civil matters.

The Archbishop of New York has a primary and immediate obligation to Roman Catholics as the chief teacher of the doctrine of the Church in the Archdiocese. As I see it, he has a broader obligation to the wider community in which he serves. He is a public person. Given the visibility and potential influence of his position, he has an obligation to communicate what the Church has to say about social issues: public policy, justice, immigrants, the poor, the hungry, the homeless, the ill-housed, racism, abortion, personal responsibility, civic virtues, and a wide variety of concerns that we generally relate to what Catholics call the "Social Gospel." From a purely informational perspective, the Archbishop has at least a modest obligation, as well, to let the entire community know what the Church is up to at any given time.

The Mayor, of course, directly or through agencies established for the purpose, has the obligation to inform citizens about an endless number of things vital to their well-being. Such information is quite apart from his personal political interests or aspirations. Undoubtedly people have a *right* to know the latter. Whether they consider such vital to their well-being is another matter.

If, then, both Archbishop and Mayor are obligated to communicate, the question becomes *how*.

The Archbishop has a variety of channels for internal communications among Catholics. He has 411 parishes staffed by some eight hundred priests. Hundreds of thousands of Catholics attend Mass in these parishes regularly. Our Catholic school system makes access to hundreds of thousands of young people, and, through them, to their parents, relatively simple. The Archdiocese of New York owns and operates an elaborate instructional-television facility (ITV). Each day, for example, my 8:00 A.M. Mass in St. Patrick's Cathedral is presented to a broad spectrum of viewers by way of our own ITV. It includes a three- or four-minute homily applicable to needs of the day.

152

Then, of course, there is our own Catholic newspaper, *Catholic New York*, and an entire Office of Communications. In other words, the Church is highly structured, with built-in opportunities for communicating.

The Mayor, too, has a vast and highly structured organization through which I am sure he communicates a variety of messages to City employees and others.

There is clearly only one way to reach the "masses," however: the mass media.

The Mayor and I both get a lot of exposure in the media. He gets much more than I do. He should. A certain amount of the exposure simply goes with the job. Where he goes, the media go. They should. The people have a right to know of any significant activities in which he is involved. He's the Mayor. Such exposure he doesn't have to seek.

An Archbishop of New York receives an unusual amount of exposure for a churchman. Some of it is simply traditional to New York, almost automatic to given events: the Christmas Midnight Mass in St. Patrick's Cathedral, the Saint Patrick's Day Parade and other happenings. Some of the exposure comes through impromptu press conferences that I do not seek, but which I am ordinarily grateful to have. For example, during most Sundays of the year, September through June, media representatives gather in the Cathedral immediately after my 10:15 Mass. The subjects are of their choosing, and I never really know what they're going to ask me.

Then there is the exposure I deliberately seek. If I'm launching a new low-income-housing program, for example, I ask the media to come hear about it. I want the world to know, not so it can see what a wonderful fellow I am, but because I believe the public has a right to know, particularly those in need of such services. Further, it is my hope that other private-sector agencies will be stimulated to do the same thing. The media are generous in coming to such conferences.

Or the media may invite me: to be interviewed on radio or TV, to do newspaper or magazine articles, to meet at off-the-record editorial luncheons.

With the exposure go many opportunities and many problems and risks. The opportunities lie in the potential for reaching thousands or even millions of people I could never reach otherwise, in order to offer them—not "impose" on them—the teachings of the Gospel as understood and articulated by the Church. The Gospel means "the Good News." It is my responsibility to try to offer the good news to as many people as I can. It is up to them, of course, to listen or not, to accept or reject. I try to present Church teaching honestly and straightforwardly, neither distorting it nor varnishing it. That's my job, whether the "good news" as I understand it is popular or unpopular.

When I came to New York for a day of preparation prior to my eventual arrival and installation as Archbishop, I met with the press. I was astonished by the turnout. I had never seen so many cameras, microphones, tape recorders and note pads in one place. I had absolutely no idea of what I would be asked, and was amazed by the number of questions and the effort of each reporter to get his or her question answered.

I tried to be very honest that day, as ever since. I wanted to be particularly honest in telling the media representatives present that every opportunity they offered me would be accepted if possible, that I would *use* them, not exploit them, but use them to reach as many people as I could. I said I would like to shake hands with every individual in New York, downstate and upstate, and that the only way I could do this would be through them.

Since then, I have, in fact, tried to respond to virtually every request, and to seize every opportunity, not to present *myself*, but the teaching of the Church, through the media. I will continue to do so. Yet the problems and the risks have been great, so much so that every day I ask myself if I would chance them if I had to do it all over again.

My predecessor, Cardinal Cooke, generally avoided media exposure. He loved people, traveled extensively throughout the Archdiocese and the world, and considered New York second only to heaven. Lest it be thought he was unknown, I have been Archbishop of New York for more than four years as I write these words, and not a day goes by without someone's introducing me as Cardinal Cooke.

In the waning hours the story of his gallant suffering was told in headlines throughout the world. Only then did the world learn of the years he had been battling cancer, struggling with constant pain without ever losing his gentle smile. Few were aware, for example, that he was so weak at times that he would have to be given blood transfusions, always secretly, *between* appointments. Yet, until his strength failed completely, he maintained his daily, demanding schedule. It was not until the final days of his life, however, that Cardinal Cooke became a media presence. Respecting him as I do, I have obviously had to ask myself repeatedly if I should simply have followed his example of reticence.

Suppose I had never given Gabe Pressman the interview *The New York Times* used to introduce me to its readers? Would I have come to town as the "controversial" new Archbishop of New York? Would segments of the Jewish community have felt threatened by the coming of a man "insensitive" to the meaning of the Holocaust? Would women's coalitions, proponents of the ERA, abortion-rights associations and others have been able to accuse me of comparing abortions to premeditated mass murders? Would politicians have been alerted to this ecclesiastical maverick who calls them "hypocrites"?

Suppose from the moment the Vatican announced that I had been appointed Archbishop of New York, I had decided that I would not, under any circumstances, talk to *anyone* in the media? Suppose I had never once appeared voluntarily on TV, or in the newspapers, or on radio? Suppose anything but what has been the reality of the past four years. Would the Church be better off? Would its teachings be better known and respected? Would the broader community have been better served? Would the Good News, the Gospel, be more warmly welcomed? How can I answer such? I simply don't know.

Why, then, have I chosen the course of both complete openness to and actual pursuit of media exposure? Because, as stated above, I believe I have a grave obligation to preach, to teach, to reach as many people as I possibly can. Which is another way of saying I believe I have an obligation to truth itself; hence an obligation also to try to counterbalance what I see as distortions of truth. That means using the media in every appropriate way I can.

So the opportunities are there. What are the problems and the risks of extensive media exposure, apart from being so frequently embroiled in controversy, and subject to so much criticism that could reflect adversely on the Church?

First, since I travel too much, am too busy, have too many irons in too many fires, read and think and pray too little, often talk too much, too thoughtlessly, about too many subjects, give so many interviews, am approached so frequently by so many reporters, on such a wide variety of issues and asked so many unexpected questions, I am quite capable of giving confusing or misleading answers to serious questions. This is a real risk. It can provoke serious problems. If on

TV, I'm trying to think through a question, find the answer in my mind and express it not only clearly but *carefully*, conscious of the wide diversity of backgrounds of viewers, and of the difficulties I can create if I say something stupid, misleading or unduly provocative. Yet at the same time I insist on trying to be honest and straightforward. If I'm not on a "talk" show, or being interviewed live, I am conscious of the fact that a five-minute statement on my part may be reduced to a ten-second TV clip, or that a taped interview can be edited. I try to answer a question making every word or phrase able to stand on its own, unable to be taken out of context. The result can be to mix people up, to misinform them, rather than inform them, about what the Church teaches.

Does the opportunity to present the truth, particularly the good news of the Gospel, justify the risk of embarrassing the Church, misleading people and perhaps provoking unnecessary controversy? That's a continuing question in my mind.

I'm not the only one with problems in communicating accurately. The media themselves have their problems.

I wouldn't want to be a reporter for anything in the world: deadlines to be met, severe space limitations, perhaps ten seconds to be aired out of a ten-minute interview, editors' blue pencils and rewrites to be confronted, bizarre and misleading headlines to distort a story. I'm sure it all makes for ulcers and nightmares.

Obviously, every profession has its incompetents, and there *are* occasional journalists and reporters who are not only ignorant of Church matters, but complacent in their ignorance. I always feel bad about complacent ignorance relative to religion. It strikes me as a sign of contempt, an implication that religious issues aren't really important, or that there's nothing complex about them. I found it difficult, for example, that a *religion* reporter covering a rosary service in the Archdiocese of New York didn't know what a decade of the rosary is. It would be like a reporter covering the Yankees who doesn't know what a double play is. Occasionally, too, one encounters prejudice or hostile ideologies among reporters and editors. It's frustrating, but again limited.

I know that reporters are often sent on assignments at the last minute and have to meet deadlines. So some come unprepared through no fault of their own, and are required to reduce highly sophisticated theological concepts to a handful of lines. Unfortunately, there is an occasional editor who knows even less theology, or a headline writer who hucksters the most sacred mysteries as though he had just uncovered a ring of prostitution in Buckingham Palace. Against unprofessionalism there is simply no defense. We are all at its mercy.

Unprofessionalism is as inexcusable in the New York press as it would be on Broadway. Aspiring actors and actresses, dancers and performers of every type all over the United States hunger for a shot at Broadway. It's the Great White Way. The Big Time.

The New York Press is obviously blessed with more than a fair share of professionals. There are dozens I could name who are tough and uncompromising and do their homework. I never know what they're going to ask me, but I know they will have briefed themselves thoroughly, and that they will *understand* my answers and give them a fair hearing, whether they agree or not. Such professionals make it possible for me to communicate Church teaching on public policy to huge numbers of people. They are often very difficult and professionally very "proper." They are sharp, probing, not infrequently painful in their questions. But they are honest, they know what they're asking, and the answers they report are *my* answers, unedited, undistorted. If I fail to communicate Catholic teaching clearly, it's my fault, not theirs.

I mentioned meeting the occasional ideologue. Fortunately, it doesn't happen too often, but I would be less than honest if I pretended it never occurred at all. An illustration is germane to my hypothesis: that the press constitutes a third dimension in Church-State relations. A classic example of ideological reporting on a public-policy issue did occur in respect to the Wilder Case in New York, spelled out in a previous chapter.

During the proceedings, the Archdiocese of New York rebutted so thoroughly the allegation of discrimination against minorities, and gave such irrefutable figures demonstrating that minorities constitute the overwhelming *majority* of those in its care, that the charge of discrimination was actually dropped.

As certain sectors of the press reported the case, however, the unproved, rebutted charges that had been dropped because unsupportable were *headlined* as indisputable fact! The public was "disinformed." *The New York Times* contributed to the error in an editorial ironically called FAIRNESS FOR FOSTER CARE. The editorial stated: "Catholic and Jewish agencies that dominate the [foster-care] system have resisted taking increased numbers of Protestant black children."[2] The error, published twice by one major newspaper, has yet to be corrected, despite the newspaper's having been informed of the truth.[3]

In my judgment, the press, with exceptions, was not at its best in helping the public understand the complicated but extremely important Wilder Case. Too frequently it ignored or brushed off the notion that the Church could legitimately claim any jurisdiction separate from the State's. It treated the issue almost as a question of "eminent domain," so that the State could simply override any pretended jurisdiction on the part of the Church. Much of the press was equally arbitrary in regard to the questions of purpose and values. It was as though Caesar had spoken, and the Church's reasons for taking care of children in the first place made no difference whatever.

That kind of thing is difficult to contend with, and it extends to many issues. For example, there are sectors of the press strongly hostile to the pro-life movement. They editorialize almost fiercely against even the mildest effort to reduce the annual number of abortions. They simply ignore various pro-life activities, yet seem to rush their cameras to the site of a bombed abortion clinic, and editorialize in a manner that strongly suggests that pro-life "rhetoric" is responsible.

Television can be quite as misleading. I recall a demonstration of protestors outside St. Patrick's Cathedral one Sunday. The leading newspapers estimated between 150 and 250 protestors. The police calculated a similar number. I watched on television. The TV reporter, watching the same news footage I was watching, informed the world that "thousands" of demonstrators protested outside St. Patrick's Cathedral. I was embarrassed for the reporter, and wondered who had written the script, and why.

I watched that bit of irresponsible nonprofessionalism annoyed, but not thinking it worth calling the station to complain about. How many such breaches *should* the public shrug off, however? How much is it safe to ignore?

2. *The New York Times*, Saturday, July 2, 1988. (We present elsewhere in this book the precise percentages. A majority of youngsters in foster care in our Church system are minorities and not Catholic.)
3. The incident is reminiscent of one some years earlier involving another major newspaper. The newspaper purchased records of Catholic Charities, available in the courts, and set two investigative reporters to work for many months searching for violations of law or misappropriations. They found nothing because there was nothing to find. In a more civil world, that fact might have merited one sentence in an editorial, but it never did.

The formation of morally sound and socially beneficial public policy depends in large measure on the public's receiving and responding to reliable information. It was because of my honest belief in the importance of the press in informing all of us and in contributing to the debate on public-policy issues that I involved myself in trying to help prevent the demise of the *New York Post* in 1987. (That and my concern about the prospective loss of jobs and the meaning of that loss to individuals, families and the City itself.) We need a wide variety of media options. The loss of a major newspaper in a city the size and complexity of New York is at minimum a reduction in variety, at worst a loss of a particular editorial viewpoint.

No one can dispense the "working press" or media officialdom of its responsibility to try to assure that information is reliable and that editorial viewpoints are fair. There is simply no room for complacent ignorance, unprofessionalism, prejudice or intransigent ideology in the New York media. Much of what happens in New York is far too important to the world at large, as well as to New Yorkers themselves. And much of what *will* happen is the result of what is reported. A story Donald Trump tells in his book, *Trump: The Art of the Deal*, offers a good example.

Mr. Trump describes his efforts to win the City Planning Commission's approval to build Trump Tower, a difficult task. Taking a "calculated risk," he invited Ada Louise Huxtable to look at the model of the Tower because "perhaps no one had a more powerful influence" as chief architecture critic for *The New York Times*, "one of the most influential institutions in the world." Mr. Trump's gamble paid off. The title alone of the article she wrote, A NEW YORK BLOCKBUSTER OF SUPERIOR DESIGN, in his estimate, "probably did more for my zoning than any single thing I ever said or did."[4]

He adds a postscript that credits the Huxtable article with influencing the City to amend its zoning laws to prevent others in the future from doing what it authorized Mr. Trump to do.

Back now to *The New York Times* editorials with which I began. How much of my future effectiveness as Archbishop of New York was affected by those editorials, particularly the first one, that implied that Genghis Khan had been reincarnated and was marching toward the City, breathing fire and slaughter? Who will ever know?

4. Donald Trump, *Trump: The Art of the Deal* (New York: Random House, 1987), p. 115

In any event, the *Times* taught me a lesson I needed to learn.[5] I still don't always *heed* that lesson, unfortunately, but I did learn it. It is that the Churchman or the Statesman, much more than the press, must assume the responsibility to be crystal clear in what he says, and to expect no quarter from the press for his own blunders. A professional press does not create a public individual's errors; it reports them. A professional press does not generate ecclesiastical or political corruption; it reports it, or not infrequently uncovers it. A professional press does not create public villains; it exposes them.

All of which I applaud about the professional press, even when an honest reporter or editorial writer thinks me a villain and portrays me as such. The Churchman has no more claim than the Statesman to privacy. Each is a *public* servant. Nor does either have the right to proclaim error, however pompously. If the Emperor wears no clothes, he can't complain if the press reports his nakedness.

5. I quote *The New York Times* more frequently than other publications, not to fault it, or carry out a personal vendetta, but because its stories go all over the world, and bring me fan mail or hate mail accordingly. It *does* say nice things about me, too, if not quite so frequently as my nephews and nieces think I deserve them!

V

THE MAYOR
EDUCATION

THE CARDINAL
EDUCATION

THE MAYOR

I am a product of the public-school system. Although I was born in the Bronx, at an early age I moved with my family to Newark, New Jersey. I went to elementary and high school there. After serving in the Second World War I returned to the City and attended the City University of New York for two years before entering New York University Law School. I won't say that everything I have achieved is a result of my public schooling, but I do credit the quality of that education for giving me the proper background for law school and the confidence in myself which has allowed me to go as far as my abilities will take me.

I'm sure it's no surprise to hear the Mayor of New York City cheerleading for public education. But I also provide more than verbal support. My mandate includes making the public schools as competitive as possible with the best education offered in the private sector. In a larger context my role goes beyond being responsible for the public-school system along with the chancellor. As Mayor I must also concern myself with the City's entire education network. That network is made up of a variety of institutions that combine to create the capacity and diversity necessary to provide every child with the opportunity to reach his or her individual potential. Libraries, museums, public and parochial schools at all levels of education are part of that matrix. Unless this amalgam delivers the basic skills necessary for our future labor force, it jeopardizes the very viability of our City.

Consider the fact that without major corporations carrying the lion's share of the tax burden the City would not be able to deliver the required level of essential services. Further, recognize that without workers who have received the educational background necessary to do a competitive job, corporations would move out of the region to find such a suitable labor force.

We need not deal strictly in hypotheticals. The New York Telephone Company not too long ago had to test over forty thousand applicants in order to recruit about four thousand new hires who had the basic educational skills required. That's a frightening proposition. The regional telephone provider has little choice but to recruit here. Other companies are not so committed and some, thankfully few, have left for what they think are greener pastures. They may be in for a surprise.

All along the presidential campaign trail the contenders spoke of education as a national priority. "We have lost our competitive edge," or similar words, were used to focus the nation's attention on the essential task of revamping our educational system. It's clear that American education is not what it once was. We didn't need the 1983 study of American education, A Nation at Risk, and its warning of the "rising tide of mediocrity" in our schools to learn of the danger at hand. It became clear to most educators who had foreign students in their classes that many societies around the world were better preparing their young to compete. To regain a once unmatched level of excellence in both public and private schools is perhaps the most urgent issue facing the new president.

New York City could not maintain an adequate public-school system without the supplement of the private schools. The total school-age population, elementary through secondary, is about 1.3 million. That's a population near the size of Detroit, the fifth largest city in the United States. More than 250,000 of those students attend private school, with Catholic parochial schools handling by far the largest segment of this group.

For many years, the parochial schools have shouldered a large share of the responsibility for educating our children. New York has always been the gateway to the United States for new immigrants. For the last 150 or so years, the majority of those new immigrants have been Catholic. The parochial schools offered religion-based, value-based education at an affordable price. Today, over one quarter of New York's population continues to be foreign-born. Unlike yesterday, the parochial schools now serve a much broader population; in some schools, there is even a majority of non-Catholic students. Tradition and religion were once the determining factors in the choice between public and parochial school attendance. Now, for many in the inner city, the question turns on quality of education and school environment. In too many instances, our public schools fail to make the grade—not because we don't have good teachers; we do; and not because of inadequate resources, either. But working parents seek a value-based education for their child that is not always available in public-school classrooms.

It's not a search for the Ichabod Crane approach: "Spare the rod and spoil the child"—thankfully, corporal punishment left both public and private classrooms long ago. However, along with a new era of student rights came confining rules and a proliferation of lawsuits. Is it any wonder, at a time when the New York City Board of Education is using metal detectors in our public high schools as a way to keep guns and knives out, that our teachers aren't willing to take the risks associated with teaching a value-based curriculum? More has to be done to encourage teachers to take those risks, to support the teachers who do and to give the guidance necessary so that the curriculum is best constructed to reflect our values as a nation. Fortunately, we have the right person to do the job in our new City Schools Chancellor, Dr. Richard Green. Chancellor Green is credited with turning around a deteriorating educational system in the city of Minneapolis. The challenge here is similar in nature but the dimension and scope of the problem increase the degree of difficulty tenfold. It is clear that we have the potential in our students, with more Merit Scholarship winners than anywhere in the country. We also have talented teachers. Leadership toward a return to a value-based education is a key to any solution.

Relatively minor atmospheric changes in the classroom can have a dramatic impact in support of value-based education and to a lesser degree, student conduct. Dress codes seem to some an unnecessary vestige of times past. Not so. If thoughtfully implemented—meaning that consideration must be given to even marginal additional economic burdens that might be placed on a child's family—dress codes would contribute to the authority and respect attributed to both the school administration and teacher. Such regulations also serve as the great equalizer among competitive student groups.

I recently proposed an experiment with dress codes in the City's schools. I asked Moe Ginsberg and Emile Tubina, two major figures in the fashion business, to donate school uniforms for a pilot program at P.S. 175. Fayva Shoes also agreed to provide shoes to the 408 students there. Chancellor Green and I were delighted not only with the response from the business community but also with that from the kids. The uniforms clearly gave them a sense of pride and purpose.

Isn't it strange that one of the most prominent issues of the 1988 presidential campaign was whether or not our children should be required to say the Pledge of Allegiance? While as a lawyer I understand the legal arguments against compulsion, I don't think the average American can accept the notion that the Constitution stands in the way of beginning the school day by formally recognizing the love of one's country. There are those who will claim that waving the flag and waxing patriotic only obscures the real issues at stake. Yet no other controversy better crystallizes the externally created tensions that push our public-school teachers away from teaching values. In my own city, I asked Schools Chancellor Richard Green to review the Pledge controversy to determine whether or not there wasn't some solution. Upon closer examination he discovered the state law requiring the Pledge to be given at the start of each school day was routinely being ignored in our schools. He said he would correct that.

Prayer in school or, alternatively, the notion of a moment of silence is an even thornier matter. Gallup polls have indicated that eight out of every ten Americans favored a constitutional amendment proposed by the Reagan administration that read:

Nothing in this Constitution shall be construed to prohibit individual or group prayer in the public schools or in other public institutions. No person shall be required by the United States or by any State to participate in prayer.

Yet the amendment never gained any momentum in the Congress. While I don't oppose such an amendment, I believe it is not worth the energy, struggle or consternation a passage fight would necessarily entail. If a child has the inclination to pray during the school day, I am sure he or she will find a suitable, albeit not an organized, way to do it.

Next door in New Jersey, the legislature battled with the courts to provide for a moment of silence at the beginning of each school day. It seems ironic that in a country that so prides itself on free speech and independent thought we find ourselves knotted up both legally and emotionally in this rather simple proposition.

For some, it is all-consuming. They see the obvious. A moment of silence is just a legalistic way around what they consider a constitutional prohibition against prayer in the public schools. They argue that such an attempt is a threat to individual freedom.

I don't share that view. To the contrary, I see the only danger of intrusion on individual freedoms arising out of an acceptance of the prayer opponents' constitutional construction.

It is all in the way you approach the basic doctrine of separating Church from State. Was the original intent to protect religious freedom? Were we seeking to prevent a state takeover of religious practice and ensure against a nationally sponsored set of religious beliefs that would exclude all other faiths except the Anglican Church? The answer to both questions is yes, in my judgment. However, there are certain ideologues who would expand the concept and destroy the protection it was intended to provide. They interpret the doctrine in such a way as to use it as a weapon to fend off those who believe in God, who teach their children to believe and who don't want the education their children receive in the public-school classroom in any way to undermine those values.

While I don't know the current president of the New Jersey State Senate well enough to put him in this category, his comments comparing Ronald Reagan's rhetoric at the Republican Convention to that of Adolf Hitler is indicative of the strong tensions in this area. Senator Russo took umbrage at the president's claim that the United States was "picked by God to preserve liberty." Never mind that the president equated liberty—the right of individuals to determine their own destinies in freedom—to the moral law of God, whereas Hitler rejected God and liberty. The mere mention of God, faith or religion in such a public setting as the Republican National Convention was deemed by some to be an unconscionable violation of the separation of Church and State. Dopey.

As determined as some ideologues may be when it comes to what is done in the public school, their resolve is all the more apparent when it comes to state-sponsored financial aid in any form to private-school children. One concept that has long provoked strong reaction is tax credits for those who send their children to private school. Since the early sixties I have favored such an approach. I believe in freedom of choice in education. It provides for competition. Becoming Mayor has not changed my views on federal tax credits—so long as there is no diminution of budgetary support for the public-education system as a result of such programs.

It would have been interesting to see former Secretary of Education William Bennett's suggestion, a variant on tax credits, become a reality. He issued a challenge to private schools in a speech before the National Catholic Education Association. He proposed that parochial schools take up the challenge of educating dropouts and troubled students who aren't making it through the public-school system. Under "Project Voluntas," as Bennett calls it, parochial schools would present the federal government with a bill for services at the end of each school year. While I don't think there would be much of a chance that the Congress would authorize payment of such an invoice, the gesture of goodwill toward the American public on the part of parochial schools might focus attention on the issue of tax credits for parents who pay the tuitions that educate not only their own children but also those children the public system is failing. Again, I would not oppose such a subsidy and in fact would support it if the constitutional questions were resolved.

For nearly two decades, the City of New York has offered special programs of remedial education to economically disadvantaged children. We have done so thanks to a program authorized by Title I of the federal Elementary and Secondary Education Act of 1965. We have done so without discriminating between students attending public schools and those attending private or parochial schools; this year, for instance, we spent $198 million on the program, and about one in thirteen of the students it served—25,000 in all—were enrolled in some kind of nonpublic school, parochial or private.

But on July 1, 1986, the Supreme Court of the United States handed down two rulings that have had the effect of denying many of those 25,000 students the educational help they need and deserve. In two cases—one brought in Grand Rapids, Michigan, and the other, *Aguilar* v. *Felton,* here in New York City—the Court ruled that for publicly paid teachers to visit a parochial school in order to offer remedial courses, even if those courses had nothing to do with religious instruction, was a "symbolic union of government and religion" and therefore unconstitutional under the First Amendment. The vote was 5 to 4.

168

I believe the Supreme Court's decision was a bad one. I also believe that in a democratic society such as ours—"a government of laws, not of men," as John Adams put it—it is essential that even a bad decision, lawfully made, must be complied with, as this one will be. Nevertheless, the Court's decision put us in a very difficult position. How can we guarantee all students proper access to Title I remedial-education benefits without violating the First Amendment separation of Church and State? On the other hand, how can we comply with the decision without denying the rights of some students to that remedial education just because of the school they attend? Justice William Brennan, great judge that he is, on this issue flunked the test of common sense.

From the beginning, the City has administered Title I in good faith—indeed, in their dissent from the majority, Justices William Rehnquist and Sandra Day O'Connor noted that "an objective observer of the implementation of the Title I program in New York would hardly view it as endorsing the tenets of the participating parochial schools." The criterion for remedial assistance has been whether the children in question are behind in their studies or have learning disabilities, not whether they are Catholic, Jewish, Protestant, professing any other faith or no faith at all. Under the 1965 legislation, a federal formula allocated funds to local school boards for remedial education—with specific portions for private or religious schools. Under the prior scheme, a local board could not deviate from the formula—if it accepted Title I funds for public schools, it had to accept them for parochial schools too; it could not use public-school funds in parochial schools or vice versa. The system was fair, it worked well.

I believe that a child does not forfeit the right to the best possible education just because his or her parents make the decision to enroll that child in a private or religious school. Therefore, I have always been in favor of as much public aid to children in nonpublic schools as the Constitution will allow. And I do not consider this, as some do, a "Catholic issue," just because the facts of the Aguilar case happened to involve parochial schools. Like the issue of tuition tax credits for parents of nonpublic-school children, this issue is to me much broader than a sectarian special interest: It involves the crucial question of guaranteeing pluralism and freedom of choice in American life. As a Jew and a lawyer, I recognize that this decision affects yeshivas as well as parochial schools, denying Jewish religious schools the benefits of

169

Title I instruction too, and is therefore unfortunate for that reason alone. But, more important, as an American I am for anything that keeps our nation secular, diverse and tolerant. Nonpublic education—private or religious—helps keep our nation that way; therefore, I see nothing wrong with promoting private education within the bounds of the Constitution.

A key role in the *Aguilar* decision was played by Justice William Brennan writing for the majority. He said that Title I funds could not be used on behalf of parochial-school students if the remedial education took place in a parochial-school building. His main reason for this was that "the students would be unlikely to discern the crucial difference between the classes." Justice Brennan's opinion would continue to allow the City to help students in religious schools, without violating the First Amendment, so long as it did so outside the school itself.

Therefore, we proposed an idea that we believed at the time was workable and that could be implemented in time to keep all New York City schoolchildren in Title I classes the following semester: mobile trailers, staffed by publicly paid public-school teachers and parked on the curb adjacent to the private or parochial school. When the time came for students to attend their Title I classes, they would merely have to walk from their parochial or nonpublic-school classrooms to a mobile trailer/classroom, and the distinction so crucial to the Supreme Court—the separation of Church and State—would be preserved. Whatever solution we devised would take money but under no circumstances would instructional funds be used to purchase these trailers or other equipment for whatever alternative we decided upon.

We thought there might be better ways to comply with the Court's decision, and to that end I sent hand-delivered letters to religious leaders here in New York whose congregations operate the affected schools. These letters went to Rabbi Joshua Fishman of Torah Umesorah and Dr. Alvin Schiff of the Board of Jewish Education, as well as to the rabbis or principals at 194 Jewish schools here in the city. The letters also went to the Cardinal and to Bishop Mugavero of Brooklyn, to Archbishop Iakovos of the Greek Orthodox Church and Archbishop Torkon Manoogian of St. Vartan's Armenian Church, to Episcopal Bishop Paul Moore and Lutheran Bishop James Graefe and Reverend Gardner Taylor of the Concord Baptist Church of Christ. To all of them, I offered my help "in implementing a plan that would cushion as much as possible what can't help but be disruptive effects on the education of the children."

Regrettably, no one came up with a better plan than the one we devised in which trailers were utilized. And consequently, during the 1986–87 school year, the first year of City compliance with the Court's ruling, the number of students served dropped from 20,965 in the previous year to 10,737. This drop was accompanied by a down-turn in the number of parochial schools participating in the program from 247 to 146. This past year has seen only slight improvement. The absurdity here is tragic. Even though we've developed elaborate means and spent millions of dollars satisfying the Court's ruling, children in need of special education aren't receiving it.

As relations between the United States and the Soviet Union have improved, the amount of information our two countries exchange has increased. If these two countries can mutually share their scientific, literary and cultural accomplishments, to name just a few, does it make sense to prohibit the sharing of resources by our own parochial and public schools?

Recently, I urged public officials in New York City to participate in an "Adopt a Class" program in which the official would periodically meet with a class, on a regular basis, and essentially serve as a resource and role model for the students. I think it's a wonderful program, and I am a participant in it. Yet I was told by my lawyers from the start that I must not allow any clergy to be involved in the Adopt a Class program. That makes no sense to me. Imposing artificial constraints in providing educational services under the guise of avoiding Church and State entanglements benefits no one.

THE CARDINAL

"I believe the Framers of the Constitution would roll over in their graves at the ridiculous spectacle of schoolchildren putting on their coats and galoshes in the middle of a wintry day to go outside and board a van full of desks in order to avoid 'excessive entanglement of church and state.'"

That's Mayor Koch at his most honest and commonsensical. Indeed, the entire article from which the above is excerpted reflects a statesmanship which is, in a sense, extremely frustrating because more frequently than not it is rendered impotent, not always through the fault of others, as he himself admits in the article. It's called "Lunacies of Government—Legal, Bureaucratic, Ideological."[1]

The issue the Mayor uses here to show the lunacies of government concerns remedial instruction for needy schoolchildren.[2] From 1965 to 1985 the City of New York was able to provide such instruction for all children, whether in public or parochial schools. In fact, such instruction was mandated by the federal government under Title I of the Elementary and Secondary Education Act of 1965.

In 1985, however, the Supreme Court decided that the federal funding of remedial instruction on parochial-school premises constituted "excessive entanglement of church and state." For twenty years specially skilled public-school teachers had gone into parochial schools to provide remedial instruction to disadvantaged youngsters.

---

1. As printed in the *New York Law Journal* on July 11, 1988, based on an address by Mayor Koch at the Chautauqua Institute on June 30, 1988.
2. Recall the discussion of irrationality of government and the Trojan Horse principle (Chapter III).

From now on, said the Supreme Court, if youngsters are to receive such instruction, they will have to *leave* parochial-school premises and go elsewhere.

Justice Sandra Day O'Connor dissented in the case and noted the irrationality of the majority decision. "For these children the Court's decision is tragic. The Court deprives them of a program that offers a meaningful chance at success in life, and it does so on the untenable theory that public school teachers (most of whom are of different faiths than their students) are likely to start teaching religion merely because they have walked across the threshold of a parochial school."[3]

And the Mayor agreed. As he put it, "This ruling makes no sense. . . . It takes the principle of separation of Church and State to an unnecessary and dangerous extreme."

So the Mayor has spent millions of dollars—federal, state, city—on such complicated arrangements as bringing mobile vans into the immediate vicinity of parochial schools. The remedial instruction is given in the mobile vans and to only a small percentage of eligible children.

This is a classic example of trying to solve a Church-State problem—truly a pseudo-problem—by cooperation and ingenuity. It is a most unsatisfactory solution (for example, many Manhattan schools have no yards nearby where the vans could be parked) but far better than no solution.[4] What I find fascinating about it, however, is that the Mayor would do it. He could simply have absolved himself of blame—and of responsibility. He chose not to, I think, not only because he rebels at the injustice of the Supreme Court decision, but because he believes in the value of our Catholic schools. Both as a congressman and as Mayor of New York he has argued in favor of more public aid to Catholic schools. And well he might.

I'm going to be very forthright about out Catholic school system and its relation to public policy.[5] In essence, our public policy regard-

3. A. James Reichley, *Religion in American Public Life* (Washington, D.C.: The Brookings Institution, 1985), p. 164

4. It is now possible that another "solution" has been found. On August 17, 1988, newspapers reported that the New York City Board of Education plans to lease property on the playgrounds of three Catholic schools in Brooklyn to provide a site for the remedial instruction. The report also states that a "religious liberty" group plans to fight this plan as unconstitutional. This is the same group that fought the instruction in the parochial school which led to the Supreme Court decision and instruction in mobile vans.

5. Much of what is said in this chapter about Catholic schools is applicable to private and nonpublic schools in general. I omit specific references to these in the text both because my familiarity is primarily with Catholic schools and because I would feel presumptuous in arguing for what private and nonpublic schools are much more capable of arguing for themselves.

ing education reflects one of the bitterest, most irrational and most self-defeating religious prejudices remaining in our society. There can simply be no rational excuse for the refusal to recognize what our Catholic school system contributes to New York and to the United States.

There is much to be gained by discussing Catholic schools in New York. I note two things specifically: One, as the Mayor's example points out, the subject reveals a lot about government lunacy; two, it reveals a lot about the prejudices that must be resolved if Church and State are to work together harmoniously for the common good. Both prejudice against Catholicism and an insistence on government control not only preclude government's doing a number of sensible things that would benefit society in general, but blind much of the private sector to the contributions *it* could make to the broader community. The question of governmental control raises, once again, the fundamental issue of jurisdiction in Church-State relations.

Newsday has never been accused, to my knowledge, of being jubilantly pro-Catholic, so I noted with special interest its comments of September 9, 1987.

. . . Catholic school students continue to outperform their public school counterparts. In 1984–1985, the most recent year for which state-wide statistics are available, 85% of Catholic school sixth graders read above the state reference point; in public schools, 78% did. . . .

In addition, Catholic schools are far more likely to post strong performance in nonacademic areas like attendance, dropout rates and safety. . . .

A decade ago, more than 30% of Manhattan Catholic elementary school students were white; today, less than half that share are. . . .

The *Newsday* report is supported by a number of scientific studies. For example, the reports of James S. Coleman and Thomas Hoffer (two non-Catholics): *High School Achievement: Public, Catholic and Private Schools Compared* (1982) and *Public and Private High Schools: The Impact of Communities* (1987). Their findings concerning the success of Catholic schools are fascinating. I quote from the latter:

There is a widespread assumption that private schools serve a socioeconomically elite clientele. The assumption is incorrect in a number of respects. In the first place the historically dominant form of private schooling in the United States has been the Catholic schools. These schools are concentrated in urban areas, charge relatively little tuition by middle-class standards, and were originally designed for anything but an elite, serving instead recent immigrants struggling to find a place in American society. In the second place, elitest tendencies have never found the nation's public schools to be an uncongenial stage for expression and cultivation, thanks to the joint effect of the policy of assignment to school by residence and the practice of parents to locate residence according to income [p. 30].

Among the three principal sectors [Catholic, private and public], the Catholic sector has sharply lower dropouts than either of the others. The proportion of students in the other private sector that drop out is nearly as high as that in the public sector and over three times that in the Catholic sector. The students in other private schools come from higher socioeconomic backgrounds than those in Catholic schools, so clearly something more than the differences among sectors in the average socioeconomic background of parents is involved as a determinant of dropping out. Dropping out of school is an action that results in part from the organizational dynamics of the school itself, and represents . . . failure in that organizational context [p. 100].

Catholic schools bring about greater growth for the average student in both verbal and mathematical skills than do public schools . . . [p. 212].

The achievement growth benefits of Catholic school attendance are especially strong for students who are in one way or another disadvantaged: lower socioeconomic status, black, or Hispanic [p. 213].

I meet frequently with various businesspeople who validate such findings by their own experience with high school graduates. These business people range from Wall Street partners to presidents of huge corporations. Whatever their own religious persuasion, most of them tell me the same thing about our inner-city Catholic high school graduates: They have no difficulty passing employment examinations and when employed acquit themselves superbly in most instances.

In no way do I cite these evaluations to demean inner-city public schools, or to disparage the superb public-school teachers who dedicate themselves to first-rate education under trying circumstances. I simply want to dispel the myth that the dropout rate is so low and the success rate so high among Catholic school graduates because we "skim off the best." In our inner-city Catholic schools the profile of students is almost precisely the same as it is for public-school students: The vast majority are black and Hispanic, from low-income families, a large number not Catholic. Many inner-city Catholic school students come from drug-infested, violence-ridden, inadequate-housing areas, just as do those in public schools.

Three years ago, within the geographical territory of one of our inner-city Catholic elementary schools, I am told there were sixty-five murders. The area is notorious for its burned-out buildings and drug pushers. During the year of the murders, in all grades of the school, its students, overwhelmingly black and Hispanic, scored significantly above the national average on national tests. What would the families of those youngsters have done without the oasis of the parish school?

Some 85 percent of our Catholic high school graduates go on to college. One of our Catholic high schools is significantly below this average, but for an extraordinary reason. It accepts without any entrance examination all applicants who have completed the eighth grade. It takes applicants rejected by our other Catholic high schools. Yet 68 percent of *its* graduates go on to higher education. It seems to me that here is a story that every educational system in the country would want to learn.

Now the clincher. The average cost of putting a student through a Catholic elementary school or high school in the Archdiocese of New York is less than half of the cost of the same student in public school. The average annual cost of educating a student in a Catholic high school may be fairly estimated at $2,690; estimates of the cost in a public school range up to $6,000.[6]

This is where the irrationality comes in. In a city in which Catholic school graduates can contribute so effectively to critical socioeconomic needs, our enrollment is dropping to a dangerously low

6. Cost estimates necessarily fluctuate as the result of the rise in insurance, salaries, maintenance and equipment costs.

level, making it a severe financial burden to keep our Catholic schools open. The scenario is absurd. Every student in a Catholic school is saving taxpayers substantial sums of money. Parents who send their youngsters to Catholic schools carry a double burden: They are taxed to pay for public schools, even though their children don't go to them, and still they have to pay tuition and fees to send their youngsters to Catholic schools. Surely some kind of "voucher" system could be designed to ease the financial burden for parents of youngsters in Catholic schools.[7]

In a rational world, if students are given a demonstrably better education at one half of the cost or less in a Catholic school than in a public school, isn't it reasonable to think the community at large would vote to support Catholic schools? Why must a rational community permit the Catholic schools to vanish before their eyes?

I really don't understand why the only democracy in the Western world that denies help to Catholic schools cannot design a constitutionally acceptable method, if only for selfish financial reasons, of preventing those schools from failing. Even Japan, with a radically different religious culture, subsidizes the salaries of teachers in Catholic schools, recognizing the contribution such schools make to society. In my judgment, the problem is not really one of constitutionality. In large measure, it's the deep-rooted anti-Catholicism that still seethes in certain sectors of society: what Harvard historian Arthur Schlesinger once called the oldest major prejudice in our society. It seems to me a classic example of Barbara Tuchman's *The March of Folly*: Irrationality (lunacy) is permitted to deprive society of a vital resource.

I have had strong disagreements with the Mayor, as noted throughout this book, yet he is fair enough to state publicly what many politicians shy away from in terror: that the way government treats Catholic schools is lunacy.

Why is the cost of Catholic education threatening its survival? I'm one reason. My father was a union man. Talk union corruption and

---

7. To its credit, New York State has repeatedly proposed programs to assist nonpublic elementary and secondary schools. These programs have all been declared unconstitutional. Yet United States Supreme Court Justice Byron White argued that tuition reimbursement and tax-deduction plans should have been approved. He said: "Under state law, these children have a right to a free public education and it would not appear unreasonable if the state, relieved of the expense of educating a child in the public school, contributed to the expense of his education elsewhere." (Reichley, op.cit.)

abuse all you will, the right to collective bargaining is spelled out with indisputable clarity in papal encyclicals. My father knew something about the charter document of those encyclicals on labor, *Rerum Novarum (Of New Things)*, and revered its author, Pope Leo XIII. I cut my eyeteeth on the doctrine of the dignity of the worker. As kids in Ireland may have been reared on stories of the Black and Tan, I was reared on stories of strikes that lasted for months, while families starved, so that wages might rise a penny an hour.

Our Catholic schools could not be what they are and contribute what they contribute without our teachers, religious and lay. We cannot expect those teachers to teach Catholic values, among which justice is basic, if we don't demand justice for the teachers themselves. That has required that we do everything humanly possible to assure a just wage, decent working conditions, security for the future. We're not there yet, but we're moving toward it as rapidly as we can. It takes money. Where does it come from? One way is to raise tuition. That can be self-defeating in a number of ways, chief of which is that we can price poor families out of a Catholic education. This would be disastrous. I am convinced that if we are truly to "empower" the poor, we *must* give them the very best education available, and that includes value education. Otherwise, we make it almost impossible for them to break the cycle of poverty.

Everything else about our Catholic educational system has skyrocketed except tuition, which has increased at a rate lower than the rate of inflation. Insurance costs virtually doubled between 1987 and 1988. Building-maintenance costs, teacher-training costs, practically all conceivable costs have escalated. The same has been true for public schools, except that their costs are defrayed by increased taxes paid by parents of public and Catholic school children *equally.*

It is shortsighted to argue that parents don't *have* to send their youngsters to Catholic schools, so they deserve double taxation. Many parents send their youngsters to Catholic schools because they believe that too many public schools don't provide what the State actually *owes* students: a disciplined environment, drug free, where learning can take place and basic values are taught and respected.

I spent many of my early school years in public schools. In my day, they provided a safe environment, discipline, values and an excellent academic education. It was exceedingly difficult for some rather unusual reasons for my folks to send me to Catholic grade schools, as they did my brothers and sisters. But I suffered little. My formal religious teaching was at home and in an after-school setting by sisters. And, just as significant, the *values* in the public schools of my day were quite like the *values* in Catholic schools. Among the "values," we were taught rules, laws and even the Ten Commandments.

Today, Supreme Court interpretations, the ACLU and various adversarial groups and individuals make true value-teaching virtually impossible.[8] Yet the Coleman study finds that *the* significant difference between the failures of many public schools and the successes of most Catholic schools is found precisely in the fact that Catholic schools are *value*-oriented.[9] Moreover, from a completely pragmatic perspective, the values taught are precisely the values vital to New York's well-being and stability.[10]

Some of the businesspeople mentioned earlier in this chapter have become increasingly aware of what our Catholic schools have to offer. They have involved themselves in the not-for-profit corporation called the Inner-City Scholarship Fund. These executives, of all religious persuasions, are committed without prejudice to quality education for children of all races and creeds in disadvantaged areas of New York City. They are contributing time and funds to help such quality education survive. Some 33,000 students of all faiths attend seventy-nine nonpublic elementary and high schools in the South Bronx, Harlem and other poverty pockets of the City. A significant number of these students are non-Catholics. Over 90 percent are minorities and 96 percent of their families live at or below the poverty level. Eighty-five percent of Inner-City high school graduates go to college.

Cardinal Cooke initiated the program to save our schools to the benefit of both our civic communities and our industries. He was de-

8. At times the ACLU will not even agree that there *are* shared values in our country. In a letter dated May 26, 1988, the California Legislative Office of the ACLU gave its reasons for opposing a Senate bill concerning a particular form of sex education in public schools.

"It is our position that teaching that monogamous, heterosexual intercourse within marriage is a traditional American value is an unconstitutional establishment of a religious doctrine in public schools. There are various religions which hold contrary beliefs with respect to marriage and monogamy."

How could educators ever hope to teach even the most basic values traditional to our nation given that kind of position on the part of the ACLU?

9. The Coleman study actually speaks of "social capital" on which our schools draw, which includes family and community life, moral and religious values and related factors.

10. Graduates of the fourteen Catholic colleges and universities in the Archdiocese of New York contribute immensely to the continuing growth of the City, in part because their education has been rooted in values.

termined to provide for the poor of all faiths an opportunity to break the cycle of poverty through quality education in Catholic schools. When neighborhoods were breaking up and families who could were moving to the suburbs, he recognized that only good schools could keep inner-city neighborhoods alive. Even then, however, costs were becoming prohibitive. The Cardinal asked a small group of executives of various faiths to address the problem. The result: the establishing of the Inner-City Scholarship Fund, which over the course of ten years has raised a substantial amount of money, which is spent in the schools as rapidly as it comes in.

Such an effort is wonderfully gratifying, but terribly frustrating. The money these friends of our schools raise represents a lot of hard work, and I am exceedingly grateful for it. It is also a long way from meeting the needs of the Archdiocese's several-hundred-million-dollar educational program.

Yet representatives of firms that pay huge taxes for our public schools tell me they can't find enough qualified basic-entry-skill employees from among public-school graduates, but have no problem with graduates of Catholic schools. Moreover, they have great difficulty in attracting to New York and then holding on to high-quality management types because many of these people don't want to put their youngsters in the local public schools in New York. I am told this is one of the reasons that many industries are tempted to move out of New York.

One still hears a lot of nonsense that Catholic schools are *divisive* in our society. They are *different*, therefore suspect. This view was advanced even as early as 1875 by President Ulysses S. Grant,

> who believed that authoritarian tendencies within the Catholic Church made Catholicism inherently antidemocratic. [He] called for a constitutional amendment to ensure that "neither state nor nation, nor both combined, shall support institutions of learning other than those sufficient to afford every child growing up in the land of opportunity a good common school education, unmixed with sectarian, pagan or atheistical dogmas."[11]

Famed Harvard educator James B. Conant was no more subtle than President Grant. "The greater the proportion of our youth who fail to

11. Reichley op.cit., p. 164

attend our public schools and who receive their education elsewhere, the greater the threat to our democratic unity."[12] (It's funny; I had never thought of Harvard University as a public school!)

Purportedly in a democracy everyone should be a product of the same basic educational system. This is apparently required for better understanding of one another and of the "American Way of life." Do we really believe that? If we believe it, do we want it? Do we, in fact, treat and teach everyone in precisely the same way in our local public schools? Of course we don't. We recognize and allow for all sorts of individual differences, abilities and disabilities.

What really seems to be happening, in my view, is that our Catholic educational system is one of the last bastions against an encroaching government monopoly that would require everybody to be educated in the same secular way. What is especially ironic, here, is that the same government courts and bureaucrats are stripping public schools of all right or requirement to teach what we have generally called our "traditional American values," values taught for almost two centuries in schools, churches, homes and various public institutions.

It is fascinating that people in the Soviet Union like Mikhail Gorbachev—whatever their true motives—are publicly arguing for a relaxation of certain restrictions on religion because society critically needs "ethical values," while in the United States there are people apparently intent on sterilizing our public schools of such values. I do not consider the secularization of schools truly "American" in any way. Paradoxically, Catholic schools are committed to the teaching of the very best of "traditional American values." To accuse Catholic schools of being divisive, then, is really to accuse them of being "American."

I believe we see in the secularization of schools a classic example of Church-State conflict waged on the grounds of both jurisdiction and values.

Clearly, for their good and its own, the State has the obligation to see that all its citizens are educated. Increasingly, however, the State has moved beyond providing education opportunities to *controlling* education itself. One way of controlling is to deny funding to private educational systems that insist on teaching religious values or refuse to teach certain offensive secular values of the State. An excellent exam-

12. James Conant, *Education and Liberty* (Cambridge, Mass.: Harvard University Press, 1921), p. 81

ple of "offensive secular values" may be found in certain approaches to school-based health clinics. Why must Catholic youngsters be exposed to health clinics which are used as a means of indoctrinating school-children in abortion and artificial birth prevention? We have no objection to the concept of health clinics in themselves. We do object strenuously to what we consider their misuse.[13]

Welfare Research, Inc., has evaluated school health clinics. One finding as reported by the Coalition of Concerned Clergy (Jewish and Christian) is that in 148 out of 198 case reports reviewed, children visiting the health clinics were given birth-control counseling. "It's clear," said the coalition, "that the staff of these clinics believe their primary mission is birth control." Yet 91 percent of the parents interviewed said they want their children counseled in sexual abstinence. Over half the parents had reservations about making birth-control supplies and prescriptions available to children, and most said, if they *are* made available, it should be only with parental consent.

Even were one to brush off moral or religious convictions as irrelevant when it comes to reducing teenage pregnancies, the Welfare Research findings raise serious questions in my mind about even the pragmatic value of the health clinics' approach. The report reveals that one can't make any prediction as to whether the birth-control services will affect the rate of pregnancy. There are no data showing that the rate of pregnancy is reduced by such clinics.[14]

Perhaps because of the special shock we all experience when a child or an adolescent commits suicide, I myself was particularly distressed to learn the report's finding that the attempted suicide rate is almost three times higher for "sexually active" children than for sexually inactive children. The coalition observes that sexual promiscuity is a symptom of a much deeper problem and of a very troubled child. The

13. The Roman Catholic Bishops of the United States issued an important "Statement on School-Based Clinics" on November 18, 1985. It reads in part: ". . . School-based health clinics that clearly separate themselves from the agenda of contraceptive advocates may provide part of an effective response to the health needs of young people. . . . We object to the campaign to provide contraceptive services through school-based clinics on both moral and practical grounds. . . . Many school-based clinics do even greater harm by facilitating abortion in cases when a teen-age girl becomes pregnant." Parents, educators and public officials will find this document exceptionally informative.
14. In the Bishops' "Statement on School-Based Clinics" previously cited, we read an even stronger assertion. "It is now well established that knowledge of and access to contraceptives do not ensure prevention of pregnancy among teen-agers. Some studies even claim that access to family planing clinics is associated with an increase in sexual activity, pregnancies and abortions." (The Statement quotes 1986 studies on the subject conducted by Weed and Olson.)

question obviously must be asked, therefore, Is contraceptive counseling in a health clinic simply going to address symptoms and mask the underlying deep problems of these youngsters?

One further question must be asked in regard to clinics. The State has a broad responsibility for the health of *all* children. Why should health services be provided by health clinics in public schools alone? Should health services be less available to youngsters in Catholic schools? Or will someone dare argue that the State may not finance health services in Catholic schools unless children are taught abortion and artificial birth prevention? That's not birth control; that's government control—of the worst sort. What was it the Supreme Court said about *privacy?*

The Church maintains its own education system today for at least four reasons: as a vehicle for explicit Catholic teaching; to provide a morally acceptable climate for students; to prepare students for the socioeconomic demands of life; to enhance learning itself.

It was the same Archbishop John Hughes mentioned in the first chapter of this book who saw the need back in 1842 and established the Archdiocesan Catholic School System of New York. What was called the public-school system in the days of Archbishop Hughes was actually operated by the Public School Society, a State-funded, *private* organization established to take care of youngsters not educated in denominational schools. The Public School Society strongly opposed any and all claims to a share of public funds by denominational schools. Archbishop Hughes argued forcefully but in vain:

> . . . Give us our just proportion of the common school fund and if we do not give as good an education, apart from religious instruction as is given in the public schools, to one third a larger number of children for the same money, we are willing to renounce our just claim. [15]

Archbishop Hughes's primary problem was not with the refusal to share State funds, however. It was that the public-school system was teaching Protestantism and anti-Catholicism. The Protestantism was at best vague: Protestant hymns and prayers and a Protestant (King James) version of the Bible were used. The anti-Catholicism, how-

15. Richard Shaw, *Dagger John: The Unquiet Life and Times of Archbishop John Hughes of New York* (New York: Paulist Press, 1977), p. 144

ever, was frequently explicit. Of all places, for example, it was in a geography book that one found such a gem as this:

> Superstition prevails not only at Rome but in all the states of the Church. The inhabitants observe scrupulously all the ceremonies of religion omitting nothing connected with form or etiquette, although apparently destitute of true devotion. Confession is a practice which all follow more from custom than from Christian humility, and rather to lull the conscience than to correct vice.[16]

Public-school textbooks were all shot through with such anti-Catholic sentiments, some even more vicious. It must be remembered that Catholics were still widely treated as second-class citizens. The Nativist riots were in full force. Catholic churches in Philadelphia had been burned to the ground.

The old St. Patrick's Cathedral at Prince and Mott streets and other Catholic churches were threatened. Archbishop Hughes called out the Ancient Order of Hibernians. A thousand strong, they surrounded the Cathedral, warding off with their muskets the Nativist would-be incendiaries.

So the Archbishop had good reason to be sensitive about the climate in the local public schools. The Church of the day was a thoroughly immigrant Church, very largely Irish, but including Germans, Italians, Slovaks and other "foreigners." Memories were long and fears high. It had not been that long since a flag had flown in New York inscribed "No Popery." In the previous century, a law had been passed against priests. A priest was to be "deemed and accounted an incendiary and disturber of the public peace and safety and an enemy to the true Christian religion."[17] Life imprisonment was the first punishment for those caught. If they escaped and were recaptured, they were subject to the death penalty. To harbor a priest was to be fined and pilloried. Catholics couldn't vote, hold office, bear arms or serve on juries.

Never mind that such laws were colonial, and that they were rarely enforced. They did create a climate of fear and of bitterness that was to last for a long time. It is difficult for a Catholic even today who

16. Ibid., p. 141
17. *Documents of American Catholic History*, John Tracy Ellis, ed. (Milwaukee: The Bruce Publishing Company, 1962), p. 119

knows the history of this his native land to be completely free of anxiety. I took note in an earlier chapter, for example, of being warned by a prestigious newspaper that accused me of becoming too "political" in the 1984 presidential campaign, that I was threatening the status of Catholics in political life hard won by President John F. Kennedy! Need anyone be reminded that Mr. Kennedy did not become president until 1960, and that, in essence, he had to promise the world that his Catholicism would never influence his political positions? In other words, we Catholics were on probation until 1960, and even today could presumably lose our tolerated status!

In my view, these were the sentiments that activated New York's first Archbishop, the insightful John Hughes. He obviously did not believe that Catholic children, particularly as immigrants, would ever be free of harassment and attacks against their beliefs in the public-school system. He made the fateful decision to establish a Catholic school system for the Archdiocese of New York.

Billions of dollars and all these years later, with a crucial obstacle to hurdle if its schools are to continue, we believe that the Catholic school system is now more important than ever, not only for Catholics but for our entire society. It is therefore a grave loss to society at large that the number of Catholic schools and the numbers of students are diminishing, overwhelmingly because of financial problems. It's a loss in terms of producing students better equipped to help society pragmatically and better equipped to help society maintain the values on which this nation was founded. I am therefore strongly opposed to closing any school unless closure is demanded by the most urgent circumstances.

Have our Catholic schools graduated any thugs, hoodlums, downright crooks, whether blue or white collared? Unquestionably. Is every youngster in a Catholic grade school, or every student in a Catholic high school, college or university a Mary Poppins, a Sir Galahad, or a Saint Francis of Assisi? Who ever said so? But as a system? Try to beat it. And for the cost? One would think that any cost-conscious government or any practical-minded businessperson would be urgently designing constitutionally legitimate ways of helping to ensure continuance and expansion of our Catholic school system.

Indeed, I believe that government, business and society at large owe an immense debt to the religious sisters, brothers, priests and laypersons who have sacrificed so much to make the Catholic school system

185

possible. With due deference to all others, in this regard, the count-less legions of religious sisters at every level of education, elementary, secondary, college, have made an incalculable impact on literally hun-dreds of thousands of lives in New York. We no longer speak pa-tronizingly of "the good nuns." We have come to recognize that their "goodness" is of a much higher order. Even today, some of our finest Catholic colleges are under the guidance of women religious as presi-dents.

A word about the fourteen Catholic colleges and universities in the Archdiocese of New York. Not everyone is aware that St. John's Uni-versity, with campuses in both Queens and Staten Island, is the larg-est Catholic university in the United States. It would be only a minor exaggeration to say that hardly a law firm or a court bench in New York has not had its share of St. John's and Fordham's Law School graduates.

The contribution to the intellectual life of New York on the part of our Catholic colleges and universities is extraordinary, and has been so for years. Yet our Catholic college and university administrators, faculty and staff have had to compete with secular institutions on whom there are few limitations in terms of government support. Thanks to the Blaine Amendment,[18] even the limited government support that comes the way of our Catholic colleges and universities has strings attached.[19] (It is perhaps not amiss to note here that our seminary system, which has prepared priests intellectually to serve both the Church and the community since 1896, receives no govern-ment support.)

Those of us dedicated to Catholic schools, and to the conviction that all parents should have the constitutional right to choose such for their youngsters, do not underestimate the public-school system's con-tribution to American society. We are convinced, however, that par-ents must have choices based on their beliefs.

New York Governor William H. Seward was not Catholic. From

18. James G. Blaine was Speaker of the House of Representatives. The amendment named after him was enacted in New York in 1894. It prohibited state aid to "any school or institution of learning wholly or in part under the counsel or direction of any religious denomination, or in which any denominational tenet or doctrine is taught." [Reichley, op.cit., p. 164] This amend-ment has created serious chronic problems for our Catholic schools in New York, problems not experienced in many other states.
19. St. John's University has consistently refused to accept any government funding whatever for this reason.

1840 onward, however, he fought for true equality for all school-children and for funding for private as well as public schools. Historians generally believe that his support for Catholic immigrants lost him the nomination for the presidency of the United States, which at one time seemed to be his for the asking. Perhaps it is well that he did. In God's Providence, a gentleman from Illinois won the nomination in his place, a man named Abraham Lincoln. But the reason why Governor Seward lost will remain a blight on the escutcheon of New York politics. To say nothing of "the ridiculous spectacle of schoolchildren putting on their coats and galoshes in the middle of a wintry day to go outside and board a van full of desks in order to avoid 'excessive entanglement of church and state.'" You're right, Mayor Koch, it's sheer lunacy.

VI

THE MAYOR
HOUSING

THE CARDINAL
HEALTH CARE
and
HOUSING

THE MAYOR

Middle-class families and families struggling to become middle-class are the backbone of New York City, indeed of the whole country. But without decent, affordable homes to live in, families of all kinds will become an endangered species. As it is, families are having a hard time hanging on. Divorce, drug abuse, and the rapid change in our economy from manufacturing to service jobs, which has uprooted many families from their traditional communities: These are the perplexing social phenomena that seem to mark the times we live in and have contributed to the decline of the family as a great American institution. Other institutions that have traditionally bolstered the family, like church, synagogue and school, for whatever reasons, seem unable to lend the family all the support it needs.

No one has failed the family in more deliberate and dramatic fashion than the federal government. It is a sad and troubling paradox that the Reagan presidency has managed to withdraw the federal government from creating affordable housing, even as it has sought to promote a conservative moral agenda. I'm all for traditional values; but they don't mean a thing if there are no families to adopt and teach them. But without housing there can be no families. Families need a place to live. Why has the federal government forgotten this?

Once it was quite different. The federal government used to be the biggest housing developer in the country. Starting in 1933, Washington built millions of housing units across the country—over 170,000 units of low-income public housing in New York City alone. That housing, which is still run by the New York City Housing Authority, is a model for the whole country and is the single largest resource in

191

the nation for low-income families. But the Reagan administration abandoned this national commitment to housing—and to families. In the past seven years, for example, the federal government has allocated only 800 new units of public housing to New York City. At the peak level of funding in 1980, Washington spent approximately $30 billion nationwide in various housing-assistance programs. In 1988, that outlay had dropped to $8 billion, a 240 percent reduction. Nowhere has the impact been harder than in New York City. In 1981 we received $2 billion from the federal government for housing assistance; in 1987 we received only one tenth of that, and it was not for new housing, only for repairs to old housing stock.

The housing crunch is especially severe and the need for federal assistance so great in New York City for a variety of reasons that are often hard to grasp. Part of the problem is our increasing population. According to the 1980 census, New York City's population supposedly fell during the 1970s. But this was a false conclusion. The census counters did not do a thorough job. Even if they were partly right, the trend is now quite clearly in the opposite direction. A robust economy and the fact that New York City continues to be a haven for refugees from around the world has contributed to an indisputable increase in the number of people who live here. We're now up to around 7.2 million people. There simply are not enough apartments to house everyone.

One of the most important tasks I've had as Mayor has been crafting a response to the overwhelming housing problem and the attendant problems of family disintegration and homelessness that flow from it. As a result, New York City now has made the largest commitment to housing of any city or state in the country. In 1986, I made a ten-year commitment to spend $4.2 billion to build and rehabilitate a quarter of a million housing units. In 1988, I went even further. The Ten Year Plan, as we call it, now totals $5.1 billion, most of which, $4.4 billion, is City funds. That might seem like a lot of abstract numbers. But when you consider that we used to spend $25 million (not billion) a year on housing production, $5 billion is astronomical—probably the size of the budget of some entire cities, states and even countries.

The Ten Year Plan is more than just government spending, however. It is a creative partnership involving the City, the private sector and not-for-profit organizations. A key player in this coalition of diverse interests is the Catholic Church. The Church's role in housing in the City was epitomized by the creation of the Northwest Bronx Community and Clergy Coalition (NWBCCC) in 1973. The Coalition was originally formed to work with tenant associations and local neighborhood groups to prevent the abandonment of buildings and stem the widespread deterioration of the housing stock in the Bronx. By the late 1970s the Coalition's efforts had evolved into devising ways to involve the private sector as well as utilizing the City's rehabilitation-loan programs to upgrade this housing. And today the City and the Coalition are full partners in this activity. In fact, over the past ten years the City has renovated over 20,000 units with a total dollar investment of $270 million in neighborhoods where NWBCCC has been active. Throughout the last decade, we have established similar partnerships with other religious groups. Very often we provide the financial resources and the technical building know-how while the religious organizations provide the commitment and the compassion needed to own and successfully manage housing for the poorest population. Yet still more needs to be done, and I am confident that religious groups across the City will continue to play a major role in working with us in building, owning and managing the housing units in our programs.

Obviously, the decision to commit $5.1 billion to housing is just the first step. We must also ensure that these funds are allocated in the most effective way. Our plan has as its major focus the abandoned housing that is located all over the City, but particularly in parts of the South Bronx, Harlem, the Lower East Side and many parts of Brooklyn. Anyone who has driven through these neighborhoods has to be appalled by the devastation they see: Blocks and blocks of burned-out, dilapidated buildings that should be decent housing are instead havens for drug dealing and other criminal activity, wasted opportunities taken over by blight. A key part of the Ten Year Plan is to rehabilitate those blighted buildings that are owned by the City and which are still structurally sound. That's 5,000 buildings that will be turned into affordable housing for people making $32,000 a year or less. In total, we expect to create 47,000 units out of vacant buildings from what is referred to as our "in rem" stock: buildings taken over by the City because the owners didn't pay their taxes. All of the units that come from in rem buildings will be affordable to low- and moderate-income New Yorkers. We will take one third of the units and commit them to the homeless, an $800 million commitment, another one third to people making below $19,000 a year, and one third to people making between 19,000 and $32,000. That's 47,000 housing units that don't exist today, that today are blight. We will turn that blight into an opportunity. We are already under way. By 1993 every one of our vacant in rem buildings will be in a rehabilitation program.

Religious groups have played a major role in rehabilitating housing and will continue to do so. Hundreds of the units being created through the various City "gut" rehabilitation programs such as the Vacant Building Program, Local Initiative Support Corporation and the Housing Trust Fund/Enterprise Program have involved religious groups. As one specific example, in the past several years, a consortium of forty churches in Brooklyn, known as the Brooklyn Ecumenical Cooperatives (BEC), has been in the process of rehabilitating vacant City-owned buildings in that borough. This development, which BEC calls the New Communities Project, will create housing for local residents of a wide range of Brooklyn neighborhoods including Bushwick, Crown Heights, South Park Slope, Fort Greene, Red Hook and Clinton Hill. BEC is currently undertaking the rehabilitation of a 113-unit project with hundreds of additional units planned for later stages.

On a larger scale, the Archdiocese of New York was recently selected to own and manage twenty-two of the City's most visible abandoned buildings situated in Highbridge, along the Cross Bronx Expressway, an area of particular concern to the South Bronx churches. The renovation of over seven hundred apartments in these buildings will provide new housing opportunities to a mix of homeless, working-poor and moderate-income families. By rehabilitating these Cross Bronx buildings, the City, together with the Archdiocese, will be transforming symbols of blight into emblems of hope and rebirth for the South Bronx and the City. Significantly, this will be the Archdiocese's largest entry into the ownership and management of housing in New York City. These buildings represent an investment of $57 million in City funds, and will be turned over to the Archdiocese, debt and tax free, so that the apartments can remain permanently available to low- and moderate-income New Yorkers, and to the homeless.

Another major part of our Ten Year Plan is to rehabilitate the occupied housing units in the City. The City had become—for far too many people—"the landlord of last resort." Through the Department of Housing Preservation and Development, we are the second-largest landlord in the United States. The first is the New York City Housing Authority. We did not plan it that way; but as landlords abandoned their buildings in neighborhood after neighborhood, we became the owner of 4,000 occupied buildings. There are probably no other private landlords with as many buildings to manage as the City of New York. And these buildings have one thing in common: They are all in terrible condition. That's the way we got them. That's not the way they are going to remain. We are determined to turn them around and make them into a viable long-term housing resource. The people who live in these buildings generally are the poorest people in the City and if this housing disappears as a result of our failure to invest in it, there will be no choice for these people but the City's shelter system, and that's unacceptable. So we have chosen to invest $1.3 billion out of our Ten Year Plan to rehabilitate *every* occupied housing unit that we own—both the 50,000 that we own today and the approximately 30,000 that we expect to acquire over the next ten years. That's a commitment to 80,000 housing units that we will rehabilitate and make into a viable and affordable housing resource so the people who live there can stay in them. The rents for these units are even below the shelter allowances and they give housing to people who have no options.

Here, too, there is a major role for religious institutions. The South East Bronx Community Organization (SEBCO) is successfully managing occupied low-income housing that used to be owned by the City, and has done a superb job of it. Father Louis Gigante has been able to succeed where so few others have. These formerly in rem occupied buildings are not only attractive homes now, but they are graffiti free, too, in sharp contrast to their surroundings. We have called upon the nonprofit community to assume the ownership of more and more of these occupied housing units. And they are responding with caring, local on-site management that is proving to be hugely successful.

Obviously, housing the homeless is a major component of our housing program. In fact, we are using both occupied and vacant in rem buildings to help the homeless. Every year we rehabilitate 4,000 permanent apartments for families living in temporary facilities such as welfare hotels. So far, we have provided over 15,000 such apartments for the homeless. Most of these have been provided through the renovation of uninhabitable vacant units located in occupied buildings. But more and more, we are turning to the renovation of wholly vacant buildings. Our new plan provides for $800 million of City funds for the creation of 15,000 additional housing units for the homeless in buildings that are totally vacant today. These buildings are being rehabilitated from scratch—at a cost of more than $65,000 per apartment—with new roofs, new windows, plumbing, interior walls, you name it, for the exclusive occupancy of families coming out of our hotels and shelters. No other city is building the permanent housing for the homeless that we are. And while it may never be enough to satisfy the advocates, it's an astronomical commitment of City resources to provide for those in greatest need.

Besides building permanent housing for the homeless, we also build transitional facilities with private rooms for families who will ultimately find apartments on their own but need a place to stay for a short period of time as they try to reestablish themselves. By mid-1988, we had 1,425 of these transitional units and we are planning to have another 1,700 in operation by the middle of 1990. These facilities, coupled with the permanent housing that we are building, will enable us to get everybody out of the welfare hotels by 1990. Families who have been without homes for extended periods will now have homes and will be able to raise their children and lead their lives in a normal setting.

The Church has a major role to play in helping the City care for the homeless. For example, recently the City and State spent over $4 million to buy the Congressional Hotel, which will provide permanent and transitional housing for people coming out of the welfare hotels. The Congressional Hotel will be run by the Archdiocese of New York and will provide social services as well as housing facilities. Run by the West End Intergenerational Residence, the renovated hotel will provide permanent housing for singles, and an innovative educational program for mothers with small children. Fordham University, Phipps Houses and other nonprofit institutions and organizations will, in association with local community groups, provide the services to the residents. In addition to this project, in Brooklyn a subsidiary of Catholic Charities, the Progress of Peoples Development, has sponsored the rehabilitation of three sites (two former Catholic schools and one former convent) to produce over 200 new units of single-room-occupancy (SRO) housing.

But our program is not limited to the in rem stock or providing for the homeless. We believe the survival of private housing is a key component of housing preservation and consequently we are also working to rehabilitate privately owned buildings, as well. We have committed $600 million through the Ten Year Plan to various programs aimed at preserving and improving this stock. We provide low-interest loans which are often matched by private developers to promote rehabilitation of occupied units so that the housing doesn't become the kind that the City ends up taking over. We provide these low-cost funds so that landlords can put in new windows, new roofs and new boilers without imposing substantial rent increases that could force out tenants. The repairs are needed to maintain the housing as a legitimate private resource, which we obviously prefer. We are not looking to be the landlord of all the housing stock in the City. In fact, we are looking more and more to return housing to the private sector, provided, of course, that we can be assured it is economically viable and will be well managed.

And finally, we are committed to building new housing from scratch. Our biggest new construction program is the one that we have developed in conjunction with the New York City Housing Partnership, a group of leading businesses committed to improving New York City. All together we expect to create 23,000 housing units over the next decade through this middle-income program, and we are well on our way toward reaching that goal. There are already nearly 5,000 Partnership units in various parts of the City, which are occupied, under construction or currently going into construction. Moreover, over 1,000 of these 5,000 units have been sponsored by religious groups.

Some other new construction programs are also Church-sponsored. One is the well-known Nehemiah Project in the Brownsville section of Brooklyn. Run by a coalition of religious groups known as East Brooklyn Churches, the Nehemiah Project has already produced over 1,000 new homes sold at "cost" to moderate-income people at a price of only $50,000. This low price is made possible by a City subsidy of $20,000 a unit. In total, more than 5,000 units are slated for construction under the City's Ten Year Plan over the next decade.

The Nehemiah Project is named for the Old Testament prophet who led the Jews out of Babylonian exile and rebuilt the walls of Jerusalem. It came about when the Bishop of Brooklyn, Reverend

Francis J. Mugavero, approached me on behalf of the East Brooklyn Churches group. Bishop Mugavero said: "Mayor, we've managed to raise eight million dollars from local churches and parishioners to build homes for families in Brownsville. If you can arrange for the City to donate enough land and condemned property, we can build them well and sell them cheap. Just help us cut through the red tape." How could I refuse? From that exchange a unique model of State-Church cooperation was born, one that is reviving a dying community and helping shore up beleaguered families.

Just as the name Nehemiah is associated with the Jews' rebuilding their city in ancient days, it is now aptly associated with the rebuilding of a community in Brooklyn that had been "exiled," so to speak, to one of the most blighted, and some would say godforsaken, ghettos in all of urban America. A "miraculous" change is under way. If you were to journey out to the Nehemiah site, you would discover row after row of neat brick houses with green lawns, white fences, backyards and carports, where until recently there stood only burned-out buildings and abandoned cars on rubble-strewn lots. Sad reminders of what the area was like before it became a neighborhood again remain half a block away, but they are quickly losing ground to the bulldozers and construction crews.

Typical Nehemiah homeowners earn on average $26,000 per year. None of them have ever owned homes before; 40 percent lived in public housing prior to Nehemiah. In fact, one of the incredible benefits that Nehemiah brings to the entire city is that it helps create room in public-housing units where none existed before. For every one hundred Nehemiah homes sold, forty publicly subsidized apartments become available for others who might be doubling up or, worse, living on the streets. The benefit is as dramatic in terms of dollars as it is for people. Without Nehemiah, $1 million would buy only eight additional units of public housing; with Nehemiah $1 million buys two hundred houses and creates eighty vacancies in public housing.

Space permitting, we have every reason to hope that Nehemiah can accomplish throughout New York City what it has already done for its first eight hundred homeowners, like a husband and wife a member of my staff learned about while recently touring the site. I'll call them Jim and Mary.

Jim is a subway conductor and Mary is a city employee. They used to rent an apartment in the East Flatbush section. During work each day, Jim could observe the Nehemiah Project's early stages of construction from the window of his subway car. After work he would come home and tell Mary about the progress of the construction crews and they would joke about "that crazy project over in Brownsville." They joked with good reason. Brownsville was blown out and broken down. You'd almost have to be crazy to build a house there. Who would want to live in such a place? But as it turned out, Jim and Mary were desperately looking for a house to buy and raise their growing family in. And as they began to realize that Nehemiah was not just one or two houses, that in fact a whole new community was springing up, they decided to make a closer inspection. To make a long story short, Jim and Mary have not only realized their dream of owning a home, they and their children are part of a strong and growing community that is revitalizing a part of New York that many had given up for dead. Recently, Jim was elected to the Board of Directors of the Nehemiah Homeowners Association. It's a story that I expect to hear throughout the city's five boroughs in the next ten years.

In the Bronx, another pilot program is under way with the Archdiocese of New York to build new homes for families with an income between $24,000 and $34,000 a year. These first homes are being sponsored by SEBCO. Subsidized by the City and the State to the tune of $25,000 a unit, this program could eventually yield as many as fifteen hundred new homes.

We also have a new development program with major builders who have made a lot of money in New York. People like Sam LeFrak, Paul Milstein and the Real Estate Board of New York, who know that if they want to protect their investments, they have to give something back to the City, and they are. They are building—on a nonprofit basis—thousands of housing units. Over the next decade, we hope to produce nine thousand units of multiple-dwelling housing, high-rise and mid-rise buildings, through developers who are going to make their housing resources and their housing know-how and their money available to us.

All together our program is a balanced one. We are spending most of our money where the need is greatest—for low-income people. Sixty percent of our housing money is focused on persons making below $19,000 a year. We have help for people of moderate means, too: Twenty-six percent of our money has been allocated for people making between $19,000 and $32,000 annually. But we have tried not to neglect the middle class, either.

Some housing advocates will always claim we should take care only of the homeless. They say the middle class—and we define the middle class as people making roughly between $30,000 and $50,000—can take care of themselves. I say that would be great if it worked. Ideally, persons with that income should not need the government to provide housing for them. But that ideal is no longer possible. The private sector in New York City, for a variety of reasons, doesn't produce housing for anybody making less than $75,000 a year. What are people to do under these conditions? We could pretend that the middle class can take care of itself. But if we did, it would mean middle-class families would leave the City in droves. If that were allowed to happen, the City's tax base would go with them, neighborhoods would become unstable and we would lose a great source of the funds and resources need for housing low-income people. Everyone would suffer. A balanced housing program avoids this disaster. Ours is balanced. Eighty-six percent of our housing money is committed to programs for low- and moderate-income people. But the fact is that, really, we probably aren't doing enough for the middle class. I often think they are penalized for their hard work, while others get rewarded because they don't work at all. That is not say that poverty and homelessness are proof of someone's inherent tendency toward laziness and debt. No one believes that old Calvinist saw anymore; I certainly don't. But I must say there are times when I think we are misguided to go out of our way to help some people as much as we do. It's not that they aren't deserving; it's that our help doesn't do them much good and our energies might be better spent elsewhere. Their problems are at such a profoundly deep level that government can't necessarily reach them, and when it tries, its efforts have only slight results.

Let me give you an example of what I'm talking about. Outside of City Hall for the past several months there has been an encampment of homeless people. They say they won't leave until I agree to give every single homeless person in the City his or her own one-room apartment. Originally, they were trying to influence the outcome of the City budget negotiations. That's why they camped in front of City Hall. But the budget process passed them by and, as of this writing, they're still there. Now they say they're going to "stay forever." I said, "Sure, stay forever"; but I can't really let them do that. Once the first snowfall comes, I'll have to do something. They can't freeze to death while waiting for next year's budget negotiations.

In any event, I decided one day as I was walking out of City Hall and they, as usual, were yelling at me, that I would offer to try to help them obtain jobs. I called my commissioner of the Department of Employment, Lilliam Barrios-Paoli. She said there were plenty of jobs to offer and that she would bring her staff over to City Hall. So along with Lilliam, eight of her staff members, Pat Mulhearn, who was then my counsel, and a security guard, I ventured into the homeless en-campment in City Hall Park. With twelve of us and twelve of them, it was sort of like a one-to-one personnel service. They weren't surprised to see me—they heckle me every day, after all—so I started right in. "How many of you want a job?" I asked. Nine of them raised their hands: four guys, four women and one transvestite. To this group I said, "We're going to give you clean clothes and carfare, and we're going to give you the name of prospective employers who are waiting to meet you." Then I had them fill out résumés with the help of the staff from the Department of Employment.

As for the three who hadn't indicated they wanted jobs, I asked them again. "Don't you guys want jobs?" The leader of the group, one of the three, says, "We have jobs, Mayor." I say, "You do? What's your job?" He says, "I'm in charge of all these people." "Don't you want a paying job?" I ask. "Not at this time," he replies. He then begins trying to convince the nine others who do want jobs not to fill out any forms. "Don't cooperate. It will ruin the demonstration."

They didn't listen to him, they kept filling out the forms. And soon after, we sent them on interviews. But, you know what? In the end not one of them took a job. One guy was offered nine dollars an hour as a security guard. Nine dollars. He didn't want it. It's true that the transvestite was not offered work from the two businesses that inter-viewed him; but that was most likely because he was reluctant to give up cross-dressing. We continued to provide him job counseling and encouraged him to adopt appropriate attire, at least for job interviews, but he just couldn't get it together.

My critics insist that I'm insensitive to the homeless and the poor, that I don't do enough for them. But, really, what can you do for people like the homeless protestors in City Hall Park who don't, ap-parently, want help?

In the meantime, hardworking people struggling to build middle-class lives for themselves want and need every break they can get. But we don't always give it to them. For example, we've made a commitment to get everybody out of the welfare hotels over a two-year period. But to do that we have to put the people in the hotels ahead of 200,000 families who are signed up for low-income housing on a ten-year waiting list. There's no waiting list for the people living in the hotels; they go to the head of line. I'm glad that we are going to be able to help them, the welfare hotels are not good places for children; but I'm not sure that we're doing it in the most equitable way.

My uneasiness crystallized last summer when I dropped in at a site in the Bronx to announce a new housing project. We were starting rehabilitation of fourteen buildings that had stood as abandoned wrecks for fifteen years, creating nine hundred new apartments to house approximately 3,000 people who, as of December 1988, are living in the welfare hotels or staying in our shelters. But across the street from this project is a privately owned building that is deteriorating. Really, it's in terrible shape. The residents of this apartment house are black and Hispanic working poor. They have struggled to get to where they are and struggle still in the hopes of getting farther. But along comes the City and provides nine hundred new apartments with modern kitchens and fancy parquet floors, rent free, right across the street, to people living in the welfare hotels. The residents of the privately owned building must be in bitter shock, because what we're doing is not fair to them.

I'm also afraid that the message we're sending these people is that hard work and the deferment of short-term luxuries for long-term goals is a hoax. I'm worried that the lesson we're teaching is that you're better off as a ward of the government than being on your own. What I'd like to do is find a way to remedy the situation, to still build housing for those in desperate need who, for example, are now living in the welfare hotels, but at the same time not penalize those who are struggling to make it on their own. Ideally, we would have a housing "ladder" whereby the people living in the dilapidated building would get first dibs at the new apartments we're building across the street, and the residents of the welfare hotels would move into the apartments the others have vacated. I honestly don't know if it's a feasible plan, but I intend to try and find out.

In the meantime we are forging ahead with the Ten Year Plan, of which I remain quite proud.

Some people say, ten years is a long time, what are you doing now? Well, our program is already under way with dramatic increases in both spending and production. In fiscal year 1985, the City committed $25 million of its own funds for housing. By fiscal 1988, that figure had soared to $450 million. In fiscal 1989, we expect to spend over $600 million and by 1990 over $800 million of City resources. That is exponential growth of almost thirty-five-fold in a five-year period.

All told, by next year we will have 17,000 housing units under construction. This is a level of activity that the City has not seen in nearly two decades. In fact, in the fiscal year that ended in June 1988, our housing-activity levels surpassed all annual City-assisted production levels since the early seventies. New York City on its own, without federal help, will be doing more than the feds did when they were pouring a substantial amount of money into New York City and other localities.

Our housing initiatives are beginning to bear fruit. The latest Housing and Vacancy Survey demonstrates some of the remarkable progress the City has recently made in the housing field:

- For the first time in twenty-five years, we have had back to back increases in the number of net housing units added to the City's total housing stock. In fact, the increase over the last three years more than tripled the increase in the previous period. Between 1981 and 1984, we gained 11,000 units, while we gained 37,000 more units between 1984 and 1987.
- Housing abandonment has declined dramatically. For the first time, between 1984 and 1987, the number of abandoned and lost housing units that were subsequently restored to the housing stock has actually exceeded the number of units lost over that period.
- The condition of the City's occupied rental-housing stock also improved dramatically between 1984 and 1987. The number of dilapidated units fell by 25,000 between 1984 and 1987 and the rate of maintenance deficiencies fell by nearly a third.

We have stepped into the housing breach in a major and unprecedented way. We are providing enormous housing subsidies. Private groups and religious institutions are providing the technical knowhow, management skills and commitment to complement our program. But obviously those of us in New York can't do it ourselves. The federal government will have to get back into the housing business. Washington must gain an understanding that housing is critical to the nation's well-being.

I am convinced that our next president will not be able to shirk this issue. The state, too, will have to increase its commitment to housing. Alone we can still make an important difference; together, and with the private sector and religious institutions, we can effectively deal with one of society's intractable problems. The challenge is enormous, but the consequences of not meeting it are immeasurably terrible. We simply must succeed in building affordable housing.

THE CARDINAL

I'm told we're not supposed to do it, and my union sympathies are such that I understand why—under normal circumstances. But imminent death from an aneurysm is not a normal circumstance, and human life transcends even union contracts.

The patient had been brought to the emergency room of one of our Catholic hospitals. Emergency-room workers were on strike throughout the City, so ours was badly backed up with patients. He had to be rushed to another hospital. The ambulance driver who had brought him was apologetic, but firm. "Sorry, this patient's on Medicaid. They won't pay us for another ambulance ride."

Our hospital called one of our own ambulances off a less urgent run and rushed the patient to another of our hospitals. On time. We will never be reimbursed for that second ambulance ride or for countless similar initiatives. That's very much all right.

Our Catholic hospital system began almost a century ago, when the Sisters of Charity opened St. Vincent's. There are now well over fifty Catholic hospitals within the territory of what was then the Archdiocese of New York. Eighteen of these are in what is *now* the Archdiocese of New York. Every one of them is devoted to works of *charity*, before, above, beneath, beyond everything else. God knows that's needed as much as ever—more than ever.

Somewhere near 40 million people have no health-care insurance. In New York the numbers who go without adequate health care are probably incalculable: the homeless, many of the elderly, the mentally or emotionally disabled, many persons with AIDS and AIDS-related problems, countless numbers of drug abusers and alcoholics.

The City itself does a certain amount of "charity." Many non-Catholic hospitals, nonsectarian, sectarian and private, provide a good bit of quality health care. They don't discriminate against Catholics or anyone else. As we ask about Catholic education, then, so we can ask about Catholic health care: Why? Why not leave all health care to government and other elements of the private sector?

The basic "why" is the Church's unconditional belief in and commitment to the sacredness, the dignity, the priceless worth of every human person, because every human person is made in the Image of God. That can sound awfully trite. It's precisely why the Church in New York engages in an enterprise that, with third-party payments, runs somewhere around a billion dollars a year, a good chunk of which must be raised by the Church in New York from the private sector. If we didn't believe what we believe, undertaking that enterprise would make absolutely no sense. It's too great an obligation to undertake for any lesser reason.

One with the belief in the worth of every human person is the Church's commitment to the poorest of the poor. It is so very often that the very poor need care, in both acute and chronic illnesses. So quite apart from a responsible effort to pay lawful bills and make ends meet, Church health care must put the patient first—always—and worry about reimbursement later, often knowing the "later" will be in the next life.

Our commitment to the human person requires that we put the patient first, not the cost, the convenience of doctors, nurses or staff, or even the sophisticated equipment and technologies that mark our health-care system. This is the one thing I ask above all that the faculty at the New York Medical College teach their students. (The College is sponsored by the Archdiocese of New York.) It's what I ask of administrators, staff and board members of every one of our health-care institutions.

Why does this conviction require an extensive health-care system? For several reasons.

We want Catholics and people of every religious persuasion to know that they can come into a Catholic health-care facility and be treated in accordance with the highest moral/medical standards. They need not fear. The Catholic Health Association in concert with the National Conference of Catholic Bishops provides guidelines that we take very seriously.

Further, we want peoples of all races, colors, backgrounds or status to know that they have a refuge, regardless of their illness. Leprosaria have long been a Godsend to the outcast. Plague victims of every description have been ministered to by sisters, brothers, priests, Catholic laypersons from time immemorial. Rose Hawthorne Lathrop, Nathaniel's daughter, mentioned earlier, chose as her special vocation not only the cancerous—considered hopeless at that time—but the cancerous *poor*. Catholic Relief Services, the Catholic Near East Welfare Association and similar agencies have sped medicines and medical personnel to disaster areas all over the world. The largest single source of help to persons with AIDS in New York, outside City government, has been the Catholic Archdiocesan health-care system.

Health care, I suppose, we do in part because we know how to do it and have done it for so long. The Church's theology of suffering— uniting one's sufferings with those of Christ on the cross to generate spiritual power for others—is a priceless reminder to many patients, but forced upon none.

So we feel quite comfortable in providing health care at every point in life: for unborn infants and their mothers, for the postnatal, for the retarded, the blind, the lame, the halt, the dumb, for the elderly, the handicapped, the wheelchaired, the cancer-ridden, the person with AIDS. We do what we do well, and have no desire to withdraw from it.

Unresolved Church-State conflicts, however, could very severely impede, or even prevent our continuance, and not simply because of problems of inadequate reimbursement against escalating costs. Why? Again it's a question of jurisdiction, values and purpose. There is perhaps no other area of public life in which the conflict could become more acute.

Any doctor, any hospital or nursing-home administrator of any religious persuasion will jump at a chance to ventilate about government regulatory procedures in health care. As these multiply (and they are veritable rabbits), and increase in complexity, the burden on any health-care institution becomes prodigious. Many of the procedures are understandable and designed to protect patients. Many are maddening exercises in bureaucracy, and make patient care extremely difficult. This situation prevails for public and private health-care facilities alike.

As costs escalate and regulations multiply, many health-care facilities find themselves treading water to survive. One result is the temptation to reduce pure charity to a minimum, and to ignore the poor. That's not good, but it's not the worst danger for our Catholic health-care system. The worst danger comes in the imposition of requirements that violate our moral and ethical positions. And in this regard we are in double jeopardy. First, we can imagine a day when we won't be funded if we refuse to practice certain procedures (abortion, sterilization, euthanasia, etc.). Secondly, we can imagine yet another day when we won't even be permitted to open our doors or engage in institutional health care at all, if we refuse to practice such procedures. I think it could happen that government would remove our credentials. In my view this is a grave threat.

This is one reason why we fight for recognition of an "institutional conscience," and the right of a health-care facility to refuse to accord with any requirements in violation of its institutional conscience.

Perhaps in no area does the State tend to intrude itself more pervasively. Besides the fears registered above, the "doing" of charity is becoming increasingly difficult for this very reason. I remember writing to a governor of a state other than New York to invite to his attention what I had read in a newspaper. The story was that a woman was taking into her own home a number of pregnant women with no place to go while awaiting the births of their babies. It seems the homeowner was in violation of one of the endless restrictions imposed by the State, and was ordered to cease and desist her charity. I hoped the governor would intervene in favor of the home owner. His reply was as bureaucratic as the restriction.

The system is filled with absurdities. Many patients would be better off in their own homes, in a familiar environment, rather than in hospitals or nursing homes. Moreover, home-care cost is a fraction of hospital costs. Reimbursement regulations are such, however, that for very many patients home care is precluded.

In instances in which home care may be authorized, there is often another problem: gross underpayment of home-health-care workers. In working with Health Care Union 1199, I have found City and State beginning to respond to this critical need, but there's a long way to go. At least half of these home-health-care workers receive income below the poverty level. That's simply immoral.

Health-care problems for New York City are overwhelming, and tremendous resources are needed. As a man who spent much of his life with highly professional and highly dedicated military personnel, I don't like oversimplifications about defense spending. However, I must in conscience reiterate something I have said elsewhere. It is heartbreaking to see the inadequacy of health care in this and in other big cities, knowing of the huge national expenditures for research, development and production of weapons systems. I'm not smart enough to know the answer. I *am* experienced enough to know both the complexity of military budgets and the continuing need for a militarily strong defense, sad though that need is. Yet there simply *has* to be a restructuring of priorities to the degree possible and a consequent reallocation of funds. It distresses me that in sayingthis I can't offer neat answers, but it would be irresponsible not to ask: "Is anybody in public office really *thinking* about it, really trying to fix it?" This is the kind of frustration I talked about in an earlier chapter concerning the hungry, the homeless and other critical problems. We *know* there is something radically wrong, but the system cannot seem to respond. Indeed, at times the system seems to be completely out of any human control.

Cooperation between the Archdiocese of New York and the City (and other cities and counties and the state) has been generally positive. I am never sanguine, however, about what any of these political entities *may* do. Public health care is demanding and complicated, but in my judgment, it becomes more so when your ready answer to critical pregnancy problems is abortion, to perplexing long-term-care problems is to "pull the plug," to AIDS problems is condoms and clean needles. In the latter case it is particularly clear that you're not thinking of *persons* with AIDS, but only of the disease itself. Persons with AIDS can thus be too readily thought of as killers, rather than as "die-ers."

The demands of public health care can generate a mind-set not in the ultimate best interest of either individual patients or society at large. I believe many public-health officials, although basically fine and dedicated persons, will live to rue the day they let themselves be lured out of desperation into a condom or clean-needle mind-set.

It is in part because of this mind-set on the part of so many public-health officials, that I am worried about the future of Catholic health care. The Church knows what it's doing in health care and contributes immensely to the good of the overall community without discrimination. It would be hard to imagine a more self-defeating course of action on the part of the State than to tax, harass, restrict or just generally hound Catholic health care into oblivion. It *could* happen. And sadly there may be some who might like to hasten the day.

In the meanwhile, my good union friends will understand that given our sense of the sacredness of every human life, we will have to send our own ambulance to prevent a death every time. No reimbursement required, thank you.

That same sense of the sacredness of every human life, in my judgment, should prompt us to expand our notion of health care to include the question of decent housing. I suspect that if we thought of decent housing as indispensable to the overall well-being of the human person, we might treat bad housing and homelessness as crises— health crises. Such a notion might give us the sense of urgency we need.

I am well aware that housing problems are among the most complicated problems in the world and yield to no simplistic solutions. Nor do we really solve the housing problem in the long run by actions that could wreck our free-enterprise system, work real injustices on land-owners or developers, or otherwise frustrate the kind of economic investment and initiative needed for long-term solutions. Housing problems are not solved by mere sentiment, allegations of corruption, or handwringing. They are tough problems. They can be solved only by realists—realists with *hearts*—but realists.

My primary concern is that housing problems seem too often to be treated as chronic, rather than acute. It's as though we have adjusted our collective psyche to take bad housing and homelessness for granted; since it doesn't affect most of us personally, we find it quite tolerable. There are, of course, those who will forever insist that most of the people in bad housing situations are there through their own fault. "They could move to another city, if they don't like it here. They should go back home, or wherever." It's hardly news that we have long had a middle and upper income class custom in the United States of blaming poverty on the poor. More recently we have come to blame homelessness on the homeless. And worse: to confuse poverty with homelessness or vice versa. They can be intimately related, but are not necessarily so.

Has the sad state of housing always been such in New York? Not according to old-time New Yorkers, or to statistics. Roger Starr, in his excellent work *The Rise and Fall of New York City*, [1] says that New York City had more rental apartments than any other city in the United States at the beginning of World War II. Indeed, he says: "At the beginning of the war, the city had a substantial surplus of housing and a comfortable vacancy rate."

Following the war, however, Mr. Starr notes, the highest priority problem for City government was the housing shortage. The second highest, however, was the poor quality of apartment houses lived in by those who could afford nothing better. More than a million people survived in tenements, walk-ups, with tubs for bathing in the kitchen, toilets in the common hall and no heating system. For most blacks and other nonwhites, things were even worse. [2]

Jill Jonnes, in her remarkable *We're Still Here: The Rise, Fall and Resurrection of the South Bronx*, speaks of early-warning signs of what was to become a nightmare. [3] In the years 1969–1970, she says, "The Whole Place Was Caving In." The state's Urban Development Corporation testified that the "total stock of housing in New York City was diminishing for the first time in a century. Landlords abandoned their properties. Almost one hundred thousand apartments were already 'boarded up, vandalized, burnt-out or otherwise unfit for occupancy.'" [4]

Ms. Jonnes goes on to say that few "could have imagined that entire neighborhoods, one after another, would soon come to resemble wartime ruins." She quotes Robert Esnard, then a graduate student, at the time of this writing deputy mayor for policy and physical development, as amazed at what he saw in Bedford-Stuyvesant. "'We had never seen such a thing. No one had ever heard of a property in New York City that no one wanted.'" [5]

We'll return to Jill Jonnes for the brighter side, and particularly for what the Church has been doing in the South Bronx, much of it, I

1. Roger Starr. *The Rise and Fall of New York City* (New York: Basic Books, 1985), p. 85
2. Ibid., pp. 84–88. Mr. Starr blames much of the problem of housing on rent control.
3. Jill Jonnes, *We're Still Here: The Rise, Fall and Resurrection of the South Bronx* (New York: The Atlantic Monthly Press, 1986)
4. Ibid, p. 199
5. Ibid., p. 199

must say honestly from my own experience, with the help of the City. But she has a lot more bad news before she comes to the good. The fall must be complete before the resurrection begins. She tells, for example, of the fires of 1957—fifteen hundred of them, four and five a day, to escalate to three thousand in a year before the arson began to abate. In the meanwhile, junkies were ripping out plumbing, families had no running water. "As the neighborhood became poorer and crazier with drugs and violence, the abandonment escalated, as did the fires."[6]

Need I apologize for speaking of housing in terms of "health care"?

I was not here when the warning signs were being given and the devastation was beginning, so it may seem unfair of me to ask, but I really must: "Where were the City's political and economic leaders?" Was it another case of good people throwing up their hands over "unsolvable" problems, problems too big, too overwhelming? I don't know, but I do know the number of pictures of presidential and lesser political campaigners I have seen, posed in the South Bronx, promising its weary people a new life—if elected.

On March 7, 1985, I appeared before the House Subcommittee on Housing and Community Development in Washington. In reviewing my testimony, I note what I have come to believe even more firmly since that date, but with a certain modification. In the testimony, I said: "I honestly don't believe it [the housing crisis] is a matter of budget." I should have said that the housing crisis is not *merely* a matter of budget; it's a matter of attitude and leadership. Nonetheless, the budget itself is crucial.

> I spent some 27 years of my life in the uniform of this country that I love . . . serving those who were trying to protect the human person here and all over. I respect the effort of government to provide the defense that we need and deserve. I want to go on record with a plea that every dollar budgeted for weapons systems be scrutinized with excruciating care, not only in terms of the morality of any intended use of such systems, but in terms of the urgent needs of some 35 million people in our society, hundreds of millions throughout the world, who are homeless, who are ill-housed, who are desperate for a restoration of the dignity, the sense of worth and sacredness that can come only with proper housing.

6. Ibid., pp. 229–230

That testimony was not directed against any administration or member of the Congress. It was testimony born of the conviction that political leadership is essential, whether Democratic or Republican, and that if such leadership is passionate enough about housing, it will find a way both to defend the nation against military force and to defend human beings against housing indignities and homelessness. That same leadership must inspire economic and industrial leadership across the board, not to sloganize, but truly to rebuild America's housing.

I was fascinated by a New York Times editorialist's saying that polar bears have "the best-planned housing in New York City." He was writing of the new Central Park Zoo, "that took eight years and $35 million to complete." He considered it "wonderful," and "light years away from the smelly old jail of yesterday. . . ."[7]

I take no issue with the enthusiasm of the Times editorialist. Almost certainly, millions will enjoy themselves no end in visiting the zoo, and they will deserve the enjoyment. Man does not live by bread alone. I wish only that the editorial could have been about a new and huge and wonderful apartment or housing complex for the poor. That would take a real sense of urgency on the part of leadership.

This takes me to a host of clergy, sisters and laypersons of the Catholic Church and other churches who have been struggling for years, sometimes in partnership with the City, sometimes alone, to help restore dignified housing for the poor and lower-income groups. At times, their successes have been spectacular—witness the rebuilding of the neighborhood around St. Athanasius Church in the South Bronx as well as the Nehemiah Project, in Brooklyn, cooperated in by clergy and people of many churches. At times, on the contrary, months and years have dragged on, with little to show for the pain.

Jill Jonnes writes appreciatively and strikingly about the work of the Church in the Bronx. For example, she describes an effort in the Morris Heights section. Morris Heights was 70 percent black and Hispanic. Enlisting the support and leadership of Auxiliary Bishop Patrick V. Ahern, episcopal vicar for the Bronx, the clergy launched a three-day workshop at Fordham University called "Strategies for Ministry in

7. The New York Times, August 10, 1988, p. A-26

213

the Urban Struggle."[8] Cardinal Cooke opened the conference with a fervent address that the parish must provide stability in the midst of the turbulence of change, and that it must not pull out of burned-out areas. (This was the same Cardinal Cooke, as we note in our chapter on education, who insisted that the way to save the inner city was to save the inner-city schools.)

Out of it all came the Northwest Bronx Community and Clergy Coalition. Bishop Ahern visited every parish and preached: "If the Bronx dies, then the hope of a million and a half people for justice and a decent life, here and now, will die with it."[9]

There was no question in Bishop Ahern's mind about the desperate need for leadership on the part of City officials. To one, he wrote:

What contempt City government exhibits towards neighborhoods and committees such as ours! In our view this is only the most recent in a series of evasions, deceptions, broken promises and buck-passing dating back to December, 1974, when we first dared to submit a proposal. [10]

To another:

I would like to be able to understand how you expect communities in desperate and justifiable need of governmental support to stand alone and fight the wave of deterioration that threatens to engulf them, while monies specifically allocated for this purpose are misdirected in the useless patronage of ineffective city agencies. [11]

And to yet a third:

[O]ur neighborhoods are at a critical stage of transition and every month's delay brings irreparable damage. I ask you once again to reconsider our requests and direct some assistance to this area. Now, before it's too late, is that too much to ask?[12]

---

8. We cite Bishop Ahern, without naming the legion of laypersons, sisters and brothers involved, only because we cite his letters below and they require attribution. Bishop Ahern would be the first to insist that he was but one of many who have engaged in such activities over the course of the years. I regret that prudence requires me not to list any of these magnificently dedicated people, no matter how deserving, lest I omit many, or even one, unsung hero or heroine.
9. Jonnes, op. cit., p. 350
10. Ibid., p. 355
11. Ibid.
12. Ibid.

"Yes, as it turned, out, it was," says Jill Jonnes.

In the meanwhile, the clergy and others forged ahead. The South East Bronx Community Organization (SEBCO) was born. Before the end of 1976, 360 SEBCO housing units were completed in the South Bronx, and work was begun on another 615 units. Others were working with equal vigor, among them the Northwest Bronx Community and Clergy Coalition.

Efforts were under way to obliterate the drug traffic that made house building and the maintenance of safe, dignified apartments a thousand times harder. "South Bronx People for Change" came into being to encourage leadership among laity of all religious faiths and empower people to renew community life. Later, a coalition of clergy and others of many faiths formed "South Bronx Churches." Its battle cry on behalf of the people was to become: "We are taking charge!"

Groups like these are still vitally operative, as are many others, like LESAC (Lower East Side Area Conference) that helps support the "sweat equity" rehabilitation of over twenty abandoned buildings utilizing the donated labor of volunteers.

The Archdiocese of New York has put well over $1 million into long-term, no-interest revolving loans to make it possible for the poor to get mortgages. Another $3 million have been dedicated to help finance at no interest the building of fifteen hundred housing units for those with low incomes, in the South Bronx. In this latter project, the State and the City have cooperated by providing the land, "write-down" subsidies and other support so that new homes can be made available to families who otherwise would be locked out of the dream of homeownership.

The Archdiocese has put even more millions into other projects, such as the refurbishing of apartment buildings. One of the latest projects, in cooperation with Fordham University, the Foundling Hospital and others, is exciting. It's the renovation of a building that will house a deliberate mix of young and old, single mothers and elderly people. The single mothers, recruited from the City's shelter system, will live there temporarily until they can move elsewhere on their own. All these young mothers will be involved in skill training for jobs, and will resume their education in a specially designed program at Fordham. When ready for jobs, they will move on. The elderly permanent residents will be involved in child care and may even wish to go back to school themselves. Most projects of this sort are carried out for the Archdiocese under the overall supervision of the Archdiocese's director of Catholic Charities, and of my special assistant for housing.

It was my staff that urged me to appear before the City Council to seek a moratorium on the destruction or renovation of SROs. Single-room-occupancy apartment buildings are generally among the worst housing units in the City. But they provide roofs over the heads of thousands of lonely people, many of them very elderly, and most having nowhere else to go. In recent years these SRO buildings have fallen under the eye of developers who know that with renovations they can be turned into high-priced apartments. I have made it my business to walk through neighborhoods where I have been told that apartments that once rented for one hundred dollars a month or less now may cost a thousand. We won the moratorium.

Generally speaking, however, we find ourselves not fighting the Mayor and his deputies, commissioners and other associates but working with them closely. We are as aware as the Mayor is that Church funds for housing, although very substantial in our budget, are a drop in the bucket. The housing needed can be built only with government funds, federal, state, county, city. We believe that our role, as Archdiocese, is to try to meet the needs we *can* meet, and simultaneously to try to encourage others in the private sector to join us or follow us.

One of our greatest frustrations, besides not having the money to do a lot more ourselves, *is*, in my judgment, a City problem. I have spoken elsewhere of the bureaucratic red tape that drives us crazy in trying to renovate or build. It takes months and months and months to get the various permits needed, before a single shovel of dirt can be turned over. It's maddening. It *has* to be fixable.

I am further frustrated that I haven't seen more ingenuity on the part of more developers to help provide dignified housing. We have some exceptionally fine people in the building and real-estate business in New York. I know that some of them are quietly devoting a lot of time and money to try to help solve the problem, but not nearly enough is being done. I wish we could stir up an all-out effort, with City officials and developers at every level. I believe that union officials and members would be cooperative if they saw that *everyone* was really ready to revolutionize the housing situation.

Too much more could be said than space permits. The City has proposed some new plans for the next five years, I am aware. I am heartened by them, and the Church stands by to help. But we have to be serious about it—*now*. We have to look at the housing problem as a critical illness and an unutterable disgrace.

There is *some* good news for the homeless families who have been living in unspeakable conditions in welfare hotels. A new U.S. Department of Housing and Urban Development regulation requires federally subsidized housing authorities to give priority to homeless families applying for public housing. As of this writing, Mayor Koch has announced that the approximately 3,000 families in welfare hotels will gradually move to transitional shelters and City-owned apartments. The entire move is expected to take two years. Unfortunately, the regulation does nothing for thousands of single persons who are homeless. And while it's a step in the right direction, it's the smallest fraction of what's needed.

Anne Donahue is director of the Covenant House Outreach Program in the Times Square district.* Covenant House is surrounded by City welfare hotels. Ms. Donahue is quoted as saying: "Very frequently at one or two in the morning we'll run into 7-, 8- or 9-year-olds playing or panhandling in the streets. One time we saw a group of boys and girls playing. When I asked what they were doing, a young boy said, 'I'm a pimp, and I'm watching over my [girls].' When you take kids and put them in the Times Square hotels, well-known pimp hotels, they are in the worst possible environment. You're asking for trouble."

In the meanwhile, what of those who roam the streets at night, sleeping over grates, against buildings, on park benches and rooftops and under cardboard tents? Whose concern are they? What are our plans as a City?

We do have one problem hard to blame on any city, state or federal official. It's a problem born, ironically, of one of our most cherished freedoms: the freedom of mobility. We prize having no boundaries, being able to move from city to city, state to state. There is no doubt but that the lure of jobs and a whole variety of other fascinations bring people to New York. Some are naïve, many unprepared, a significant number with no housing arrangements, no promise of housing

*Since the writing of this book, Anne Donahue was named executive director of Covenant House/Los Angeles.

before they leave wherever they come from. It's the nature of New York. But blameworthy or not, it's still a problem. Do we take it seriously?

Which brings us full circle. I am convinced that decent jobs and decent housing are critical to the well-being of individuals and society alike. At this point, we are doing pretty well in jobs. A lot of thought, money and concern go into providing jobs. Elections—national, state, county and city—can be won or lost on the basis of the employment issue. I have never heard a serious political campaigner *not* talk seriously about jobs. I'm afraid I have rarely heard a serious campaigner talk seriously about housing.

I want to add one note to the efforts of the Church in New York to help. No property in the Archdiocese may be sold, no matter how alluring the price, until I am convinced that it cannot be used for an alternate Church purpose such as a residence for people with special needs. If this is not practical because of the circumstances, special consideration must be given by the developer to affordable housing for a portion of the project. It may be only a small plot of land or an unpretentious building, but if we can envision any portion of it as a dignified home for a human being or a family, that's the route we must follow. Developers are hereby invited to help us turn such visions into brick and mortar.

This is one area in which neither differing jurisdictions, nor values, nor purposes preclude Church-State cooperation. This is fortunate. Too much is at stake: the lives and dignity of human persons, God's most precious creation.

Earlier in this chapter I suggested looking at housing as a health-care problem. I conclude by extending such a concept even further, to include the total environment. Most people spend only a portion of their day in their own homes, with a significant amount of time spent in other kinds of "housing": subways and buses, streets, parks, office buildings, beaches, shops, hospitals, etc. In all of these environments we live out the only lives we have on this earth. They need far more attention than they receive.

I have mentioned Roger Starr's book, *The Rise and Fall of New York City,* and I return to it because I believe it offers an incisive analysis of the deterioration and decline of this great city, its infrastructure and its spirit. Mr. Starr sees it as essentially a moral problem, a loss of the sense of moral values that made the building of the City possible in the first place. I don't believe Mr. Starr's book has been a best seller. That's the City's misfortune. I would make it a primer for any elected or appointed official, and I should probably urge it on all my own clergy. A few sentences alone would be worth the price:

Whatever religion's inadequacies, and they are many . . . it is the institutional expression of an idea: that in the face of life, a sense of awe is not irrelevant. Whether worldly or religious, civic leadership that treats its problems with a sense of wonder is the city's need.[13]

The New York Times could have done a lot worse than give this member of its editorial board a year off to write a book.

13. Starr, op. cit., p. 241

VII

THE MAYOR

AIDS

THE CARDINAL

AIDS
and
DRUG ABUSE

THE MAYOR

In the summer of 1981, an obscure medical publication provided the first sketchy details of a disease that would soon take lives, break hearts and make headlines all across America. A unique kind of cancer, reported the National Centers for Disease Control's *Morbidity and Mortality Monthly*, was afflicting, then killing young men. Six diagnosed in California, twenty in New York. The episodic quickly became epidemic.

Since its first appearance in the United States, acquired immune deficiency syndrome—AIDS—has killed 44,071 men, women and children, of whom more than 9,800 were residents of New York City.

And the toll keeps climbing. In December 1986, municipal hospitals in New York City cared for an average of 329 AIDS inpatients a day. By December 1987, they were caring for 427 AIDS inpatients a day. A year later they were caring for 570 inpatients. Another 3,317 were in private hospital beds in the city on a typical day.

This year, the City of New York will spend at least $118.6 million in local tax dollars to care for AIDS patients. Next year we will spend at least $135.2 million in local dollars. And the year after that, we'll spend millions more. Whether in human terms or dollars terms, AIDS inflicts an enormous cost.

AIDS is a disease for which there is no cure and against which there is no immunization. Medical and scientific experts are not optimistic. Neither is likely to be developed in the near future. Until then, an AIDS diagnosis will be a certain sentence of death.

It is also a certain source of fear and irrational feelings for many Americans. I am among them. Every Thanksgiving morning since I became Mayor in 1978, I have set aside three or four hours to visit city workers who aren't enjoying the holiday with their families, eating turkey and watching parades and football games without end on television. Usually, I go to at least one police station, firehouse, senior center, jail and hospital. At each stop, I always provide a box of freshly baked chocolate-chip cookies. I say they are prepared by the chef at Gracie Mansion under my careful supervision.

A couple of years ago, Victor Botnick, who was then my special adviser on health matters and who would always accompany me on my holiday journeys around the city, went with me to St. Clare's Hospital in Manhattan. It is operated by the Archdiocese of New York. Until a few years ago, it was in very serious financial straits. It then decided to shift its focus from providing general medical care to caring primarily for those with AIDS. On an average day, some 80 AIDS patients are in its care. Its financial fortunes have been reversed and, even better, it has become one of the leading providers of care to people with AIDS to be found anywhere in the nation.

As was true of every other visit that morning, at St. Clare's, I tried to take as much time as I could with each patient. On so special a day, I like to ask whether they've been visited by their family or friends, whether they're receiving good care, and whether the food's any good. No matter who I ask or where I ask it, it seems institutional food everywhere is judged lousy by those who eat it. No one ever volunteers compliments to a chef at a hospital or a jail, and institutional chefs must be among the least appreciated cooks in America. That's why I bring cookies. I know they're delicious.

On this particular Thanksgiving morning, I offered cookies to each of the patients I met. Despite the fact that the best medical evidence proves that AIDS is transmitted from one person to another under only the most specific and intimate of circumstances—sexual intercourse or the sharing of hypodermic needles—a sense of fear gripped me as I handed out the cookies. "What happens," I worried irrationally, "if one of the patients touches my hand?" Not surprisingly, whether because they wanted a cookie or just wanted to shake the hand of their Mayor, a number of patients did.

After a visit of about half an hour, it was time to head on to my next stop. As I was walking down the hallway of the ward, I couldn't shake the fear that had gripped me moments before. I asked the sister who accompanied me if there was a rest room I could use. No, I did not have to urinate. But I realized that I would be very uncomfortable if I went down to the car without washing my hands. No matter the medical evidence. I'd be afraid to touch my unwashed hands to my face.

"Over there, Mr. Mayor," the sister replied, pointing me to what looked like a closet door. In I went, locking the door behind me. Even in private, a Mayor must be aware of his public image. I knew that if the only sound heard while I was inside was of running water, those who might be within earshot would put two and two together and my irrational fear would be exposed.

So before turning on the water, I flushed the toilet, hoping to drown out the sound from the tap and suggest I was making full use of the facilities. The sister wasn't fooled. "Was the water hot enough?" she asked when I walked out of the rest room. I was very embarrassed.

Especially since I know there are thousands of dedicated people who provide direct care to people with AIDS who do not allow such irrationality to interfere with the jobs they do. They are cautious and careful, sure. But they are also very considerate of how those they treat are viewing and interpreting the way in which the care is provided. Being treated as a pariah on one's deathbed doesn't make an already difficult transition any easier.

And some providers are nothing short of saintly in their work. In December 1985, Mother Teresa opened a hospicelike facility in Greenwich Village for prisoners with AIDS who have only a short time to live and have been released from jail into Mother Teresa's care so that they may die with dignity. During a conversation, she told me she and her sisters will sometimes lay their bare hands on the sores that are manifestations of the disease. Neither the patient nor the sisters expect a cure. But it does offer hope and comfort. "They want a ticket to heaven," Mother Teresa said, "and we give them that."

Mother Teresa is a saint. I am not. I am a mere mortal who happens to be the Mayor of New York City. To those who have the misfortune to suffer from this disease, I know an apology is probably due for the impolitic reaction and irrational fears I displayed that Thanksgiving morning. My behavior cannot be excused, only explained.

A mysterious and deadly disease seems to give rise to the worst in many people. Throughout human history, leprosy has struck fear into generation after generation after generation. That fear has brought out the worst side of human nature. Christ's example notwithstanding, thousands upon thousands of lepers have been brutalized, banished and even burned.

Even today. Just two years ago a medical clinic in Alviso, California—a community just north of San Jose on the shores of sophisticated San Francisco Bay—announced plans to provide outpatient care to some 170 lepers who had immigrated from Mexico, Southeast Asia and South America. The community erupted. Staff members at the clinic threatened to quit and, in the words of one health expert, "mass hysteria" swept through a community meeting, overwhelming his explanations of why modern drugs and the low incidence of communicability made fear of leprosy irrational. Ultimately, the plans were dropped. Leprosy didn't play in biblical times. Nor does it now.

AIDS victims are modern-day lepers. As we have come to know more about AIDS and the needs of those who suffer from it, the City of New York has increasingly recognized the importance of providing long-term-care facilities where a person with AIDS can spend his or her last months and weeks in comfort and with dignity. In 1985, we decided that an underused city-run nursing home on the beach in the Neponsit section of Queens would provide a perfect setting for a long-term AIDS facility.

The Neponsit community decided otherwise. Picket lines were formed, demonstrations were held, and lawsuits were threatened, all in order to prevent people with AIDS from moving into their neighborhood. On one occasion that I visited the facility, in fact, I was greeted by a group of very upset elderly women.

"If men with AIDS live in Neponsit, they'll be able to use our beaches and swim in our ocean. If they do, we'll get AIDS if we swim there too."

"No, no, no," I tried to assure these women. "The only way to get AIDS from the young men who will be in this facility is to have sexual intercourse with them or to share a hypodermic needle with them." Hardly likely, I thought to myself afterward.

The fears of these women may have had no basis in fact, but was a real fear to them anyway. Thanks to a decision by the Archdiocese of New York to have Mother Teresa open her facility in Greenwich Village, use of the Neponsit home was no longer necessary and the risk to the AIDS patients who would have received care there was eliminated.

But fear is always just beneath the surface of any public-policy discussion about AIDS. As a private person, of course, I have expressed some of the same fears, no matter how irrational and how unfounded they are. But as a public official, I cannot and will not give in to such fears.

At the beginning of the 1985–1986 school year, for example, the New York City Board of Education announced that seven children with AIDS wanted to attend classes on opening day. Once again, the fear of AIDS gave rise to ugliness. A lawsuit was filed by a local community school district demanding to know the names of the children and the schools they would be attending and some parents even withdrew their children from school.

We could have given in to that fear, not fought the lawsuit, and released the names of the children. That, of course, would have subjected the children with AIDS to a lifetime of fear, castigation and isolation. "Not to worry," some would have replied. "The rights of the majority always take precedence over those of the minority." Regrettably, throughout history that has been a powerful, often prevailing argument. Only after the damage is done to a minority are regrets expressed to those whose lives have been ruined because a society gave in to its dark side.

Fortunately, the City of New York did not give in. AIDS is not transmitted through casual contact and the Centers for Disease Control had earlier issued findings that the risk of AIDS transmission from one child to another in a classroom setting was very remote. Based on these findings, a protocol was developed to evaluate all children diagnosed as having AIDS. If they were too ill to attend school, alternative educational arrangements were to be made. If they were otherwise fit, they would be permitted to attend classes. And their names and the schools they attended would not be announced.

I was very proud of the position my administration took in this very controversial matter. First and foremost in our minds as we met one weekend at Gracie Mansion to develop the protocol were the rights of the children with AIDS. In our view, those rights, and not the fears of the community who did not want them in its midst, took precedence.

"We are very concerned," I said at the time we announced our protocol, "about the physical and mental welfare of the small number of school-age children who have AIDS. In the absence of valid medical and scientific reasons, we cannot simply say that we're going to exclude them as though they were lepers. That will cause the child and the parents of that child to be terribly scarred, harmed and hurt. They're already going through a terrible trauma," I said. "Let's not make it any worse for them."

Our protocol was challenged in court. But we prevailed. Based on the advice of medical experts and on our commitment to making sure the rights of a minority, even a minority of one, are not trampled by irrational panic and unfounded fears, the City of New York stood tall and stood firm. I am proud of many things I have done as Mayor. I am particularly proud of what we did to protect the rights of innocent schoolchildren whose lives could otherwise have been ruined because they had AIDS.

The public policy that guided us in Queens guides our approach to AIDS today. As Mayor, my commitment has been and must continue to be that, based upon the best available medical and scientific advice, we do all within our power and our resources to help prevent the spread of AIDS and to care for its victims. The ways I have gone about meeting that commitment have sometimes put me at odds with my friend John Cardinal O'Connor.

A few years ago, Dr. David Sencer, then health commissioner, recommended that the city begin a program to distribute sterile hypodermic needles to intravenous drug users. His recommendation was very, very timely.

As educational efforts by New York City's gay community have had an increasingly positive effect on reducing high-risk sexual activity and, as a result, reducing the spread of AIDS among gay New Yorkers, an increasing proportion of our AIDS caseload has been comprised of intravenous drug users. Users in a shooting gallery often share needles. When they do, traces of blood from one user go into the veins of another. If the blood of the first carries the HIV virus, that of the second, third and fourth user with whom the needle is shared probably will too. Especially if the sharing occurs again and again.

New York is one of the very few states in the country to require a prescription for the purchase of sterile hypodermic needles. For Dr. Sencer's proposal to go forward, a change in state law would have been required. Since I knew that a bill changing the law would spark controversy, and that state legislators would want not just Dr. Sencer's expert medical opinion, but also several legal opinions, I shared his proposal with district attorneys and other law enforcement experts. If they approved, I was sure the Legislature might be receptive. But the reaction of the law enforcement community was a loud and unanimous no. It would lead to an even greater incidence of drug abuse, they argued. I knew Dr. Sencer's proposal would go nowhere until and unless the climate changed. A few months later, the prestigious National Academy of Sciences/Institute of Medicine revived the idea, proposing a demonstration project to test whether a limited needle-distribution program would lead to increased drug abuse and whether it would reduce AIDS transmission. Dr. Stephen Joseph, my new health commissioner, agreed, and in fact submitted a proposal for such a project to Dr. David Axelrod, the state health commissioner, who had authority to approve a limited project. After many months and many discussions, Dr. Axelrod offered his support for Dr. Joseph's proposal.

His Eminence Cardinal O'Connor, however, offered his opposition. "It is a quick fix that ignores the dignity of the human person," he said one Sunday morning following Mass at St. Patrick's Cathedral. "It's not going to accomplish its avowed purpose of saving lives. It's only going to demean people and drag society down some more. It's a bad word to talk about values in education," he concluded, "so we're always dealing with quick fixes."

I see it more like a patch on a tire. The patch will get you to the service station. The condoms, the clean needles, these are the equivalent of patches; condoms may help prevent infection; needles may be a bridge to treatment. Reality forces us to come to grips with the fact that an addict not in custody or a successful treatment program is going to use drugs; and prisoners are going to continue to engage in sodomy, in both cases despite the risks.

Let's say we were simply to take the money, which is a very modest amount, that is being used to advance the use of condoms and clean needles, and apply it only for subway placards and public-service announcements that admonish: "Don't have sex out of wedlock" and "Don't use condoms" and "Don't use used needles" if you're addicted to heroin. Some might say that was terrific, a moral program. But would this have any practical effect beyond saving us some criticism?

While some may decry the "danger" that by "promoting" the use of condoms and clean needles we will be encouraging some people to engage in sex or minimizing the horrors of drug addiction, I just don't believe this to be dealing responsibly with the problems of the real world. We're not advocating easy sex. We're not promoting consensual homosexuality in prison. We're not pushing drugs. And I do believe that there are other jurisdictions that are employing both of these initiatives with some success, however modest.

Besides, these initiatives are hardly the bulwark of the City's AIDS-prevention effort, which must be targeted at the broad spectrum of New Yorkers, some of whom do and many of whom don't adhere to moral imperatives. These are, rather, only small components of much larger programs on which we are spending hundreds of millions of dollars. Among these programs, we have devised campaigns—targeted particularly to adolescents—to point out the dangers of drug use as well as to advocate abstinence. Cardinal O'Connor is among those who applaud that particular facet of our effort.

But what should we do, for instance, about the youngster who is sexually active, and who will be sexually active no matter what? What about those who are seized by the terrible compulsion to shoot smack? What about their wives and partners who may not share their drug appetite but do share their beds? We are compelled to confront the fact that 2,100 women and 366 babies—90 percent of whom are black or Hispanic—have already contracted the HIV virus, a direct result of sexual relations with infected drug users. We would be remiss if we did not at least attempt some strategy to promote some tactics that might save the lives of other women and babies who are at risk. Have we no responsibility to try to reduce future instances of AIDS in innocent women and even more innocent infants? And let's state the obvious: In addition to preventing human suffering, the more we do now to prevent the spread of the AIDS virus, the less strained an already overburdened municipal hospital system will be as the scourge of AIDS manifests itself, as predicted, in more and more victims.

Virtually every public-health expert in the country, beginning with the Surgeon General of the United States, has stated that condoms, while not a panacea, are still among the only weapons we have in our arsenal to block the transmission of the HIV infection. If we really wanted to do the job correctly we would be out there telling people in a very public way how to use condoms. We don't, because in our society it is still unacceptable to become that graphic.

The needle controversy is odd, in a way, because only eleven states in the entire union even require a prescription for needles. You could go to, say, Florida and walk right into a pharmacy and purchase a hypodermic needle without a prescription. In point of fact, these needles retail for maybe twenty cents on the black market. If you're a user you can rent or buy so-called "works" for five dollars, and there's a good chance you'd be buying AIDS as well; your friendly neighborhood dealer is throwing this in as a little extra. So is it wrong to supply some addicts with clean needles and maybe prevent them from becoming contaminated with the AIDS virus?

Consider the estimate that upwards of half of the approximately 200,000 IV drug users who call New York home are already infected with HIV, primarily through sharing "works." And most heterosexually transmitted cases of AIDS, and instances of AIDS in newborn babies, are spread as a direct or indirect result of drug addiction. Even if the woefully inadequate number of drug-treatment slots were to be tripled (an unlikely event, considering the limitations on state and federal funding), over 100,000 of these addicts would remain out in the cold. And only half of the IV drug users on waiting lists for treatment ever actually enter a program; the rest lose motivation and hope and continue to seek barter for a fix by hustling and stealing.

Cardinal O'Connor has one institutional role. I have another. He is principally concerned with saving souls. I am principally concerned with saving lives. His view is that the needle project won't save any lives. Medical experts tell me otherwise. I think it is worth a try. After all, my Bible says that if we are able to save just one life, we have saved the world. And, as I said at the time of Dr. Axelrod's announcement, if the experiment doesn't save lives and only leads to increased drug abuse, it will be ended.

Nor will we neglect efforts to try to educate the intravenous community to stop sharing needles. Indeed, the city has a contract with ADAPT—the Association for Drug Abuse Prevention and Treatment—to conduct anti-sharing outreach and education campaigns among addicts.

The chances for success? Well, it isn't easy to get the attention of an addict on the nod, no matter how life-or-death the issue. An addict, after all, is committing a form of suicide. But, again, if we are able to save just one life through our educational campaigns, those campaigns will have proven worthwhile.

AIDS education has proven successful among communities not intent on destroying themselves. The educational work, for example, of outstanding organizations like the Gay Men's Health Crisis has helped reduce the rate of HIV sero-position conversion—the year-to-year rate of increase in AIDS infection—among gay men to less than 1 percent.

Those kinds of successful efforts have led us to greatly expand our educational campaigns. We've developed television, radio and print campaigns targeted at specific, at-risk groups and even made them available to media outlets at no cost. The ads are provocative. But if provocation is what's necessary to get an idea across, provocation is the order of the day.

Probably the most controversial aspect of our educational efforts has been the City Health Department's distribution of free condoms to at-risk groups. According to many, distributing condoms only promotes sexual activity. What we should be doing, they argue, is to find a way to discourage sexual activity.

Given the huge consequences AIDS is having on our society, I'd like to think there was a way we could discourage sexual activity outside of stable, monogamous relationships. But I think I know enough about human nature to know how hard that is to achieve; that the words of elected officials, religious leaders, editorial writers or anybody else probably don't have much effect on another person's libido. But of course, it all depends on who is speaking and who is listening.

What we can do, of course, is to encourage people to engage in sexual activity that doesn't put their lives in danger. For a while, it was argued by some that use of a condom was a way to have safe sex. Just as condoms are not a surefire method of birth control, however, they also aren't a surefire way of preventing the exchange of body fluids that can transmit AIDS. Condoms leak. While sex with condoms may be safer than sex without them, condoms still don't offer 100 percent protection against AIDS. Abstinence is truly safe-sex behavior. Condoms can only offer safer sex.

The Cardinal certainly has a compelling reason for opposing our distribution program: the traditional opposition of the Roman Catholic Church against birth control of any sort, including condoms. As Mayor, however, I will continue to support the Health Department's distribution of free condoms. The medical experts believe it can promote safer sex and help reduce the chance that AIDS will be transmitted from one person to another. As has been the case with other issues involving AIDS, I will take the advice of my experts. For me, this is an issue of public health, not of morals or faith. As Mayor, therefore, it is the only responsible course for me to follow.

AIDS has not crept quietly into the public imagination. At each new turn in the epidemic, with each new finding, controversy has erupted. Strong words are spoken, and strong positions taken on both sides of any AIDS issue. In my view, that has been healthy, for it has helped educate people and move our society along in developing a comprehensive approach to the problems AIDS presents. Cardinal O'Connor and I may have disagreed on specific measures to address the epidemic, but I am quite certain he believes that I am committed to dealing with those problems. I know he is.

What is regrettable is that sometimes the controversy gets in the way of reaching agreement on solutions. In the fall of 1987, Pope John Paul II visited San Francisco, a community with an AIDS caseload second only to New York's, as part of his North American pilgrimage. As he prepared to offer Mass at the Mission Dolores, chants could be heard from a group of demonstrators about half a block away. "Curb your dogma," yelled one. "Pope go home," said another. "Nazi Pope!" screamed a third. The demonstrators were described by one newspaper as "good-natured." I wonder how His Holiness would have described them.

"God loves you all," he told the audience, "without distinction, without limit. He loves those of you who are sick, those who are suffering from AIDS and from AIDS-related complex." Following his speech, he strode down the aisle, greeting those who had joined him in celebrating Mass, including some sixty-two AIDS victims. "He is someone to roll back centuries of hatred for us gays," said one victim. "I don't always agree with him, but I think he cares." "If they," said another victim in referring to the demonstrators outside, "had heard what I had heard, they would not be protesting."

One event. But two completely different versions of it. Cardinal O'Connor suffers from the same kind of mixed reviews. Sometimes I think that if people who are so critical of what they think he is saying about AIDS would only listen, they might not be so critical. Some time ago, he was appointed to the Presidential Commission on AIDS. I supported his nomination. In fact, until he was named, I was afraid the commission would be a moribund body, offering no new ideas, no real solutions of the crisis we face.

The Cardinal's critics, of course, rushed to condemn his appointment. I still don't really understand why. After all, here is the head of an Archdiocese that, since his arrival, has opened a hospice facility for prisoners with AIDS, has seen St. Clare's Hospital transformed into one of the leading AIDS hospitals in the country, has helped find placements for "boarder babies" stricken with AIDS so that they do not have to spend their first weeks, months, even years in a hospital ward, and has offered to help the city establish more long-term-care facilities for people with AIDS. And, he told me recently, he has done voluntary duty at St. Clare's Hospital more than one thousand times.

Is this a man who, as some say, is an enemy in the battle against AIDS? I don't think so. He is a friend. His Archdiocese does more than almost any other religious institution in this country to help people with AIDS. That's not the behavior of an "enemy." Certainly, there are occasions when his faith requires that he oppose a particular method, a specific program to deal with the public-health crisis this nation faces. But there are probably some things the City of New York is doing to deal with AIDS that you might not support.

No, John Cardinal O'Connor is a friend, an invaluable ally for those of us concerned about AIDS. Controversies may arise between us, but a common bond will always unite us. He cares not just for the soul but also the lives of those who have AIDS. He has shown that in the pulpit, in his writings, on the Presidential Commission, and most significantly, every time he has walked through the doors of St. Clare's Hospital to offer comfort and care to those who have the misfortune to suffer from this terrible disease.

THE CARDINAL

Christmas of 1987. The Midnight Mass in St. Patrick's Cathedral had been magnificent. Mayor Koch had his customary front-row seat. Overflow crowds packed the side aisles and the steps outside. The brilliant lighting provided by WPIX that annually televises the Mass throughout the United States turned the countless poinsettias surrounding the high altar into a symphony of color. Under the direction of John Grady, the Cathedral choir and Metropolitan Opera star David Rendell were dazzling. It was a night of nights, when even my homily seemed to please at least the less discerning. The wheelchair presence of the incalculably courageous Steve McDonald, police officer paralyzed by a bullet in the spine, and his beautiful blond and equally courageous wife, Patti Ann, was the ultimate Christmas gift. I went through the Mass euphoric from start to finish. It seemed the most beautiful Christmas I had ever experienced.

Until the dawn. It was after not much sleep that I went to make my customary rounds of the AIDS wards in St. Clare's Hospital. Christmas broke apart in the first room I visited.

I never check the religion of the persons with AIDS I visit, nor color, nor sex, nor "life-style," nor the way in which the virus was contracted. I visit *persons*, persons who happen to have AIDS. The sobbing lady standing beside the bed of her son was clearly not Catholic. It was equally clear that her son was dying. I waited, praying. He died.

His mother's sobs became convulsive. The sixth sense that comes of years in the presence of suffering and death told me her grief was even greater than the immediate tragedy. I waited. The rest of her family arrived. Then I learned that the twenty-four-year-old son who had just died of AIDS acquired by intravenous drugs was the third in the family to die within the year. A twenty-year-old daughter had been first: drugs. A thirty-four-year-old son had been second: drugs. And now the twenty-four-year-old. On Christmas Day.

I completed my rounds, including the locked ward, where prisoners with AIDS had been sent by the state. I tried to be cheery with every patient, especially with the prisoners. I smiled and wished Merry Christmases all around, while my heart was a lump in my belly. They would all die as the twenty-four-year-old had died, wasted to the bone, burning with fever, almost all desperately lonely, however many people may surround them or love them. I went home. The Magi wouldn't come today. The Christmas Star was a dull glow. The mother of the twenty- and the twenty-four- and the thirty-four-year-old will be my own suffering Pietà for a long time to come.

AIDS won't go away for a long time to come. Before it does, short of divine intervention it will ravage our society. God alone knows how many people will die, how many will live in a torment of uncertainty, how many families will be shattered, hearts broken, loves lost. In the meanwhile, we calm ourselves with platitudes, armor ourselves with ignorance, posture with self-righteousness, pretend that only the misbehaving will die.

Let there be no misunderstanding. The City of New York is spending more and doing more than any city in the United States, offering more voluntary testing, providing more treatment centers, more hospital beds. The Church in New York has committed extraordinary resources to the same end. Yet neither is scratching the surface of the needs. Nonetheless, in no area of public concern have City and Church worked together more cooperatively, in an attempt to serve the people of New York. The problem is that the needs so exceed the resources. We both seek refuge in the belief that we're doing all we can. That belief must be modified radically.

In the summer of 1987 I reluctantly accepted a White House request that I become a member of a Presidential Commission on the Human Immunodeficiency Virus Epidemic (better known as AIDS). My reluctance was rooted primarily in the demands of an already impossible schedule. I accepted because of my conviction that my hands-on experience as sponsor of eighteen Catholic hospitals and visitor of persons with AIDS would permit me to generate a sense of urgency in the commission, particularly concerning patient care. I pretended no medical, scientific or research expertise.

During my year on the commission I learned a great deal. More than six hundred witnesses gave testimony before the commission: some of the most prestigious scientists in the country, representatives of the National Institutes of Health, the American Medical Association, the American Academy of Sciences, the surgeon general of the United States, pharmaceutical companies, persons with AIDS, relatives and friends of persons with AIDS, volunteers working with persons with AIDS, social workers, lawyers, drug-enforcement agents and many, many others. They offered us opportunities for invaluable insights. They provided us with voluminous reports, statistics, scientific studies. They frightened us.

Not a single witness, however, affected me as did my Christmas Day mother of anguish. During my entire time on the Presidential Commission I continued my visits to persons with AIDS, visits that I had begun before becoming a commission member. It is far from a boast— much more with a sense of privilege—that I am able to say that I have sat with, listened to, wiped the brow of, soothed the lacerated, bleeding skin of, or emptied bedpans for more than one thousand persons with AIDS. In many cases I have talked with their families and friends. Some I have buried. None has ever heard a word of judgment from my lips. All are persons, sacred persons, made in the Image of God, persons of infinite worth and dignity.

The Presidential Commission members worked together with extraordinary harmony. Widely differing philosophies, experiences, religious and moral beliefs—and prejudices—had to be reconciled.[1] Commission members had to listen not only to witnesses but to one another. Initially, and then sporadically as the months went on, each member had to risk insults, jeers, catcalls from hostile or skeptical observers, attacks often born of fears that the commission would be insensitive to the needs and sufferings of persons with AIDS.

Some observers were particularly hostile to me, personally, resentful that I served on the commission. I believe a number of them were surprised, however, by positions I took in favor of rights of patients

1. The commission was made up of a retired admiral, a sexologist, a nurse, an insurance executive, a businessman, a public-health official, four medical doctors (one of them a drug-abuse-rehabilitation expert), a research scientist, a self-identified homosexual, a state representative and myself.

with AIDS, compassion for them and their families, hospital, hospice and residential facilities, decent housing, sharp reductions in the cost of medications. They heard me argue with public officials that red tape had to be cut, that we are fighting a war that allows of no halfhearted measures. They were perhaps especially surprised by my urging health-care professionals and counselors to resist efforts to force them to disclose that a person coming to them in confidence had AIDS, and to resist involuntary testing. And they knew that I voted in favor of antidiscrimination legislation to protect those with AIDS. From my viewpoint there should have been little cause for surprise. I was simply arguing from the perspective of Church teaching on social justice and Gospel values. If I contributed anything constructive, it is the Church that deserves the credit.

Many representatives of homosexually oriented groups who served as observers at Presidential Commission meetings were courteous and obviously recognized the complexities of our task. At the same time, I know that my personal effort in relation to persons with AIDS was and is difficult for those who have not understood the distinction I make, the distinction the Church makes, between homosexual *behavior* and homosexual *orientation* (discussed elsewhere in this book).

I have entered hospital rooms, even in Catholic hospitals, where some patients have been deeply resentful because of my reputation in opposition to homosexual behavior. I was therefore not the slightest bit surprised when I was excoriated occasionally as a commission member, or when my position as a member was protested and picketed both within and outside St. Patrick's Cathedral. My refusal to reply in anger made some protestors even more furious. They asserted that I didn't even care enough about them to be angry. Nothing could have been further from the truth. Despite almost incessant and strident pressures, the Church will not, cannot, change her teaching on homosexual behavior. But the same Church demands that I, and every Christian, treat every human being as a person, with dignity and respect.

It is the same teaching about the sacredness of every human person that motivates me in my approach to persons with AIDS. Once a person has acquired this frightful disease, my concern is with the fact that a person *has* AIDS. Regardless of how the disease was acquired, he or she deserves every bit of care and, indeed, love, that I would try to offer a cancer patient, or anyone else who is desperately ill and almost certainly terminal.

This was the mind-set I wanted to offer the commission; I found its members most receptive. As a matter of fact, it was largely the willingness of all commission members to listen, to question, to argue with witnesses and with one another, and to compromise when principle was not at stake, that made possible a final report that seems to have met with remarkably broad acceptance. It seems to me an outstanding example of what this book is about—that public officials and churchmen, if both of goodwill, can together achieve for the broader society what neither can achieve alone, and that no constructive public policy can be formulated without the combined efforts of the public and private sectors.

This returns me to the multifaceted problems related to the AIDS epidemic in New York and the grave obligations of Church and State to address these problems together, with a true sense of urgency.

I leave to the Mayor a detailed description of what the City is doing, except to say that it is not enough. This is not necessarily to determine how much more the City can do alone, without state and federal funding—big, big monies. But I don't like to read about City officials quoted as saying that future needs will be so great we can't even *plan* for them—we'll never be able to meet them. That attitude is deadly.

Nor can I accept for a moment the wholesale condom or clean-needle approach. As I note elsewhere, apart from other moral aspects of such approaches, I believe their use to be immoral because they pretend that AIDS can be handled by a "quick fix." They excuse us from being serious about the problem, because to be serious calls for a lot of agonizing self-appraisal.

Indeed, the *Los Angeles Times* reported on August 10, 1988, that the federal government has been doing an about-face on the use of condoms for preventing AIDS. The story notes that the government has cut off funding from a UCLA study of condom effectiveness in respect to AIDS, the only major study under way. A National Institutes of Health representative whose agency was funding the study is cited as stating that the cutoff stemmed from concern that the chances of transmission of the AIDS virus were too great because of the risk of condom failure and the high infection rates. New York is one of the cities named in which unacceptably high infection rates put volunteers at too great a risk, given condom failure.

In the Archdiocese of New York we have been repeatedly quoting studies of condom failure as high as 50 percent. The City has consistently rejected such concerns in favor of its condom-distribution program. I believe such a program exceedingly shortsighted.

I embarrassed the Mayor when he got on the condom bandwagon to save New York from AIDS. Nothing would do but that the television stations hawk condoms to kingdom come, that they be scattered around "shooting galleries" like campaign leaflets, and all but stashed into cereal boxes for little kids to discover as prizes. I can't accept that.

I believe the "quick fix" approach is unworthy of the mayor of a great city, and an effort to *evade*, rather than *confront* the real problems. (As mentioned earlier in this book, I discussed this with the Mayor at dinner.) I believe that those with AIDS or in danger of either receiving or transmitting this killer disease deserve more than condoms. Real monies are going to have to be spent, residential facilities made available, serious educational programs developed, hospital beds provided, medications offered at affordable costs, and a whole variety of other needs met.

But the Mayor is often open to a degree to reasonable persuasion, especially on the part of someone who really knows what he is talking about, in this case, my astute auxiliary bishop and Vicar for Education, Bishop Edward Egan.* In the midst of the Mayor's "condom program," Bishop Egan had a rewarding lunch with him and some fruitful follow-up talks with the Mayor's associates. The bishop, as always, had done his homework and knew the facts. The Mayor caused some outstanding videotapes to be made stressing abstinence. He began changing the emphasis in the talks he gave, as well, rejecting the "safe sex" propaganda that had become a dangerous but popular cliché. He did not, however, call for canceling the widespread condom-distribution program, so I could not end my criticism, even though I didn't enjoy embarrassing him. Indeed, a small group purporting to represent one of the homosexual organizations passed out condoms in front of St. Patrick's Cathedral following one of my Masses. I'm sure they didn't get them from the Mayor.

A similar scenario was played out in regard to drugs. The Mayor decided to experiment with providing addicts with clean needles, to prevent transmission of AIDS. As so frequently, his motive was good. I thought the idea atrocious and told the press I considered it a desperation move on the part of the City. I argued, once again, that it was

---

*Since the writing of this book, Bishop Egan has been appointed the Bishop of Bridgeport, Connecticut.

an evasion of responsibility not only toward persons with AIDS and others at risk, but toward the entire drug-dependent community. It evidenced a gigantic failure on the part of government to come to grips with one of the most monstrous problems of our society. It *encouraged*, rather than *discouraged* drug abuse. It demonstrated complete ignorance of the drug culture and the meaning of sharing needles and equipment. It ignored the incalculable dangers of abuse. It was illegal. In my judgment, it was immoral and irresponsible.

Monsignor William O'Brien, founder and president of Daytop Village, knows more about drug abuse than almost anyone I know. Here's what he has to say about the clean-needle approach:

> A program of free-needle distribution to those doomed to die soon from AIDS, or to die a little later from lethal dosages of drugs under the banner of AIDS curtailment, proceeds upon some fundamental miscalculations and represents an assault on what we are about as a caring society. Morally as well as programmatically, it is an outrage. The program is wrong because the message is wrong: "We'll help you die! Just don't bring AIDS to our doorstep!" The program is wrong because besides syringes, heroin addicts share both the cotton and the "cooker" (bottle-cap)—all of which are contaminated. Of what value, then, are antiseptic needles alone? The program is wrong because 200 addicts cannot provide scientific data. Expert testimony and strong data are readily available at Daytop from former habitués, who would be happy to share their reaction in terms of the program's content and its potential for achieving its goals. Once again, government leadership rings all bells on consistency, i.e., never discuss a proposal with the people who might provide facts. While we wipe away the tears of parents whose kids cannot get a treatment bed until December, the program instead offers clean needles to prolong their agony. We are a sorry lot if this is the best we can do![2]

My anger is only partially fair, perhaps, since everybody is grasping at straws and the City is doing more than pushing condoms and clean needles. Nobody, however, is doing enough, State, Church or other elements of the private sector, and we all feel it. The frustration level is high. I just wish that the City would stick to trying to find real solutions to these very real problems, and not resort to gimmicks.

2. *New York Daily News*, August 24, 1988

The more time I spent on the Presidential Commission on AIDS and the more personal hands-on experience I accrued with persons with AIDS, the more convinced I became of the frightening role played by drugs. New York's own Dr. Beny J. Primm, president of the Addiction Research and Treatment Corporation, and I urged, with other commissioners, that the commission spend a large part of its time on this issue, and devote a significant portion of its report to President Reagan on recommendations related to drugs. The commission did so. The final report calls intravenous and other drug abuse "a major port of entry for the [AIDS] virus into the larger population."[3]

I am not at all sure that with the emphasis on the homosexual factor in AIDS transmission, the public at large yet appreciates the monstrous role played by drugs. Let's check the record, as compiled by the commission.

[Seventy] percent of perinatally transmitted AIDS cases are the children of those who abuse intravenous drugs or whose sexual partners abuse intravenous drugs. . . .

Most of these children die in their first few years of life. Many never leave the hospital. . . . By 1991 there are expected to be 10,000 to 20,000 cases of AIDS among infants and children.

But they represent only the beginning of the tragedy if this nation does not move to address its entire drug abuse problem. . . . The United States continues to have the highest rate of illicit drug use among young people of any country in the industrialized world. Our drug problem pervades all elements of society. A recent study has demonstrated that drug abuse is a problem for both suburbs and inner cities, for all races, and at all income levels. Without a coordinated and sustained response, America as a whole faces a bleak future.

In addition to the devastation that drug abuse represents for the individual, the family, and the community, the purely financial cost of drug abuse—in terms of providing health care, reduced productivity, law enforcement, plus theft and destruction of property—is estimated at $60 billion annually. This remarkable figure does not include the staggering costs of providing health care for drug abusers with HIV infection.[4]

3. *Report of the Presidential Commission on the Human Immunodeficiency Virus Epidemic* (Washington, D.C.: June 24, 1988), p. 94
4. Ibid., pp. 95–95

To curb intravenous and other drug abuse, the commission asserts, requires a comprehensive *ten-year* strategy. This demands that "individual drug abusers take personal responsibility for their own well-being. . . . It will also require a major commitment from federal, state, and local governments, as well as parents, educators, and community leaders to work together to initiate new prevention and education programs and to build community support for eliminating drug abuse and drug trafficking."

Such a program must include "increased treatment capacity, increasing research into treatment modes, strengthening primary prevention and early intervention programs, and conducting aggressive outreach programs in HIV-related education and prevention."

Obviously, I support the commission's recommendations, yet I know, realistically, that even if they *are* carried out, at the rate we are moving on this national catastrophe it will take every day of the ten years projected. We do not have that kind of time. Even had we no AIDS epidemic, drugs are ravaging our nation. The crime, the violence, the general destructiveness have become unspeakable.

The Presidential Commission report notes that temporarily alleviating the health effects of symptomatic HIV infection can cost as much as $100,000 per person. To say that drug-abuse "treatment on demand" is too costly is foolish by comparison.

I appreciate particularly the commission's emphasis on prevention and treatment. I again quote Monsignor William O'Brien of Daytop Village. And again he argues forcefully:

> The Federal Government, after years and billions of dollars expended on interdiction, crop eradication and international trafficking on the premise that supply reduction is at the heart of the solution of America's drug crisis, while paying lip-service to treatment and prevention, must reverse its priorities to Main Street, USA! The 90% of allocations now must go to demand reduction (treatment and prevention) as well as to local law enforcement which propels addicts into treatment.[5]

Those last few words should become the battle cry of an aggressive program in New York. The limitation of drug-treatment facilities is a

5. By personal letter of May 4, 1988, from Monsignor William B. O'Brien to author

243

disgrace. [6] Legislatures pass budgets with tidy sums for abortion on demand. How many heartbreaking stories are there of families who have begged and pleaded that a loved one "turn himself in" for treatment—only to have him turned away when he does so. No room. Come back in four months. It is estimated that a minimum of thirty thousand new treatment beds are needed. I suspect that the estimate is modest.

While I have listened to and appreciate Mayor Koch's emphasis on interdiction, I see its potential as severely limited. The complexities of bureaucratic control and congressional watchdogging of foreign aid, as well as the cold-bloodedness of every nation's "enlightened self-interest" is known even to those who are politically naïve. What happened with the threats made to General Noriega in Panama was a simple illustration. In Bolivia, the rage against the United States—witness the burning of the American flag—reached the boiling point during Operation Blast Furnace, the effort to seek out and destroy crops. The reason given? Cocaine production is the "only way out of poverty for peasants."

Whatever the potential of interdiction, however, without extensive treatment and rehabilitation facilities, little progress will be made. The City is simply not providing them. Nor will significant progress be made without an intensive and comprehensive education program. This is another instance in which I believe prejudice rears its ugly head.

It has become a platitude to call for massive education against the acquisition and transmission of AIDS. Obviously, education is always a *must* against ignorance. Much of what I have seen offered as education, however, is superficial: the mechanics of how not to contract or transmit AIDS.

What is the crucial element in education concerning AIDS? In my judgment, it's motivation. And the motivation must be more than to avoid acquiring or transmitting illness, however useful such may be. Such motivation is simply not enough. For the question remains: *Why* avoid AIDS? Perhaps it is sufficient for some people to answer that it

6. Monsignor O'Brien cites case after case where lack of treatment facilities has put the lives of countless human persons in jeopardy. In the dry language of case reports, we learn, for example: "A 17-year-old arrived for her interview [to enter Daytop's treatment facility]. She reported that her mother had sold her (sexually) to two crack dealers for vials of crack." "An undomiciled 38-year-old homeless man arrived at the Far Rockaway site for an interview. He was sick and was bleeding internally as a result of his lifestyle. He blacked out on the third floor and an ambulance had to be called to take him to a local hospital."

can kill them. This is not necessarily sufficient motivation for them to worry about transmitting the disease to others, or even, in *itself* sufficient to deter them from risking acquiring it themselves. *Unless.* Unless they have a sense of the priceless worth of every single human life, the sacredness of every single human person.

If I really believe I am sacred—priceless and irreplaceable—that belief is an extraordinary deterrent to doing something that may spell my death, not a heroic death, or a sacrificial death, but a totally useless and unnecessary death. If I believe the same about others, the same applies. I will discipline myself in every way I can to avoid contributing to the death of another.

That's called "value" thinking. Tragically, educational systems all over the United States have rejected the teaching of values, even the most fundamental values of life, as unconstitutional. Fear of imposing one's values on others has become a fetish. But if educators have the right to say "You shouldn't kill people," why are they forbidden to add "because human life is sacred"?

During 1988 I conducted a series of workshops for chaplains, priests, sisters, ministers and rabbis, for pastoral counselors, laypersons and anyone else who wanted to attend. The subject was the care of persons with AIDS. My whole sense of the response from participants was that of everything I said, what made the real impact was my insistence on the sacredness of the human person, at whatever stage of illness. In my view, this should permeate and dominate the education of medical and nursing students, doctors, social workers and everyone else committed to the care of persons with AIDS.

The Archdiocese of New York has both an in-school and an "extracurricular" drug-education program that could be vastly expanded in our own schools and communities had we the funds, and could be effectively used in public schools and the broader community. The in-school program is called ADAPP (Archdiocese of New York Drug Abuse Prevention Program) and is coordinated by the Archdiocesan Department of Education. The out-of-school program, directed through the Office of Substance Abuse Ministry, is called DARE (Drug, Alcohol, Rehabilitation, Education).

The exceptional results of ADAPP and DARE speak for themselves. I am proud of both programs, both the vision of my predecessor, Cardinal Cooke. ADAPP provides prevention services to 23,031 students in the Archdiocese of New York. In 1987, at the end of counseling services for students referred because of their substance abuse, 88 percent were able to remain in school and significantly reduced or eliminated abuse; 75 percent demonstrated a significant improvement in grades and school attendance; only 1.9 percent of students referred were expelled or dropped out of school.

DARE is unique in both its operation and effectiveness. The uniqueness is largely in the 37,000 peer-group substance-abuse workers who have given 10 million volunteer hours to encourage their peers to stay away from drugs, or to seek help if they have become involved. In 1987, DARE handled 3,835 referrals, conducted over two hundred community events involving some 330,000 people and continued and expanded its anti-drug advocacy media campaign.

If any single problem within health care needs and lends itself to an all-out cooperative efforts on the part of Church and State, it is the drug scourge. Drugs know no creed, no color or sex or ethnic background. Heavy government spending is a must, but without motivation nothing will happen. Without a sense of values, nothing will happen. Without a recognition of the urgency of the problem, nothing will happen. I would hope that by the time this book is published, the Mayor and I will have agreed that this is one area in which the goodwill of Church and State can make New York a model for the world.

We do have the potential to become such a model. Our cooperative effort regarding "boarder babies" is illustrative.[7] At supper one evening, the Mayor was talking about boarder babies, a number with AIDS. I asked how many needed care. His deputy, Stan Brezenoff, answered. There were forty-two. I told the Mayor we would take all of them and any others that come along in the future. He took me up on the offer, and our respective staffs followed through later. This is where a good working relationship between Mayor and Archbishop is imperative and can pay off handsomely for society. No matter how often they may disagree they can do a lot more for everybody as friends than as enemies. And together, Archdiocese and City could do a lot more about drugs through a combined support of ADAPP and DARE.

In addition to continuing and expanding ADAPP and DARE, what is the Church in New York doing and what does it plan to do?

7. "Boarder babies" are children in hospitals who are abandoned by their parents.

Long ago, on October 20, 1984, I wrote to the administrator of each of our eighteen[8] Catholic hospitals, directing that no one be discriminated against for actual or suspected AIDS. The letter read, in part: "I am grateful for the sensitive concern with which you have responded to the needs of those afflicted with AIDS. . . . I know that charity characterizes all your efforts, and I want you to be aware that occasionally there are some who ask whether you discriminate against certain patients. It gives me great pride to be able to say that you do not." I have yet to receive a valid complaint of discrimination concerning any of our hospitals.

Persons with AIDS are treated in seventeen of our eighteen hospitals, and at least three treat substantial numbers of persons with AIDS.[9] St. Vincent's Hospital and Cabrini Hospital have been among the leaders. I have visited persons with AIDS in both these hospitals, examined their overall programs and am deeply gratified by what I have seen.

The hospital in which I spend most of my time is St. Clare's, which has pioneered with AIDS so effectively in so many ways. Most important of these has been the centralization of treatment for patients with AIDS, in preference to what is commonly called the "scatter bed" approach, with such patients scattered throughout a hospital.

Concentrating patients has many advantages. Persons with the same illnesses and fears, successes and failures, similar problems to face in regard to their families and friends can support one another significantly. One sees beautiful examples of such support. Families who visit, many ashamed and afraid, discover they are not alone. Medical doctors, nurses, staff, volunteers and pastoral counselors become particularly skilled in diagnosis and treatment, and sensitive to the emotional needs of their patients. The patients themselves seem to draw support from this centralized method of treatment.

Let me talk a bit about some of our patients at St. Clare's. Name changes will protect identities.

• Frank was typical. It was his third hospitalization. Once contracting full-blown AIDS, the average patient goes through three to

8. It was during the course of writing this book that the eighteenth hospital was included in the archdiocesan system.
9. Calvary Hospital is uniquely oriented to cancer victims in the terminal stages of their illness. It is not equipped to treat the broad spectrum of opportunistic infections that actually cause the death of most persons with AIDS.

four periods of acute hospitalization and dies within eighteen months. Frank was coming through his third acute illness. He would have to leave the hospital. He would not return.

I talked often with Frank. He had lived in the streets, begging for drug money. Nights were safer on rooftops than on benches, he told me, and much safer than in shelters. In times past, he was able to get drugs easily—by carrying a gun for a dealer. He told me he had used the gun before refusing to carry it anymore.

Frank had no religion, no money, no friends, no clothes, nowhere to go. St. Clare's had stretched his stay to the lawful limit.[10] The social worker had been unable to find him a place to live—one of the most common and acute problems faced by persons with his condition. He told me he dreaded going back to the streets; it meant going back to drugs.

There was only one option and Frank was afraid of it. He had been told that Mother Teresa's "Gift of Love," the little house in Greenwich Village, was a virtual prison. It was the kind of misnomer I had heard before about this simple little place that houses some fourteen persons with AIDS who have no place to go. They find a home there, some the only real home they have known, and they are bathed in love. No questions are asked. Religion, color, ethnic background are not the issues. There are only two requirements: AIDS and having no place to go while "recuperating" from an acute stage.

Permit a digression here about this special place, Gift of Love.

When I asked famed Mother Teresa of Calcutta to help me open a residential facility for persons with AIDS with needs outside a hospital setting, the Mayor was quick to support the idea. The Archdiocese provided the house, one-time rectory of St. Veronica's Church, near Greenwich Village. The City, through the Mayor's efforts, expedited permissions required by law to open such a place. The Mayor joined Mother Teresa and myself for the dedication ceremony, despite the fact that the location of the house was initially unpopular with the local community. Many have since lived and died in that little house, bathed in love by the sisters, who have little else to give them but can help them to find eternal happiness, secure in knowing that God loves them as do the sisters. Neither the sisters nor the Archdiocese is reim-

10. Various government regulations preclude hospitals from retaining patients who are no longer in the acute phase of an illness.

bursed by the city, state or federal government for a single resident. It's strictly a work of love.

I cannot count the number of times I have heard the Mayor praise this little house, Gift of Love, to the skies. As when he praises anything related to the Archdiocese of New York, some people criticize him severely. They speak sharply of what we *haven't* done; hence, belittle what we *have* done. I can understand that, but I admire the way the Mayor holds his ground and risks losing some votes.

Back to Frank. I assured Frank he would be no one's captive, and could come and go as he pleased. We gave him a new suit. He went to Gift of Love, at his own request. I visited him a few weeks later, a laughing, gentle Frank, a member of Mother Teresa's family, waiting until he would become acute again and die, but no longer afraid. He had learned about love, later than some, far sooner than many.

The Church must open more such "respices." I have asked Mother Teresa to open another such house, and one for children. The City should be doing this in spades. As far as I can see, bureaucratic entanglements, costs, and the fact that current government-reimbursement programs don't apply to such places have kept City efforts in this regard to a minimum.

In May of 1988, in St. Patrick's Cathedral, I had the honor of presenting Mother Clara Hale, a black Protestant woman, with the Pierre Toussaint Medal. Toussaint was a black Catholic Haitian slave who came to New York with his owners in colonial days. After being given his freedom, he spent his life helping the poorest of the poor. Mother Hale runs a marvelous respice for babies with AIDS (and other illnesses) who can't qualify for hospital care and have no place to go. She is a Mother Teresa in her own way. How many other such places are there? Few, if any.

• Leslie wanted her hair washed every time she saw me. The first few times she fooled me. Then I learned that staff or volunteers had already washed her hair, and did so every day. Leslie was largely in a state of dementia (often characterized by severe memory loss, staring into space, withdrawal and similar symptoms). Mostly she stared at me when I came in, rarely answering any questions. Her eyes would follow me, quizzically, and always seemed to me to be pools of pain.

Dementia is common for persons with AIDS, the result of brain damage. Motion is extremely limited. Usually the patient simply lies there, weak, tired, often having to be fed intravenously. There are other patients who hallucinate, still others who go blind. It is a terrible disease. As its very name, acquired immune deficiency syndrome, tells us, the patient is open to every conceivable "opportunistic infection." Antibiotics may help or may make things worse. AZT, the most commonly used drug at this writing, seems to make some feel better, prolong the life of others, and have a toxic effect on still others. I listened and read carefully during our Presidential Commission hearings, always hoping for the name of a miraculous new wonder drug. Nothing.

The hearings for me weren't even fractionally impersonal. I was listening for a cure for Leslie with the haunting eyes, Leslie in her dementia, wanting her hair washed while her life slips away.

• Luiz had Kaposi's sarcoma. I have seen what looks quite like it in a leprosarium in the Philippines. But Luiz is not a leper. He has AIDS. There is hardly an inch of his skin free of a lesion—open, running sores, tumors larger than fists, legs swollen with edema, feet raw and tender. Luiz never uttered a word of complaint. Always he would ask me to pray with him, to bless him. Unfailingly he would force a smile and tell me how well he was doing. Luiz is dead now. He suffered too much not to be in heaven.

I hate this disease. Writing about it is easier than lecturing about it, which I do with increasing frequency. When I describe "my" patients, I find it hard to breathe, hard to speak, hard not to weep openly.

• Jimmy was a bank robber. He robbed banks because "that's where the money is." He needed the money to get drugs, to feed a habit far in excess of his $50,000 a year salary. Jimmy went to jail, but off drugs. Five years after he last "did" drugs, the AIDS showed up.

Prisons haven't been kind to persons with AIDS. There are horror stories of men and women locked in solitary, without treatment, to await death.

Sister Antonia Maguire is absolutely fearless and as tenacious as fearless. She works in a prison. Her appeals to authorities on behalf of prisoners with AIDS were fruitless. She targeted her Archbishop. By letter, phone call and personal visit she made crystal clear that I was a no-good profligate who didn't deserve to run a flea circus, much less an Archdiocese. She assured me that if I didn't call the Mayor, the Governor, the President and the Pope all in the same day, to get

AIDS prisoners transferred from prison to St. Clare's, she would have my baptismal certificate rescinded. None of her threats worked. Making me fall in love with her did. It's a trick she uses on all prisoners, guards, wardens and everyone else who gets in the way of God's work as she sees it.

So we dedicated a couple of wards in St. Clare's, negotiated with the City, were provided with security guards and welcomed all the prisoners we could take. We have since doubled the capacity to about thirty. Prisoners with AIDS are *persons* with AIDS. They are treated with the same respect and given the same care.

Jimmy is one of these. He had been with us for a number of months now. I have seen him go from perhaps a solid 180 to skin and bones. He has a wonderful family. Their fidelity has been a thing of beauty. I travel a lot, and each time I leave I wonder if Jimmy will be alive when I return. He has had several close calls, and he hallucinates more frequently now, I notice. I will return from a trip one day and he will have died, no longer a prisoner.

Jimmy and his family are Catholic. They are not from the Archdiocese of New York, but I told him, and them, that I want to offer his funeral Mass, in St. Patrick's Cathedral. Some of these fellows get to you.

I could write of many others: the husband and wife in the same hospital room, both afflicted, the young woman struggling to protect her children from the jibes of other youngsters in school who know their father has AIDS, the children who have AIDS, the blind man who called me "John," and who always told me of the many friends he knew would be in to see him that evening. I never met any.

I could write of the fears—and the courage—of medical and staff people, of volunteers and of chaplains, not only the fear of contracting AIDS, but the fear of being feared because they minister to persons with AIDS. Will their life insurance be renewed without question? Will they be given a lease on an apartment? Will people fear touching them, shaking hands or eating with them, kissing or loving them?

It's a shadowy world, the world of AIDS, and most of us are uneasy with shadows, especially when we're not sure what causes them. Yet the way in which we as City or Church treat persons with AIDS and their families and friends and loved ones is a test of what we really believe about the human person.

The sanctity of human life is absolutely basic to sound Catholic teaching. As I understand our Declaration of Independence and our constitutional tradition, the sanctity of human life is basic to everything that we mean when we speak of the American way of life at its best.

It is because I believe in the inviolability of every human person that I have argued against doctors revealing to wives or husbands that a spouse has AIDS unless the spouse agrees. Why? Because I believe that *every* human person, whatever he or she may have done, must have *someone* to turn to in absolute confidence. Most public-health officials, a large number of doctors and probably a significant number of ordinary citizens would almost certainly disagree with me. They would believe that the transmission of AIDS is such a critical danger that revealing the information is justifiable in order to prevent it. I recognize, of course, that it's a real dilemma. Obviously there must be a balance of rights. What of the nineteen-year-old girl, for example, exposed to a man who can literally kill her? What of babies born of such unions? I am well aware that I have no right to dismiss such critical questions out of hand. More discussion is needed on both sides of the issue.

I worry about this issue for another very grim reason. Some projections for the 1990s put the number of AIDS cases in New York City at a half-million or more. Thus far, the City's answer to the threat has been to the effect that we can't take care of a half-million people sick with *any* illness, so there's little we're going to be able to do about it. With that attitude, how long is it going to take before the "death with dignity" crowd have their way? How long will it take them to mount a campaign to convince the terminally ill that suicide is a noble act that frees the world of danger and of having to take care of them? How long will the euthanasists, the "mercy killers," remain silent in the face of massive suffering? Who will be the first judge to sign a court order to begin the "mercy killing" of persons with AIDS?

There can be only one possible defense against this nightmare: an unconditional commitment to the sacredness of every human life on the part of all society. Should churchmen relax for a moment their insistence on the sacredness of *every* human life, there will be no refuge for *anyone*.

The final report of the Presidential Commission on AIDS pleads for a sense of urgency, begs for a restructuring of governmental agencies in order to speed the search for prevention and cure of AIDS, urges a reallocation of massive sums of money to take care of those who will be ravaged by the disease before prevention or cure is found. No level of government can be exempted from its responsibilities, however any other level may fail. Nor may the Church or the private sector in general refuse to share the responsibility, refuse to question its own allocation of resources.

Because it is by no means a personal accomplishment, I am proud to "boast" that as of this writing the Archdiocese has been able to announce the establishing of the first long-term nursing unit in the United States for persons with AIDS. The Terence Cardinal Cooke Medical Center is meeting truly critical needs by providing sixty beds in a nursing-care facility. This was a need I argued as a member of the Presidential Commission. I am truly grateful that one of our archdiocesan hospitals has been able to meet it, and hope similar facilities will be opened everywhere.

We are confronted with a plague of potentially unimaginable proportions. We can be terrified into hysterical and self-defeating panic. We can deny all research reports and predictions or convince ourselves that it will all go away. We can argue that there's nothing we can do about it and wash our hands of it all. Or we can design a New York Manhattan Project of the type that produced the atom bomb, only this time the best minds and hearts would devote themselves solely to trying to save as many lives as possible.

Thus far, the City has been highly supportive of the Church's efforts in trying to meet whatever needs it can for persons with AIDS and their families. As of this writing, a beginning has been made—a good beginning, but *only* a beginning. And people like Frank and Leslie and Luiz and Jimmy don't have time to wait.

VIII

THE MAYOR
RACE, RELIGION,
and
EQUAL OPPORTUNITY

THE CARDINAL
RACISM
and
PREJUDICE

THE MAYOR

It was 1931, a time of suffering and hardship for countless millions throughout the country and around the world. The Great Depression had shut down banks and factories. My father, a furrier, struggled to keep his business going. But the economy was in ruins. There was nothing to do but give up our apartment and move in with my father's brother Bernie and his family in Newark. Eight of us shared a two-bedroom apartment on Spruce Street. My brother and I slept on folding cots in the dining room. My two cousins slept on cots in the foyer.

Our neighborhood, the High Street area, had a racially mixed population. My school on Monmouth Street was more than 50 percent black. Double desks were the rule in those days. My seatmate was black. It wasn't by accident that blacks and Jews often lived in the same parts of town. Both groups were victims of systematic discrimination, especially in housing and employment. Government agencies rarely intervened. The concept of "civil rights" was virtually unknown. Blacks, especially, were denied protection against racism and bigotry. Equal justice under the law was the national ideal, but for the most part it applied only to white Christians.

Because the law was often slanted against them, immigrants and minorities tended to gather in self-protective enclaves. Newark had many large and flourishing areas where different cultures lived in close contact with each other. But they also lived in distinct neighborhoods. Blacks and Jews in the High Street area shared shopping facilities, schools, parks and transportation. At the same time we lived on different sides of Quitman Street. We were divided by the pervasive effect of the 1896 Supreme Court "separate but equal" ruling (which really meant "separate and unequal") but were joined in poverty and in our hope for better times.

I mention these facts about my childhood because some people, upset that I speak out candidly on all issues—including the sensitive questions of race and religion—assume that I come from a sheltered background where I never got to meet people of different cultures. The opposite is true. At the Monmouth Street School, and later at the Miller Street School and at South Side High School (now called Shabazz High School) I was educated in ethnically and racially integrated classrooms. I think my experiences were fairly typical. The students in my schools got along well together. The only time I ever had serious trouble was when a kid from a Polish neighborhood beat me up on my way to Hebrew school. I was twelve, he was about fifteen and didn't like Jews. But that was the exception, not the rule. I learned by experience that America's many different groups have far more to unite them than they do to divide them.

In 1941 we moved from Newark to Brooklyn. I attended classes at City College and went into the army in 1943. During my combat infantry training, I was sent to Camp Croft in Spartanburg, South Carolina. The army was segregated, but the cities and towns of the Deep South were many times worse. It was in South Carolina at age nineteen that I first came across "Whites Only" drinking fountains and segregated restaurant and bathroom facilities. It was infuriating to realize my classmates from Newark—with whom I'd been sharing drinking fountains and eating facilities for most of my life—could be subjected to the indignity and outrage of legally ordained racism (even in Newark some movies houses required blacks to sit in the balcony). Jews were treated with contempt and sometimes belligerence by this same system, but were allowed to pass through the racial barrier. I began to fully understand the desperate plight of black Americans. The law had failed them completely.

After the war I entered law school, graduating in 1948. Over the next decade, I pursued a steadily increasing interest in politics. American society had its faults, but it also provided the means—political action—by which those faults could be corrected. Progress wouldn't happen by itself, however. Inequities and shortcomings had to be confronted openly and honestly. The 1950s saw the beginnings of the civil rights revolution. *Brown* v. *Board of Education* rang the death knell for racial segregation. The integration of Central High School in

Little Rock showed that the federal government meant business. America was living up to its ideals at last.

It was a time when Americans were challenged to look around them and root out discrimination wherever it was found. In the late 1950s, as lawyer for the Village Independent Democrats, I helped to organize a picket line calling for the integration of a Howard Johnson's restaurant at Sixth Avenue and Eighth Street. The management hired blacks to work at certain jobs and whites to work at others. It was a clear case of racial prejudice. Some people crossed our picket line, but many—understanding that fundamental issues of fair play and equality were involved—did not. Howard Johnson's saw the light. It ended its practice of racial discrimination.

But the real battles were just beginning. On August 28, 1963, I took part in the civil rights march on Washington, and was among those privileged to hear Martin Luther King, Jr., deliver his historic "I Have a Dream" speech to the assembled throng. His vision of a new America at peace with itself thrilled every one of us.

"I have a dream," Dr. King told us, "that my four little children will one day live in a nation where they are not judged by the color of their skin but by the content of their character."

It was a powerful and persuasive call for equality under the law, a vision of an America that casts aside racism and bigotry. In Washington, and two years later in Selma, Dr. King made us see that only by liberating ourselves from prejudice could we ever be "Free at last!"

We were traveling down a road toward change and progress. Less than three months later we saw just how difficult and dangerous the road would be. John Kennedy lay dead in Dallas.

But President Kennedy's death didn't slow the march toward justice. If anything, the pace increased.

In August of 1964, there was a call for lawyers to go south to help in a civil rights voter-registration drive. The drive was coordinated by the American Civil Liberties Union. I went to their office and volunteered.

I was sent to Jackson, Mississippi, where the lawyer directing the effort was Marian Wright, a well-known civil rights activist.

She sent me to Laurel, Mississippi, to defend a group of civil rights workers. They were mostly college students from the North, both black and white, and included local blacks who were involved in the voter-registration drive.

259

In addition to registering voters, this group decided to hold a sit-in at the lunch counter at Kress Department Store. While they were sitting in, they were assaulted, and in a classic twist of justice, Jim Crow style, even though they had been beaten and victimized, they were the ones charged with breaking the law. My job was to defend them. My clients ranged from eighteen to twenty-two years of age and they were very dedicated to the cause, so we headed off to the courthouse.

While I was standing at the top of the staircase in the courtroom, I saw a student being assaulted. He was not one of the defendants but rather an onlooker. He was assaulted by someone dressed in rough farmer clothes, and no one came to his aid. I was shocked. I went to the sheriff's office and when I started to lodge a complaint, they shut the window.

Then the courtroom was opened. The sheriff came in and people filled the room. The sheriff made an announcement. He said, "Nigger defendants on the left, white defendants on the right, and all other niggers out of the room."

When the judge came in I said to him, "Something terrible has just happened and it is illegal. The sheriff has just ordered the Negro spectators out of the courtroom and has separated defendants based on their race. It is illegal under a Supreme Court decision."

The judge said to me, "Well, tell him to stop."

I said, "Your Honor, I can't do that. You have to tell him."

The judge told the sheriff and he obeyed.

There was a preliminary hearing, and the case was set down for trial the next day. I had been asked by the Jackson office to secure some transcripts from another court. The court was located in another courthouse not far from the Town Hall, where the court that I had just appeared in was located. With me was a young man who had been in Mississippi for a year or more. He was not yet admitted to the bar, and was there in his capacity as a clerk to help me.

The two of us left the Town Hall building and walked across the street to the courthouse. We suddenly heard hands clapping loudly in a way that was clearly threatening. We looked to the rear and saw a group of about ten men scowling and laughing derisively at us. And at the head of the pack was the man who had assaulted the student.

My companion said, "We are in trouble. This happened to me in Hattiesburg. I was kicked and pummeled. The only thing that we can do is to try to get back to the Town Hall."

I said, "How do we do that?"

He said, "We make a sharp turn, take them by surprise, and walk right through them before they can react."

I said, "Okay."

Then I started to count—one, two, three. And when I got to three, we turned on our heels and walked through the pack. I was scared to death. When we got into the building, I saw the young corporation counsel whom I had met in the courtroom a short time before.

I said to him, "You have to help us. There is a mob outside that wants to attack us."

He said, "I can't."

I said, "You must. I am an officer of the court."

He said, "I can't help."

I said, "Well, the least you can do is help me get to a telephone."

He said, "I will."

He took me into the clerk's office and said, "Let this man use the phone." I am convinced they would not have allowed me to do it without his having made the request. I called the local FBI office in Laurel.

The voice on the other end answered, "FBI, Robert E. Lee speaking." And Robert E. Lee had the thickest Southern drawl I have ever heard.

I said to him, "This is Ed Koch. I am a lawyer calling from the Town Hall. There is a gang outside, and I think they want to kill me."

He said, "Would you please spell your name?"

So I spelled it for him.

Then he said, "We are not allowed to intervene in any matter down here. We are here as observers, but I would like to have some information from you." He proceeded to ask me questions about what my purpose was in Laurel, the license number of my car, et cetera.

I interrupted him and said, "Mr. Lee, I have to get off this phone. I have to find a way to get out of this building alive. I will give you my itinerary back to Jackson to make it easier for you to find our bodies."

The young white lawyer was listening to this conversation.

Finally, he said to me, "I will try to help you. Come with me. I will try to get you out a side door."

We went out the side door from which we could see the car. Then we ran to the car and drove away from Laurel as fast as we could.

I don't mean to convey that I think of myself as a civil rights hero.

261

I'm not. Many others did so much more. And still others like James Chaney, Mickey Schwerner and Andrew Goodman lost their lives. In the first eight months of 1964, more than thirty blacks were murdered in various parts of Mississippi. It was simply a moment in American history that demanded that each of us do what we could to help over-turn racism and secure equal rights and opportunities for everyone. I was glad I could help. I have many warm memories of the time I spent in Mississippi. There was a true feeling of alliance and friendship among the blacks and whites involved in the civil rights movement. We looked ahead to a day when we would all be part of a world where people are judged "not by the color of their skin but by the content of their character." I went to Mississippi because the words I live by are found in a biblical injunction I have known all my life: "Justice, jus-tice shalt thou render, saith the Lord." When the sages commented on why the word "justice" is repeated twice, they decided it's because it's not enough to have justice only for your own, in this case the Jews. There must be justice for everybody. I've always taken that as my highest precept. It's part of my religion.

In 1966 I was elected to the New York City Council and continued to work for civil rights. During these years the ideals and direction of the movement underwent tremendous changes as America came to grips with the increasingly militant and strident nature of civil disobe-dience and protest. The riots in Los Angeles, Newark and Detroit brought demands for immediate and sweeping changes in all sectors of American society. But I don't think I really understood just how far and how quickly the original goal of racial equality had been altered until I took my seat in Congress in 1969.

In the space of five years, the laws of the land—which had once denied equal protection to blacks and other minorities—had begun a process of transformation that was reestablishing the concept of special privilege. During my years in Congress I was particularly distressed to see the laws, rules and regulations defining affirmative action undergo-ing a change for the worse. What had previously been thought of as equality of opportunity—a goal defended by Hubert Humphrey and so many other advocates of civil rights reform, myself included—had be-come something else. I found that more and more whites were coming to Washington to ask my help. College professors had bitter com-plaints about reverse discrimination. They saw themselves as victims of hiring policies based not on merit or objective criteria, but on new and sometimes hidden forms of racial prejudice.

I was both saddened and offended by this trend. To me it was a perversion of a goal the civil rights movement had worked so hard to reach. The dangerous and divisive nature of this policy shift was especially apparent in the administering of government loans to small business. White applicants were finding themselves shut out because they weren't black, Hispanic-surnamed, American Indian, Eskimo, Aleut, or Asian. I remember when several Hasidic Jews who had been denied loans came to see me. They pointed out the unfairness of the new racial standards. Not only were they a minority, they were a minority within a minority. So ill-conceived was the new policy that Sephardic Jews—who often have Spanish surnames—were granted loans while Jews with non-Hispanic names were turned down.

Because I was a member of the Small Business Administration Committee in the House, I decided to try to bring about a change in the rules that would allow everyone to be considered for a loan, based on need and the merits of individual cases. I was successful in getting my subcommittee to adopt a provision saying the government should not discriminate against applicants based on race, ethnicity or religion, or give preference to any group on that basis. But the provision was overturned in the full committee. Special privileges for special groups was now the rule. Expanding the number of special groups was not the answer because that would only compound the basic injustice.

I understood the rationale behind the new rules. For hundreds of years blacks had been held in slavery and denied the fruits of their labor. Other groups had also suffered. Since the law had previously discriminated against them, the only way to balance the ledger and overcome the lingering effects of discrimination was to discriminate in their favor. However, what might seem to be an appealing policy when viewed from a distance breaks down into chaos when examined in detail. Is it really fair for all members of favored groups—no matter what the circumstances of their individual lives—to enjoy an automatic edge over all members of nonfavored groups, who may have had to overcome greater disadvantages? Should nonwhite immigrants, who did not suffer discrimination in America, be given preferential treatment? Should white immigrants, who are not responsible for the historic wrongs of American society, be automatically sent to the back of the line?

I felt very strongly that in our commendable zeal to erase the old menace of racism and bigotry we were creating a new menace that would do incalculable harm to Dr. King's dream of a color-blind society. Putting government back into the business of racial and ethnic discrimination was like letting a mad dog into the house and hoping it bites only the burglar. We know from bitter experience that once the mad dog of discrimination and prejudice is turned loose, our entire society suffers.

Polls indicate that a majority of Americans, from all segments of our society, are clearly opposed to quotas based on race, ethnic background and religion. Militants, advocates and leaders of some radical groups often support quotas because they favor the centralization of political power and hope to acquire that power for themselves. But the average citizen recognizes that there's danger in abandoning the ideal of equal opportunity and replacing it with government-approved prejudice.

And yet strong action is clearly called for. We can't just sit around doing nothing while millions languish in a culture of poverty, a culture that is passed from one generation to the next. We must take effective action to help poor people rebuild their lives.

I believe the answer lies in placing greater emphasis on affirmative action and economic set-asides aimed directly at the problem of poverty. I am not opposed to economic programs designed to help people who are economically disadvantaged. I strongly support such programs. If job training is needed, the government should help fund the necessary projects. It is money well spent. Federal assistance to small-business people is another excellent investment in the fight against poverty. I also favor special job programs for areas that have been heavily affected by unemployment. But these programs should and must be open to all, without regard to race, religion or ethnic background. If a construction program is targeted for a black community, it's understandable if the overwhelming majority of those who apply for the jobs are black. All I'm saying is that government shouldn't exclude any nonblack job seekers from being considered for employment. Neither should black job seekers be excluded from seeking work in a construction program targeted for a mostly white community. Our goal should be to help *all* poor people. It's true that black communities suffer tremendously from poverty. It's also true that most of the people in the United States who are below the poverty line are white. The fact is that all poor people need help, and they need it now, regardless of race, ethnic background or religion.

The key to running successful social programs is to put the emphasis on good management, not on politics. If a social program is designed to satisfy special political objectives or serve a narrow political agenda, it will almost certainly fail to produce a lasting impact on poverty.

To me, affirmative action means going out and making contact with people who have suffered, or are suffering, from the effects of discrimination. It means making those people aware that jobs are available, making them aware that training programs exist, and actively encouraging them to apply for both. If they have trouble passing civil-service tests, then classes should be organized to help them prepare. We have classes in New York City to help people get ready for the police-department exam. The classes are open to everyone. When the study and preparation are finished, exams should be administered and scored on a nonpartisan basis. Fairness and objectivity are at the heart of the civil-service system.

Does this approach work? In New York City minorities were 31 percent of the workforce in 1978. Today they are more than 45 percent. We increased minority representation in city government by pursuing a policy of true affirmative action. We reached out to those who had once been shunted aside. At the same time we preserved the concept of fairness to all.

For some people, however, "affirmative action" has come to be a synonym for "quotas." They see affirmative action not as a means of advancing the concept of equal opportunity. They see it as a way of assuring equal results. Many changes have taken place in the struggle for civil rights in America. One of the most controversial is the shift away from a doctrine of "equal opportunity" and toward a doctrine of "equal results."

This doctrine holds, for example, that tests for public employment cannot be considered fair and valid unless the group that passes the test has the same racial and ethnic profile as the test-taking population as a whole. For example, if the test-taking group is 20 percent Asian, then approximately 20 percent of those who pass the test must be Asian. If the percentage of Asians is significantly lower, there are grounds for Asian test-takers to challenge the test in court as unfair. It should be noted that if the percentage of Asians passing the test is significantly *higher* than the percentage of Asians as a whole, the test could be challenged by members of other racial or ethnic groups on the grounds that the test was prejudiced in favor of Asians.

This line of reasoning has gained acceptance by the courts. It goes without saying that tests can be unfair or unrelated to the job. Such tests should be thrown out and new tests prepared. The problem comes in determining which test is fair and which is not. I believe all parties concerned should be consulted in the formulation of the test and agree in advance that a particular type of test is fair. But I am opposed to judging the fairness and validity of a test solely on the percentage of each racial or ethnic group that passes it. A fair test should be objective, job-related, and color-blind. The purpose of a fair test is to determine ability and make possible the hiring or promoting of employees based on merit, not on the favoritism that used to plague public service. What have we gained if we dress up the old biased system in new clothes? The hard truth of the matter is that although there are times when people fail because the tests are unfair, there are also times when people fail because they aren't well enough prepared. We must demand fair tests. We must also expect people who take those tests to pass them.

A statement such as this will sometimes bring an accusation of "insensitivity," or an allegation that the speaker has failed to comprehend the new goals and principles of the civil rights movement. Occasionally I hear people say that I've lost my former commitment to civil rights, that I've turned "conservative." My answer is this. My principles and goals are the same now as they were then. I have not abandoned the cause of civil rights. I simply refuse to substitute lower ideals for higher ones. "Justice, justice shalt thou render, saith the Lord." It is a terrible distortion of justice for government to engage in the practice of discrimination on the grounds of race, religion, gender, sexual preference or ethnic background.

Historians frequently ponder the question of what America would be like today if Abraham Lincoln had lived to complete his second— and perhaps a third—term. Lincoln alone had the necessary vision, determination and moral courage to bring post–Civil War America back together without allowing the evils of the Reconstruction period to generate a new climate of racial division and hatred. Lincoln might have been able to establish a course for this country that would have led us out of the nightmare of racial prejudice and bigotry more than ninety years ago. I've already referred to the Supreme Court's 1896 "separate but equal" decision that extended the rule of racism. It's not difficult to imagine that if Lincoln had lived even a few years longer his moral legacy might have influenced the Supreme Court to vote the other way, and thus challenge the conscience of this country to do away with racism at the end of the last century.

I mention Lincoln in this context because with each passing year I realize with ever greater regret just how tragic and terrible was the loss of Martin Luther King, Jr. The shock of Dr. King's death, combined with the loss of Robert Kennedy two months later, was a trauma from which the civil rights movement has never really recovered. Like Lincoln, Dr. King had the necessary vision, determination and moral courage to put an end to old evils without giving rise to new ones. During the Montgomery bus boycott, Dr. King urged the blacks of that city to be firm and resolute, but to avoid violence and retaliation. His goal was not revenge but revision. He saw clearly that we cannot expunge evil by imitating it. When the torch fell from Dr. King's hand in 1968, the light of moral leadership was tragically dimmed. It was dimmed because great leaders cannot be replaced. Dr. King's greatness was based on the greatness of his spirit, and on his understanding that true leaders don't lead just one segment of the country. They lead everyone. They advance and defend ideas that enlighten all people, everywhere. If Dr. King had lived I think the original goals of the civil rights movement would have become the permanent goals of our nation.

Instead we find ourselves mired in moral relativism, with dozens of special groups making special appeals for special rules and regulations that benefit themselves. The federal government has taken advantage of this divisive climate to divide and conquer. Washington is shamefully pushing for rollbacks in civil rights. By now it should be clear that if we ask the law of the land to play favorites, we encourage those in power to favor their private interests over the public good. If we lack a single set of standards that applies to everyone, regressive ideologues find it easier to invent their own standards, to turn back the clock and call it progress.

Some well-intentioned people support the move from equal opportunity to equal results. The struggle for a truly equal society has been long and frustrating. There are those who don't want to wait any longer for a race in which the various runners cross the finish line in a certain racial, religious or ethnic order. They want the competition to be settled by the courts. I understand their impatience. But I don't think they've thought through the consequences of taking this path. The goal of equal opportunity requires fairness, which can and should be legislated. But the goal of equal results requires force. Force can also be legislated. There was a time when racist laws forced racial and religious minorities into second-class citizenship. Our laws must be strong enough to deter criminals and defend the rights of citizens, but force should be used with extreme caution. It is the antithesis of freedom, and freedom is America's greatest blessing. If equal opportunity for all had been the guiding spirit in American society, we would never have sunk into racism and slavery. Instead we went for a system of special rights for some, and thereby allowed a form of totalitarianism get a toehold in our land.

Racial and religious quotas are made even worse by the fact that they don't work. Individual pride and public well-being come from meeting the challenge of equitably established standards. Quotas only inspire disrespect, because it's widely perceived that the beneficiaries of quotas are not the best, but the favored. Nobody respects a contest when the results are rigged.

We must not give up on the American ideal of equality of opportunity. This ideal has not failed. It simply hasn't been tried, at least not the way it should have been and not for the required length of time. A reversal of discrimination cannot be achieved by reverse discrimination. True affirmative action—reaching out to those in need and helping them develop their potential to the fullest—is the best way to strengthen the American dream.

But before we can reach this or any goal we must have the strong moral leadership that will inspire our citizens to make the necessary effort. The civil rights revolution was led by members of the clergy. Even in the midst of the 1964 anti–civil rights terrorism in Mississippi I felt safe in the black churches of Jackson, especially when compared to Laurel. But not only in terms of physical safety, because a black church in Mississippi wasn't necessarily a safe place to be. During the "Freedom Summer" of 1964, fires destroyed thirty-five black churches throughout the state. In spite of this attempt to intimidate the civil rights movement, an atmosphere of moral commitment in the churches did contribute to the sense of safety that comes from knowing you're on the right side.

During my years as Mayor of New York, I've been invited to

speak in dozens of black churches in all parts of the city. The churches have remained faithful to their mission of strong moral leadership. Fighting racism and bigotry is still a prime objective, but other dangers also threaten. The scourge of drug abuse has been taking a terrible toll, especially among young people. The added menace of AIDS, which can be spread through intravenous drug use, has made a crusade against drugs all the more imperative. Throughout the nation, federal, state and local criminal justice systems have been overwhelmed by the drug problem. Prison populations are at record levels, but drugs continue to destroy people and communities. Some people say the answer is to legalize drugs. I say the legalization of drugs would be a catastrophe for America, and would hit the poor and minority communities the hardest. Legalizing drugs would be so destructive to minorities that I question the real motives of those who suggest it.

Clearly, we cannot win the struggle against drugs by using law enforcement agencies alone. We must create a strong moral climate which communicates to our young people that using drugs is not only illegal, it is wrong. Morally wrong. Whether you get caught or not, it's *wrong* to harm yourself and your community. Establishing a moral climate has been the traditional job of religious leaders of all faiths. Never has this job been more important than it is now. Nowhere is it being carried forward with greater vigor than in the black churches throughout our nation.

As I said at the beginning of this chapter, I speak out candidly on all issues, including the sensitive questions of race and religion. I feel strongly that unless an issue is clearly and plainly stated, it's much more difficult to address it properly. So I speak out. Sometimes I can be too blunt, I admit. But my instinct is to avoid "code words" and get the issues out in the open where they can be resolved.

For this reason I am sometimes accused of "insensitivity." "Insensitivity" is a code word which, on the surface, means that someone is not sensitive to the feelings of a particular person or group. The word has been used in a racial context for some time. Years ago, if a member of a "restricted" country club brought a black or a Jew to the club as his guest, that member would have been labeled as "insensitive" to the hidden prejudices of his clubmates. He might also find his membership canceled. Today, "insensitive" has taken on an additional

269

level of meaning, one that has ominous implications. It has come to mean that while people of goodwill are expected to profess belief publicly in the equality of all races and ethnic groups, they are also expected to privately understand that minorities are not quite as able or gifted as others, and should therefore be treated with a kind of paternal protectiveness. In other words, they say it is "insensitive" to actually expect minorities to perform as well as others in school or on the job.

Educators around the country know well the destructive effects that "low expectation" can have on minority students. If a teacher doesn't expect a minority child to learn as quickly or well as the other kids, that damaging message is conveyed to the minority child in small but unmistakable ways. The child responds by failing. We see examples of this insidious form of racism at work in other areas of American society, too. People who would never dream of saying hurtful words about minorities are nevertheless "sensitive" to the unspoken understanding that minorities should be held to a lower standard. The result is to do with kind words what was once done with the rules of racial segregation—to put minorities in a special category and thus isolate them from full participation in American society.

I believe that only by formulating and adhering to fair and comprehensive standards that apply to all will we make the progress that must be made. These standards should apply not only to national issues, but to international issues and events as well. Why do oppression and tyranny in one country provoke cries of outrage when similar events in different countries are ignored? It seems to depend on which kind of political climate is found in which country. Those who assail human rights violations under the left-wing Sandinistas in Nicaragua don't seem to worry about the oppressive right-wing regime in Chile. And those on the left have similar ideological blind spots. When blacks are killed by the racist government in South Africa the world responds with condemnation, and rightly so. But where are the protests and outrage when thousands of blacks are killed in civil strife in Burundi? Israel is assailed at the U.N. Security Council when deaths occur during violent demonstrations on the West Bank. But no one at the Security Council protests when Iraq slaughters thousands of Kurds with poison gas. A social climate that allows people to pick and choose their causes according to personal preference leads to a kind of moral anarchy, and anarchy is "the rule of a thousand despots."

I believe today what I learned in my classrooms in Newark fifty-seven years ago: All people are equal, both in rights and abilities. Neither America nor the world will be free until we stop the prejudice of double standards and low expectations and stand firmly behind the ideals that lead to freedom: equal rights, equal justice and equal responsibilities for all.

THE CARDINAL

Sister Ursula sees most of my mail before I do, unless it's marked Personal or Confidential. She's a lovely person who thinks I'm wonderful, so I can never be sure she gives me every single piece of hate mail that comes in. I feel pretty certain, for example, that she thinks I'm too young to see some of the language used by some of the more colorful protestors, so I suspect she does occasionally palm a letter or two when she gives me the others.

I really don't mind, because most of my hate mail is not very original, and after I have read a handful of letters on a particular issue, I have a pretty good idea of what my nonadmirers want me to know.

I have paid special attention, however, to letters protesting two things I have done as Archbishop of New York, because they were exceptionally numerous. The first major influx came when I let it be known that I had sent a telegram to President Reagan asking him to reconsider his planned visit to the cemetery at Bitburg, in Germany. Overwhelming though some people believe my influence to be in both the White House and the Vatican, the president still went to Bitburg. But the fact that I had tried to discourage that visit brought me substantial hate mail.

That mail saddened me because I knew little was directed against me personally. A good bit of it was directed against Jews. Some of it was venomous, and despite disclaimers to the contrary, I saw its basic motivation as deep-rooted anti-Semitism.

We call ourselves a Judeo-Christian culture, but to the degree that we introduce religion into national life, we tend to "institutionalize" only Christianity. We have another tendency—if usually an unconscious one—to institutionalize anti-Semitism.

I have written elsewhere of my personal effort to introduce into the United States Navy a pennant to be used during religious services which would bear the Tablets of the Law, symbolic of the Jewish faith. The story bears brief recounting here because it's a good example of institutionalized anti-Semitism.

The only flag authorized to be flown above our national colors is called in navy language a "church pennant." When divine services are being held, this pennant, bearing a Christian cross, is run aloft. It had always troubled me that when Jewish services were held, either this or *no* pennant was hoisted.

One of my earliest actions as a new Chief of Chaplains, in Washington, in 1975, was to present a formal request to the Chief of Naval Operations and Secretary of the Navy that a new pennant be designed, bearing the Tablets of the Law. Weeks passed without a reply. Then finally it came, a blunt "No," signed by the Administrative Officer of the Navy.

Puffed up with my own importance as a spanking-new but technically senior Rear Admiral (as chief of a bureau), I called the Administrative Officer, a Rear Admiral himself. He listened to my expression of surprise and my query about his reasoning. His answer was brief and definitive. "The navy has used a pennant with a cross on it for years. It's good enough for *all* religions."

That answer was not all that long ago. It was hardly an advance over the even earlier day when the first rabbi entered the navy. His first uniform was marked with a Christian cross. He wore it in goodwill until a uniform could be approved marked with the Tablets of the Law.

For a long time we have taken for granted that Jews should appreciate living in *our* "Christian" culture and that their gratitude should transcend our ignoring their beliefs, or forgetting about them, or even our institutionalizing Christianity as our exclusive national creed. The closest some of us come to sympathetic understanding is to feel a modest sob in our hearts when Tevye sings "Tradition" in *Fiddler on the Roof.*

Catholics are not exempt from anti-Semitism, any more than from racism. Following the publication of "Nostra Aetate" ("In Our Times") in 1965, we began purging our liturgies and our religious-education texts of pejorative references to the Jews.[1] Recent popes,

1. "Declaration on the Relationship of the Church to Non-Christian Religions," by Pope Paul VI together with the Fathers of the Second Vatican Council

including Pope John Paul II, have made clear that we do not blame the crucifixion of Christ on "the Jews." When a group of non-Catholic religionists warned the top management of Universal Studios, a Jew, that its production *The Last Temptation of Christ* could bring anti-Semitic reprisals, the Roman Catholic Archbishop of Los Angeles, Roger Mahony, rejected the threat as reprehensible. So did I (although I thought the movie itself a disgrace and an insult).

We could multiply illustrations of progress, but regretfully not all Catholics have lost all prejudice.

In 1987, Austria's president, Kurt Waldheim, called upon Pope John Paul II in the Vatican. The Pope visited Austria in 1988. During the visit he met with Mr. Waldheim. The details of both visits have been too extensively reported by the press to require retelling.

For our purposes here, what is important is that some Catholics dismissed the pain and anger of many Jews as purely contentious. Even more unfortunately, when Jews desired that in his own visit to Austria the Pope would say something they could perceive as "compensatory," there were Catholics who asked in exasperation: "Are the Jews never satisfied?"

I am particularly pained when I hear a Catholic suggest that it's time to forget the Holocaust. (I have been not only disappointed but deeply distressed to hear this even from some Jews.) Remembrance of the Holocaust should be a continuing agony for the entire world. It is not enough to argue that there have been equally savage massacres in history, including the genocide in Cambodia, the purges of Stalin and similar savageries. Nor will it do to argue that millions of Christians died as a result of the Nazi scourge.

For many Jews, the Holocaust is in no small measure a summary of their history as a people, a sacred mystery, "sacramental" in character, a confluence of their centuries-old unanswered questions of God. This is to say nothing of the bitter personal sufferings of those who endured it, or barely escaped it. Their very souls were seared. Do not speak to them of parallels. Do not tell my good friend Elie Wiesel that you "understand," when he has devoted his entire life to examining and reexamining what *he* doesn't pretend to understand. His mother, his sisters, his father died for one reason only: They were Jews.

We must understand that as the Holocaust was the ultimate "crucifixion" for Jews, Israel is for many, in a sense, the "resurrection." Those who speak only in terms of national security and the pragmatic importance of supporting Israel with billions of dollars each year think too little of the spiritual reality of these people in whom we have our roots as Christians.

As president of the Catholic Near East Welfare Association, I have strong feelings about the Middle East and a degree of responsibility to its people. As a charitable agency we solicit and distribute many millions of dollars annually to the poor and needy of every religion, race, color or ethnic origin in some eighteen countries of the Middle East. In this capacity, I have gone to Ethiopia, to Lebanon, to Jordan and Israel, and will continue visits to other mideastern lands to see our hospitals and clinics, our schools and orphanages. I have come to appreciate the exceeding complexity of the Middle East and of its conflicts.

Both visible and invisible forces are always at work in the Middle East, many of them highly volatile. Some of these are the result of convoluted historical influences; others, of a variety of vested interests. There are no easy answers. No single solution will suffice. There are too many problems, each critical. My visits and studies have convinced me, nonetheless, that one problem is key to many others, and that no matter what other problems are resolved, there can be no lasting peace in the Middle East until *that* one is resolved. I refer to the desperate situation of the Palestinians. I have stated this repeatedly. The Palestinian situation must be resolved with *justice* (and, I might add, the world must stop equating Palestinians with terrorists, and recognize the richness of Arab culture). I cannot imagine justice in this case without the right of self-determination. Justice delayed is justice denied. Delaying the right of self-determination is denying the right, and denying the justice. Not every Jew has been happy with my insistence on this, yet I must go even further. I do not believe there will be a just and lasting peace as long as Lebanon is a battleground for opposing forces, particularly if they are contemptuous of Lebanon's rights or its tradition of being the one country in the Middle East in which all peoples, of all religious persuasions, could and did live together in harmony and peace for so long.

Having argued this and believing intensely today in what I have said, however, I believe further that Israel's rights to secure borders and international recognition are beyond question. Not every Palestinian or Arab may agree with me on this, but I sincerely believe it. As I understand the position of the Holy See, which I have heard explained publicly by Pope John Paul II himself, these rights are not disputed. The Holy See has questions about the current status of Jerusalem, and emphasizes the need for guaranteed free access to the Holy City in perpetuity. The Holy See is very much concerned about the security of all Christians in the Middle East and their freedom to worship. The Holy See has repeatedly and emphatically insisted that the rights of Palestinians must be recognized and their problems resolved.

It does not seem to me, personally, however—and I speak absolutely for no one but myself, and certainly not for the Holy See—that any of these obstacles to full *diplomatic* recognition of Israel by the Holy See cannot be overcome. It took time for the United States to extend formal diplomatic recognition to the Holy See.

Some things take almost infinite patience and unconditional goodwill. But neither virtue can be effective without mutual understanding. Both Israel and the Jewish communities here in New York must try to understand the Holy See's position. (There is no point in arguing, for example, as Mayor Koch and some Israeli officials have done, that there is no real reason for the Holy See's concern that diplomatic recognition of Israel could gravely affect the status of Christians in lands hostile to Israel. It's not the Mayor's responsibility to worry about Christians in the Middle East, although I'm glad he does. It *is* the responsibility of the Pope. That makes for big differences in perspective.)

Israel and Jews here must understand, as well, how the Holy See views Jerusalem, scene of the ultimately meaningful acts in the life of Jesus Christ and cradle of Christianity. Indeed, Pope John Paul II speaks strongly of the attachment to Jerusalem on the part of all three major faiths, Judaism, Islam and Christianity. His comments deserve quoting at some length. [2]

> Before it was the city of Jesus the Redeemer, Jerusalem was the historic site of the biblical revelation of God, the meeting place, as it were, of heaven and earth, in which more than in any other place the word of God was brought to men.
>
> Christians honor her with a religious and intent concern because there the words of Christ so often resounded, there the great events of the Redemption were accomplished: the Passion, Death and

2. Apostolic Letter of John Paul II, *Redemptionis Anno*, April 20, 1984

Resurrection of the Lord. In the City of Jerusalem the first Christian community sprang up and remained throughout the centuries a continual ecclesial presence despite difficulties.

Jews ardently love her and in every age venerate her memory, abundant as she is in many remains and monuments from the time of David who chose her as the capital, and of Solomon who built the Temple there. Therefore, they turn their minds to her daily, one may say, and point to her as the sign of their nation.

Muslims also call Jerusalem "Holy," with a profound attachment that goes back to the origins of Islam and springs from the fact that they have there many special places of pilgrimage and for more than a thousand years have dwelt there, almost without interruption.

. . . Indeed, insofar as she is the homeland of the hearts of all the spiritual descendants of Abraham who hold her very dear, and the place where, according to faith, the created things of earth encounter the infinite transcendence of God, Jerusalem stands out as a symbol of coming together, of union, and of universal peace for the human family.

The Holy City, therefore, strongly urges peace for the whole human race, especially for those who worship the one, great God, the merciful Father of the peoples. But it must be acknowledged that Jerusalem continues to be the cause of daily conflict, violence and partisan reprisals.

. . . The Roman Pontiffs, especially in this century, have witnessed with an ever anxious solicitude the violent events which have afflicted Jerusalem for many decades, and they have followed closely with watchful care the declarations of the United Nations which have dealt with the fate of the Holy City.

On many occasions the Holy See has called for reflection and urged that an adequate solution be found to this difficult and complex situation. The Holy See has done this because she is concerned for peace among peoples no less than for spiritual, historical and cultural reasons of a nature eminently religious.

The entire human race, and especially the peoples and nations who have in Jerusalem brothers in faith: Christians, Jews and Muslims, have reason to feel themselves involved in this matter and to do everything possible to preserve the unique and sacred character of the City.

In my judgment, it is equally important that we Catholics, in turn, recognize the meaning of Israel, not simply in nationalistic terms but as "resurrection." It is the land of hope against the despair of the Holocaust. It is the realization of a two-thousand-year dream and prayer, recited daily in the synagogue ever since the destruction of the Temple in Jerusalem. However secular its current form of governance, Israel seems to me to be in some mystical way an embodiment of the spirit of Judaism. Since the Pope's own power is surely spiritual, I wonder if we should not try to explore the spiritual dimension of Israel, and pray and work that one day two great spiritual powers of the world may find a way to extend to each other the courtesies of formal diplomatic exchanges.

I venture into this palpably provocative speculation in part because I know that in the minds of many Jews formal diplomatic recognition by the Holy See would be the ultimate sign of the Church's formal rejection of anti-Semitism. I raise the issue for another reason, as well. It is my personal conviction that, if the Holy See's concerns were met and formal diplomatic relations exchanged as a consequence, the potential for peace in the Middle East could be significantly enhanced. I have absolutely no question in my own mind about the validity of the Holy See's current position. Therefore, I would have to encourage Israel and all Jews and Christians alike to devote themselves in every way they can to a solution of these legitimate and responsible concerns on the part of the Holy See. The Jewish world accomplishes no more by throwing up its hands and asking "Is the Pope never satisfied?" than do those Catholics who respond to Jewish protest with "Are the Jews never satisfied?"

This may seem a long, unjustifiable intervention in a book devoted to Church-State relations here in New York. I believe it justified. New York includes the highest number of Jews in the world. There are Catholics and others who believe that Jews control every influential force in New York: the media, the courts, the schools, the stage and screen, the real estate, the major businesses. No matter the reality; the perception is profound.

For these Catholics, the perception is "authenticated" every time a Jewish agency protests tuition tax credits or other aid to Catholic schools, or supports a pro-abortion or pro-choice position. It is exacerbated when a Jewish-owned newspaper publishes an "anti-Catholic" editorial and so on. There are many Catholics who believe that Jewish values are totally hostile to Catholic values. Despite Archbishop Mahony's and my own disclaimer, cited above, at the time of the New York showing of *The Last Temptation of Christ*, I heard educated Catholics saying such things as: "If this were a film attacking a sacred belief of Jews, it would never be allowed in town."

The anti-Semitism is there, I believe, muted, but deep-rooted. Were I a Jew, I am certain I would be conscious of it, and resent being considered paranoid. But I believe that Jews must try, as well, to understand the Catholic position, and to try to support "Catholic" causes when they conscientiously can. The above-cited movie offers an example. The Jewish community had an excellent opportunity at least to express public understanding of how offensive the film was for most Catholics. Mayor Koch did go public, as did a small number of Jews. I believe it could have provided an opportunity for the larger Jewish community to advance Jewish-Catholic relations. Obviously, Catholics are not the only ones obliged to "work at" understanding and support. Nor do I want to pretend that anti-Catholicism is not as strong on the part of some Jews as anti-Semitism is on the part of some Catholics. Both communities must work on this divisive flaw which is bad for both communities and bad for New York.

For we *are* talking public policy when we talk about Jewish-Catholic relations, or at least how such relations can ultimately affect or shape public policy. It is possible that in this regard the maintenance of a positive working relationship between a Jewish Mayor and a Catholic Archbishop is helpful. Even more helpful is that the majority of Catholics are not anti-Semitic, any more than the majority of Jews are anti-Catholic. Thank God for *big* favors.

We are also talking in this book about the role of the Archbishop of New York vis-à-vis the broader community, and his influence for weal or woe in that regard. How do I measure the overall effect of my telegram to President Reagan about Bitburg, not on him but on my ability to influence the broader community? How should I react to heavy hate mail rooted, in part, in anti-Semitism, and how does my reaction affect my status and influence in the broader community? I cannot let that be the issue. I must listen and be sensitive to critics, of course, but I must act out of conscience at all costs and in response to the moral imperatives of my Church.

The Bitburg telegram was not the only message I sent to President Reagan that aroused the indignation of some New Yorkers. I wrote, for example, to urge an exemption of the economic embargo on Cuba in respect to medicines. My purpose was not to argue the political issue of an economic embargo, or even its long-term effectiveness in bringing the Cuban government into a more responsive posture. That's our government's call, not mine. My purpose was to propose from a purely humanitarian perspective that neither the Cuban people nor any other people should be deprived of needed medicines because of the posture or actions of their own government. I found President Reagan quite reasonable in his responses, and at the time of this writing hope to be able to get at least a partial exemption from the embargo. In the same letter, I asked that the United States facilitate visas for a large number of political prisoners that President Castro told me he would release if I could get them visas. President Reagan was likewise responsive on this issue, and processing of visas was expedited.

Not every Cuban in the United States applauded my efforts, however, as my mail attests. Some believe that in some way I sold out to Castro.

Finally, a letter to President Reagan asking him to consider issuing an executive order, if within his power, granting amnesty to undocumented Irish in this country (an estimated 125,000 in New York alone), came under fire as well. This time, critics simply read in the press that I had pleaded for the Irish. They didn't know my letter also called for amnesty for "others" and an opening of the window of opportunity to many more immigrants from various other countries. The hate mail faulted me both for thinking only of the Irish, and for risking the jobs of American citizens that could be threatened by immigrants.

I cite these incidents simply to observe that prejudice knows no monopoly. Blacks, Jews, Catholics, Irish, Hispanic—all are vulnerable to being resented, as is anyone who tries to reach out to them, especially if it is perceived as being at the expense of others.

It's the history of prejudice in the United States. Unfortunately, most of us share it in one way or another. In 1865, Abraham Lincoln noted: "As a nation we began by saying that 'All men are created equal.' We now read it that 'All men are created equal except Negroes.' When the Know Nothings get control it will read, 'All men are created equal except Negroes and foreigners and Roman Catholics.'" (New York's first Archbishop, John Hughes, could validate Mr. Lincoln's comments on the Know Nothings, as we see elsewhere in this book.)

As a quasi-student of prejudice, I should therefore have anticipated what I would stir up by some ill-fated remarks in City Hall. This brings me to the second event that precipitated a goodly share of hostile letters.

On the birthday of Dr. Martin Luther King, Jr., the fifteenth of January, I went down to City Hall to join a group of community leaders for lunch to discuss with them the many problems caused by racial tensions in this city and its general environs. Prior to the luncheon there would be a series of addresses, in which I had been invited to participate, but because of a previous commitment, had to decline. I thought I was late but arrived early, was quickly seen and was asked to join the others.

By the time I got to the little platform set up as a stage, perhaps a dozen speeches had been given. Seeing that I was about to be called upon, I asked myself what I might add to the eloquent remarks that had already been made. I must confess that I surprised myself by what I said when I got to the podium. (I'll blame it on the Holy Spirit who takes blame for so much of what I do.) "I really have nothing to say that would add to the marvelous addresses that have been given. So rather than *say* anything, perhaps I should *do* something. I receive a few thousand dollars a year in Social Security which I could do without, and therefore I think that I should put this toward scholarships for some black youngsters, whatever their religious persuasion, to go to any school of their choice." I was thinking only of the youngsters, whoever they might be, and I thought that the mechanics could be worked out later. I would simply turn the money over to some agency that could handle it and for me that was the end of the matter. I really thought nothing further about it except to arrange that it be done. Then came the letters. Two are sufficient to convey the general idea.

The first one begins rather well, "Your Holiness." It's downhill from there on, with some settling on "Mr. O'Connor."

"I read the article whereby you are organizing a fund for the poor Black students only. I and my family and friends are planning our protest in this manner. When the basket reaches us in Church on Sunday, we will throw black buttons into the basket instead of money. We must show our protest in this manner. Most sincerely . . ." and it is signed.

Fortunately I wear black suits.

Space precludes printing the many I would like to include, like the one that tells me the pressures of my job are getting to me, and that I need a vacation or retreat to collect my thoughts and return to what I was when I arrived in New York. A number were good-humored, some angry but thoughtful. The following lengthy one, however, says a great deal.

Dear Cardinal O'Connor: After reading of your surprise donation of Social Security checks to the Negro College Fund, I feel compelled to write you. Firstly, why didn't you make it an anonymous donation. Are you running for office, pandering for votes? How do you think the Hispanic community should feel? They've not received a similar bequest. If you have so much spare money, why didn't you give it to the poor parishes of the Diocese instead of asking us to dig deep again, and again. Furthermore why are you taking your federal pension? If you want to help equally, return it to the American taxpayer. I once heard there is more politics in the Catholic Church than there is in Washington. Now I know it's true. You are a tremendous disappointment. Don't mandate a policy on all parishes to preach against discrimination. You will lose more people than you realize. We have been bombarded enough from the media. Why don't you use your so-called influence on the Black community about the large numbers of Black criminals that prey on society bringing their murderous assaults, rapes and drugs with them? Preach to them about how they should be conducting their lives. We've had it. The Church should be a quiet haven where we go to pray. Don't bombard us from the pulpit unless you give Blacks and Whites equal time.

Is there no one to stand up for the rights of the lower middle classes, the very persons who have carried the country and the Church thus far? Here, where I live, we are accused of racism, a charge that is an outrageous lie. Race is not the issue. Now our lives are going to be destroyed together with our neighborhoods. No one ever gave me or my family and friends anything. We have worked, worked and are still working into our late sixties.

On the other hand, the Black community have been the recipients of more programs and tax dollars than any group in the history of our country. Tell me if you can who's going to stand up and help us here in Yonkers and other areas where people are angry and frightened thinking there is no one or no place to turn to for help.

I would be very interested to read your response in the Catholic New York real soon. Where I once had no negative feelings about race, I now have anger and dislike for the militant activists whose actions are counter-productive and will not further their cause. The atrocities perpetuated by Blacks against Whites go almost without notice and yet the media blows this racism problem all out of proportion. Decent Blacks, I know, claim they are not fairly represented by the well-known media activists. [It is signed,] Not so respectfully.

I understand the fears and anxieties of the senders and those they represent. I understand those who are terrified because they think that a lifetime of work in building their own homes and building their own lives is being threatened. I understand those who have had to work terribly hard for a living, those who have tried to accord with the teachings of the Church, who have done their best to teach their children, have made real sacrifices to send them to Catholic schools and have rarely received any extraordinary help. I understand all of that. I understand, as well, that some of these letter writers are definitely *not* racist, and others are not consciously so. Those whose letters are obviously and rabidly racist do not represent Catholics in general, by any stretch of the imagination. Again, thank God!

But it would be naïve and dishonest for us to deny that too many of us, Catholics and others, are guiltier of racism in one form or another than we would like to admit. Pope John Paul II was so conscious of this that with all of the issues he had to address when he visited in the United States in September of 1987, one of the most powerful addresses he gave was on racism. What did he talk about? The *sin* of racism. He didn't use euphemistic terminology. He didn't talk as a sociologist. He talked as the number one bishop in the Church and he said, "Racism is a sin." We cannot look at it in any other way, and we cannot simply blame understandable fears for permitting these feelings to continue.

I don't think there can be any question but that racism is still a cancer in our land. We have made progress, but not enough. I will defend the record of the Archdiocese of New York in trying to provide an education for blacks and for others when many deserted that effort. We have tried to keep our schools open to help empower the poor so that in turn they can contribute to the best of their ability to all of society.

I will defend the record of nondiscrimination in our Catholic health-care system, including our eighteen Catholic hospitals in the Archdiocese. The formal record of the Church in trying to free itself from racism, trying to help excise this cancer from *all* society, is an improving record. [3]

But we can not rest on records. We still have work to do, and we have to know what we're doing. We will not obliterate racism if we attribute *every* injustice or conflict to racism. Only a racist calls everyone else a racist. Some fears are legitimate, rooted in sad experience. For example, I repeat that some of the letters I received reflect out and out racism. Other letters clearly come from people fearful that they will lose homes that they worked for throughout the course of a lifetime, because it has happened to them before. Whether or not their fears are well-grounded, they are not necessarily grounded in racism, as such.

At the same time, it can be an easy evasion to blame our fears about desegregation on "proof" that it always brings crime and violence, always results in wrecking a community. Who *doesn't* fear crime and violence? In recent years we have had whites gang up on blacks, blacks on whites, both groups prejudiced, each group fearing the other in some way. We are *all* victims of crime, of course, but that blacks in our society are most often the victims of crime is indisputable. If some whites are poor, many more blacks are poor. The highest rate of unemployment is among blacks. Blacks, as do whites and others, want to live in decent housing. They want to rear their children as all people want to rear their children.

We speak of the cycle of poverty. Once we are in its grip, a hopelessness besieges us and to try to overcome our plight takes not only a superhuman effort, but a supernatural effort. Those of us in a position to help will do little unless we are truly convinced that every human being is sacred, made in God's Image, regardless of color. Dr. Martin Luther King, Jr., who is treated so shabbily in some of the letters I received, got it just right when he said, "If we refuse to live together as brothers and sisters, we will die together as fools."

In January of 1985 I commissioned a study that took two years to

3. See my chapters on Education and on Housing.

complete: "The Hope and Experiences of the Black Community in the Archdiocese of New York." To some the findings may seem prosaic. To me, they are highly provocative. If nothing else, the study corroborates our guesses that, for example, in Manhattan almost half of the black households are headed by females, one third of black families have poverty-level incomes, 12.7 percent of persons sixteen years of age and older are unemployed. External factors (which contribute to this) include racism, economic and demographic trends, adverse public policies. Internal factors include dysfunctional family and individual problems. The four most pressing problems given by the survey respondents are drugs—mentioned by three quarters—housing, unemployment and safety. Family and neighbors continue as the most frequent source to which people turn for assistance with problems. The large numbers of no responses to questions about neighborhood, institutional and church resources for assistance raises the question about a lack of knowledge of such resources.

The black community clearly looks to the Catholic Church for support in a variety of efforts to combat racism and affirm black traditions, and for providing quality education, including quality religious education for black children. The Church must examine its conscience every day to ensure that it is doing everything possible to provide that support. Too many nights I go to bed not at all easy in conscience in this regard.

There may never be another chance to make New York a model of racial harmony unless we change not only our words but our hearts. And it all goes back to whether or not we believe the ultimate truth in all human affairs—the priceless, sacred worth of every human person. There's no substitute. It's got to be for real.

Elsewhere in this book I quote Roger Starr to the effect that a city's problems must be addressed with a sense of wonder. It's precisely a sense of wonder that we need when we look at a phenomenon touched upon only lightly up to this point, a wonderful phenomenon, indeed. I refer to the fact that New York is preeminently a city, a state, of immigrants. It has been remarked that in the history of civilization since the time of Augustus's Roman Empire, no city has had a larger concentration of diverse language groups than we have today in New York. In both the Diocese of Brooklyn and the Archdiocese of New York, for example, we celebrate Catholic Masses in some twenty-nine different languages each week, as well as in "sign."

What should be seen as enrichment, however, too often provokes even further prejudices. It is frequently perceived only as a cause of complex problems, rather than as giving New York an incomparable richness and vitality. Some of us, for example, simply become irate at the transplanted Russian or Romanian taxi driver with an accent so heavy we can hardly guess he's speaking English. He's taking a job from a full-blooded American. He's probably a spy. He doesn't know where he's going. He needs a shave, a haircut.

We hear there are as many as 125,000 undocumented Irish in New York. Whose jobs are *they* taking? And the Haitians! Three hundred thousand of them in the New York area, it is said.

It's the Hispanics, however, who have ruined New York, says the "real" pundit. Millions of them have come to town, from Puerto Rico, the Dominican Republic, Cuba, Nicaragua, El Salvador and everywhere else below the border. According to the prejudiced: They all look alike and sound alike; they wreck neighborhoods; they frighten people on subways; they're all drug pushers and voodooists; they keep having kids, and they want everybody in New York to kowtow to them; they refuse to learn English, so they want us to learn Spanish, and teach it in our schools.

How sad, how very sad our prejudices that blind us to the wonders of diversity. The great Saint Thomas Aquinas, in the thirteenth century, described beauty as unity in diversity. That gives New York the opportunity to be the most beautiful city in the world!

I don't believe that New York City has moved aggressively enough to actualize the potential of its immigrants to the advantage of both the City and the immigrants. I do credit the Mayor, however, on his general attitude toward immigrants vis-à-vis immigration law. As far as I can see, he simply refuses to let New York police be used to look for the undocumented in order to have them deported. And despite all the understandable furor over his remark that British troops are peacekeeping forces in Ireland, he has been particularly sensitive to the needs of Irish immigrants.

The Mayor and I have together consulted officials in both the Republic of Ireland and the North of Ireland to enlist their help in getting our own government to legalize the status of far more Irish immigrants here. Together we explored the possibility of getting American industry to invest in Ireland and of opening markets here for goods produced in Ireland. In each instance, however, in which we have worked together to broaden opportunities for Irish immigrants, we have sought equally broadened opportunities for all immigrants, whatever their origin.

As I commissioned a study of blacks, so Cardinal Cooke, in 1982, commissioned a study of Hispanics. It was an extraordinarily extensive study, and the recommendations based on its findings were among the first documents given me upon my arrival in the Archdiocese. More than four years later, we are still engaged in integrating them into the overall administration and operations of the Archdiocese. We have a long way to go and are not moving rapidly enough, but I do consider the task critical and a daily priority.

What is important in our effort, however, is our recognition of what Hispanics do to enrich the Archdiocese of New York and how we can work *together* for the good of all. We are no longer a Church that asks itself simply: "What are you doing *for* Hispanics?"

It is true that we have spent a good bit of time in trying to help Hispanic undocumented immigrants (and Haitians and others) get their "green card." When the federal government established a limited amnesty program for the undocumented, for example, we established centers in some thirty-one parishes, where lawyers and others volunteered to help immigrants with paperwork and advice, free of charge and on an unconditionally confidential basis. I myself made a number of thirty- and sixty-second videotapes in both Spanish and English for repetitive television announcements, urging immigrants to come for help.

But rather than describe our various programs *for* Hispanics, I repeat that the essence of our approach is a belief in the Hispanics themselves, that they have such extraordinary potential, already offer so much and may be expected to offer even more in the future. So there can be no patronizing.

That help is needed from the "establishment," however, is obvious. As an average, Hispanic incomes, jobs and housing are only slightly higher than those of blacks. To use the South Bronx again as an example, we find that blacks and Hispanics are overwhelmingly in the majority, subject to the worst violence, drug pushing and so on. It was revealing that South Bronx churches began their efforts under the motto "We are taking charge." It is clear that both blacks and Hispanics feel disenfranchised, unable to get a hearing on the poor state of education, housing, trash removal, police protection and other basics. It is above all clear when I talk with them that they feel disenfranchised politically. They point to a relative handful of blacks and Hispanics in significant elective or appointed offices. They feel that they are successfully divided and conquered by tactically shrewd politicians, so that they cannot form a cohesive, strong political force.

In my judgment these are moral issues, including the political helplessness. The Church has an obligation to help educate for political responsibility, especially since it is only through the political system that many of the social injustices will be righted.

It is obviously asking a great deal—perhaps the humanly impossible—for *any* officeholder, candidate or other political figure to help empower those who could become political opponents. Few politicians are in business to lose elections! Nevertheless, I see it as the moral responsibility of an incumbent Mayor to help minorities, and certainly blacks and Hispanics, to prepare for and to achieve significant political status, even to help them become formidable contenders.

This may sound silly. I'm quite serious about it. We make a cliché out of "affirmative action" if we confine it to hiring a respectable number of minorities or placing them in highly visible public offices. We think it quite appropriate to encourage and help blacks and Hispanics to become doctors and lawyers and to enter other professions. What have we really done to help either blacks or Hispanics to actualize their potential to be elected to the very highest offices available and to be appointed to others almost as high? That can sound patronizing. It is not so intended. We pride ourselves on a Horatio Alger culture in which anyone who is disciplined, bright and morally sound can rise from "rags to riches" by dint of sheer hard work. I was reared on Horatio Alger maxims: "Sink or Swim," "Paddle Your Own Canoe," and a host of others—the ultimate distillation of Teddy Roosevelt's "rugged individualism."

Maybe it still works in some fields, like becoming a prizefighter or a bishop. Does it work in politics? Or did neither Horatio Alger nor Teddy Roosevelt ever think our land would be populated with immigrants?

The Church in the United States today is serious about trying to put minorities in leadership positions. Blacks, Hispanics and other minorities are still underrepresented in the ranks of bishops. In 1988 the first black became an archbishop in the United States. The Most Reverend Eugene Marino, former auxiliary bishop of Washington, D.C., was appointed by Pope John Paul II Archbishop of Atlanta (upon the death of former New Yorker Archbishop Donnellan). The Church in our country includes two Hispanic archbishops.

In New York the first Hispanic Chancellor of the Archdiocese was not appointed until 1985, Monsignor Raúl del Valle, "refugee" from Cuba. The first appointment of a bishop came eight years earlier, Auxiliary Bishop Francis Garmendia, a Basque from Spain.

It really is time for a sense of wonder.

[Postscript: I did eventually bypass the Navy's Administrative Officer and was able to get the Secretary of the Navy to approve a Jewish "church" pennant. The aftermath is interesting. Someone proposed that it first be flown on board the USS *Constitution*, "Old Ironsides," in Boston. I argued that this would give it not a "historic" tone but the flavor of being a mere curiosity, if not a museum piece. I insisted it be flown first in Jewish-led Divine Services on board an operating ship of the navy—at sea. It was off Norfolk, Virginia. I was there. I wasn't the only one who cried.

THE MAYOR
GAY RIGHTS

THE CARDINAL
HOMOSEXUALITY

THE MAYOR

I am sixty-four years old. I am a lawyer, I was a member of the City Council, a member of Congress and now I am Mayor. I served in World War II and overseas on the field of battle. I came from a poor family with a religious background. I went to Hebrew school after the public-school day and on Sunday. One of the strongest taboos that is part of a young male growing up in our society until recently is the taboo of homosexuality. Certainly one of the worst things you could ever say to a young male or about him was that he was "queer." That phrase is rarely used today. Also, one of the things that you learn as you grow up is that any unmarried individual—and years ago it applied only to men but today it applies to women as well—who remains single after the age of forty is perceived by many to be, in the new vernacular, "gay."

Further, if you are out to hurt someone in political office or someone running for political office, one of the ways to do it is to spread rumors that he or she is gay. I speak now not as a detached observer of the scene but rather as someone who has been subject to those rumors and political attacks over the years.

Indeed, I have been in twenty-four elections in twenty-four years beginning with 1962. In every single one of those elections, my opponents would seek to defame me or destroy me by spreading the rumor that I was gay. With two exceptions, I won those elections.

My first defeat was in 1962. I decided at that time, when I was running for the Assembly from Greenwich Village, that I would take on the three toughest issues of the day: sodomy, abortion and divorce. Sodomy was then a violation of the penal law and abortion likewise.

You could only secure a divorce in the state of New York only on grounds of adultery. My campaign focused on elimination of the sodomy laws, making abortion legal and adding grounds for divorce other than adultery. My supporters showed great consternation at such a bold program; nevertheless, they loyally stayed with me because they believed that I was right, although too avant-garde.

Isn't it interesting that twenty-eight years later all three areas of concern have been addressed exactly as I proposed. Today, no one thinks of the positions that I held then as avant-garde. Indeed, they are mainstream. It was not so difficult to eliminate the criminal law against consentual sodomy between adults because it was done by a court rather than by legislation. Indeed, that was the case with abortion as well. But it has been extremely difficult throughout the country and in New York City to pass legislation that would eliminate discrimination against an individual based on sexual orientation.

The first legislation to propose this was introduced in the City Council fifteen years ago. And almost every year prior to my becoming Mayor, there would be efforts in committee or on the floor of the City Council to pass such legislation. It always went down to a crushing defeat.

The gay community in New York City is large and militant. How large, no one knows. But I assume that the statistics provided by Kinsey—that 10 percent of the adult population in the United States is gay—continues to be correct, even though they have been disputed by commentators such as Pat Buchanan. In major cities like New York, San Francisco and Houston, the percentage would be even higher. Gays elsewhere in the land, seeking anonymity as well as a more accepting environment, came to these larger cities. Therefore, the percentage in New York City accepted by most analysts would be a minimum of 15 percent. That translates to over a million individuals.

The gay community, ever since the incident that occurred in 1969, is very militant. Every year they celebrate the Stonewall Confrontation with the same fervor that Jews celebrate the Warsaw uprising.

When I ran for mayor in 1977, the gays had formed a political caucus and sought to elicit the support of all of the candidates. They met with each of us separately. My meeting took place on Wednesday, July 7, 1977. It was held in the home of Robert Livingston, who had been appointed by Abe Beame to the Human Rights Commission. He was the only publicly announced gay official in government, albeit without salary. He was the son of Molly Parnis, and he was very wealthy.

That night about 8:00 P.M., I was interrogated by a committee of about fifteen gay activists. They said, in effect, "We know that you support our position." I had demonstrated that support year after year. As a member of Congress, I had joined with a small group of congressmen who introduced a national gay rights bill which had no chance of success. Nevertheless, it was used as an educational vehicle on the subject.

They asked, "How will you get it done? What will you do to ensure its passage?"

I foolishly said, "It will be easy. The mayor can certainly get the majority leader to allow the committee to vote their consciences. If they have that right they will vote it out and it will ultimately pass in the City Council."

Little did I know. One of the first things I did when I came into office in 1978 was to announce that I was signing an executive order ending governmental discrimination on the basis of sexual orientation in the fields of employment and housing. This would mean that in the future, sexual orientation could in no way adversely affect an individual applying for a City job, no matter if it's a civil service title or a provisional appointment. And the New York City Housing Authority could not discriminate against such individuals.

There was a furor and it received wide attention. The notoriety was so great that instead of its being perceived as my fourth executive order, which it was, the public and the press to this date think it was my first. Obviously, this was not a panacea since it would have such limited impact. The ultimate goal was to do what had been done in a few cities—impose by law a prohibition against discrimination in the private sector on the basis of sexual orientation in the fields of jobs, housing and places of public accommodation. That was a struggle.

I had a number of conversations with Majority Leader Tom Cuite urging that he allow members to vote their conscience. It was clear, not by his comments, which were always very oblique, but rather by his actions, which were very direct, that there was no hope of his ever allowing that to occur. The militant gays were very angry with me. They would often say to me, "You could buy him. You could get his cooperation and give him jobs or judgeships." I said, "I will never do that." And I must say, knowing Tom Cuite as I did, it is a slander to think he would have made that exchange. For him, it was an issue of morality and on that he would never budge nor would he allow it to be a matter of individual conscience.

On this issue, I believe it is defensible for those whose faith teaches that homosexual behavior is anathema, that they not surrender in any way, if surrender means that something they are opposed to will come to fruition. I believe that holds true on all matters of morality, although there are not many such issues in government that reach that plateau. The ones that come to mind are the death penalty, homosexuality, abortion, birth control, the State of Israel for Jews, and for the Irish, opposition to Great Britain in Northern Ireland. And on those issues, no one can demand that you surrender your morality because you are a minority of one or because the opposition is militant. On matters of morality, you should be prepared, figuratively and in some cases literally, to go to your death in their defense. So it was not until Peter Vallone was in contention in 1985 to replace Tom Cuite, who was retiring, that the issue again surfaced with a hope of change. To his credit, Peter would not impose his conscience on other legislators.

Peter Vallone is conservative, a Roman Catholic, very religious and someone who goes to Mass every single day. He is a wonderful man. The question was, what would his position be on this issue if he became majority leader? I asked him that question without in any way seeking to browbeat him or threaten him with opposition in his quest to be majority leader. Even if we disagreed on this issue, I still preferred him over his opponent, who was basically a surrogate for the borough president of Brooklyn, Howard Golden, with whom I have had enormous personal and public disagreements.

Peter's response to the question was "On a matter of morality, I will never ask someone to substitute my morality for theirs. Therefore, this matter will be decided by the members of the committee in accordance with their own sense of morality. I will not stack the committee."

He was true to his word, and the committee, which was chaired by Peter's opponent for majority leader, Sam Horwitz, voted the legislation out by a vote of 5 to 1. When it came to the floor, it was approved by a vote of 21 to 14.

The Roman Catholic Church was and is opposed to that legislation. Its position is that it will not support any legislation that in any way gives legitimacy to that which it perceives to be anathema. Its spokesmen go out of their way to make that point. The Cardinal has said time and time again that he does not and will not discriminate against or exclude those people who are homosexuals from jobs within his control *provided* that they do not seek to propagate that sexual approach to life nor flaunt their sexuality in such a public way as to cause the Church to perceive it as a scandal.

The term "scandal" is a technical term in the Church lexicon, which I believe connotes enormous notoriety. My own position is that one is either genetically homosexual at birth or because of environmental reasons becomes so within the first few years of life and that nothing we can do in terms of education or moral teaching will change that individual's sexuality. We cannot allow people to suffer slings and arrows that will destroy them professionally or personally simply because of the sexual nature they were born with. What purpose does it serve?

The night that I was interviewed in the home of Robert Livingston was the night that the lights went out in New York City as a result of a power failure at Con Edison. As I recall, we had to leave the apartment and walk down seventeen flights of stairs. Almost every year, a survey is taken by reporters who will ask, "Where were you the night the lights went out in New York?" I always honestly answer, "I was sitting in the dark with twenty-five militant gays discussing what I would do when I became mayor to get justice for them." I am proud of what I have done.

I mentioned earlier that I have been the subject of scurrilous rumors and gossip in political campaigns. Two incidents stand out.

One occurred when I was running for mayor for the first time in 1977 against Mario Cuomo, who is now the governor of the state. His supporters embarked upon the first visible campaign of that kind. They put posters up all over the city which read VOTE FOR CUOMO, NOT THE HOMO. When I first saw those posters I cringed, and I wondered how I would be able to bear it. Then I was asked by a reporter for the first time if I was homosexual. My response was "I would hope that if I were, I would have the courage to say so." I thought to myself, how outrageous it is that I should have to submit to such an inquiry.

I hasten to add that the governor denied all responsibility or involvement in those attacks and said that he deplored it. I won that election. I am sure that there were people then, as there are now, who believed that I was a homosexual but did not care and voted for me. Likewise, there were those who thought I was and voted against me, and the vast majority who had no thought on the matter.

The second time that I lost out of twenty-four elections was in 1982 when I ran for governor, again against Mario Cuomo. Again, in a public way, one of his major labor supporters denounced me as homosexual. It became a *cause célèbre*. But this time I was not so terrified. I thought, it really belittles those who engage in that kind of campaign. Even though I lost that election in 1982, it in no way was attributable to the scurrilous campaign. People decided that they preferred Cuomo as governor and me as mayor. In fact, that was Mario Cuomo's major television commercial. "Why not keep the two of us in office. Cuomo as Governor and Koch as Mayor."

In 1986 a militant homosexual playwright, Larry Kramer, was dissatisfied with what I was doing as mayor to deal with the overwhelming tragedy of AIDS. I believe that the City of New York was and is doing more than any other city in the country including San Francisco, which has always been held up as the beacon light in this area. He decided that he would bait me, cause me anguish or destroy me by denouncing me as homosexual. He got the so-called underground media, or so-called alternate press and radio, to take up that cause, and for the first time in print instead of being whispered, those allegations were made. What was shocking was to have *The Village Voice* participate by artfully referring to an article on this subject that appeared in the *L.A. Times*.

The members of my staff at City Hall were more pained than I was, and they were very concerned about my feelings and reactions. I decided at that point that I would stand up on this subject, not for myself but for others who had no public platforms from which to be heard and who might feel destroyed. I had the sense that at this point in my life, with my life being as public as it has been for the last eleven years, these people could not destroy me. I only felt sad for the militant homosexuals who thought they would gain some advantage by seeking to use a despicable accusation employing homophobia which normally gets an understandable response of outrage from homosexuals and heterosexuals alike.

It was interesting that none of the standard press or media picked up this objectionable material. Since this incident occurred at the time of Gary Hart's public sexual escapade, one would have thought that the restraints on decency in commentary had been removed. But not so, to the credit of the New York press.

I mention this because it reinforced my feelings on this whole matter. Whenever this issue was the subject of discussion, I had to stand up and protect young men and women who could not protect themselves from such inquiries. So I took the public position that I would not respond to such an inquiry ever again. People could think whatever they wanted to. My sexuality, just like my religion, is a private matter. I don't have to account to anyone for it, so long as what I do is private or, to use the Catholic terminology, not a public scandal.

THE CARDINAL

In retrospect, King Solomon's solution of the quarrel between the two women who both claimed to be the mother of the same baby may look a little less profound to some today than it looked at the time. The king knew human nature. When he invited the women to cut the baby in half, so both could share, he banked on the real mother's willingness to sacrifice her own desires, rather than see her baby die. As soon as she made the offer to give up the child, Solomon knew the truth. As we would say today, he gave her "custody."

If the solution seems less lustrous today than it did then, it is undoubtedly that the issues today seem almost infinitely more complex, and human nature a lot less predictable. Solomon—and certainly the baby—would have been in deep trouble had the real mother thought to herself, "If I can't have the baby I don't want anyone else to have him."

I hope that's not irreverent, or that I'm not being disrespectful to the great King Solomon, but I *am* an Archbishop of an indescribably complex Archdiocese in a day when yesterday's problems seem so very simple, if only because they are yesterday's!

In regard to the extraordinarily complicated question of homosexuality, I suspect that many bishops join me in wishing they had only the problems of Solomon. The question of homosexuality may be addressed from a variety of perspectives. I want to begin with one uniquely pertinent to this book. It's equally relevant to the question of abortion discussed elsewhere.

Recognition of the diversity of cultures is not new to the Church, nor is the effort to try to bring about a reasonable match between local customs and Catholic rituals, or to teach Catholic doctrine and moral practice in a manner intelligible to various native peoples. "Enculturation" has come to be perceived as a critical goal for the Church in any country.

There is a basic political "doctrine" in the United States, however, that has come to be virtually synonymous with America: one man or one woman, one vote. Every voter's voice has equal weight. Democracy here is politically pluralistic of its very nature.

The Church in the United States has long felt required to prove its Americanism and its freedom from control by a foreign power. In recent years there has been an increasing tendency even to speak of the "American" Church, and to argue a very significant degree of independence from "Rome."

In any event, political pluralism is a way of life in this nation. It should not be surprising, then, that a certain number of Catholics, products of this political culture, would demand *theological* pluralism, and perhaps a right to vote their choices in matters theological on a one Catholic–one vote basis. In such a situation, it would not be inconceivable that the pope himself would have only one vote, precisely as does the president of the United States!

This mind-set leads more and more to an exaggerated emphasis on the difference between what Catholics call "defined doctrine," which must be accepted by all Catholics, and those many teachings and practices that have not been explicitly defined, although many have been held by Christians since the earliest centuries. The group called "Catholics for a Free Choice," for example, have this mind-set about abortion. They aver that the Church's teaching has varied on this matter through the centuries, that it has never been in the category of "infallible" teaching, and that it is therefore subject to change. The fallacy in such arguments is discussed in my chapter on abortion, and need not detain us here. The implicit hope of such movements, of course, is that if enough people protest the Church's current "hard line" on abortion, and simply refuse to accept it, eventually the Church will be forced to modify its position. They reject the reality that certain Church teachings will never change and *can* never change.

It is fair to say, I believe, that this is the mind-set and the approach of some who argue the validity of homosexual behavior. They do not accept the position that the teaching of the Church on homosexuality is immutable. They argue that it is subject to change and *will* change if protested persistently. Again the implicit hope is that if enough people reject it, the Church's current "hard line" will be significantly modified.

The general thrust of such arguments is that the Church must at the very least accept a form of moral pluralism. The Church must be large enough, broad enough, compassionate enough and *humble* enough (read "democratic" enough) to accept a diversity of beliefs and practices on the part of those *who have the right to call themselves Roman Catholics.* This is a spirit quite different from that of reformers who have broken from the Church in the past, and either formed a particular mode of "Catholic" life, or transferred to some other religious body. For whatever reason, or however they did it, they "left" the Church.

Certain advocates of abortion, homosexuality and other "rights" today, however, explicitly refuse to leave the Church. It is as much their Church as the pope's or the bishops', they argue, and they will not be driven out of it because of what they consider the stubbornness and shortsightedness of popes and bishops clinging to outmoded teachings and practices.

In a certain sense, then, we are dealing with a Church-State problem, but one of a quite different order from those problems that have earlier preoccupied us in this book. The Church may disagree with the State's enacting legislation to liberalize or legalize either abortion or homosexual activities, but recognizes that the passage of such legislation, whatever its morality, is under the jurisdiction of the State. What the Church does not accept, however, is any implication that legalization by the State creates a moral or doctrinal right for an individual because the individual happens to be American. Again we find Church and State differing in jurisdiction, in values and in purpose. The people in a democracy can vote in support of legalizing abortion, homosexual activity or a variety of other positions. The vote does not change the moral status of any such position, as far as the Church is concerned.

This is one of the very real challenges confronted by a bishop in the United States today. The national temperament, with its very strong emphasis on the rights of individuals to decide all sorts of things for themselves, sometimes clashes with the moral absolutes he must proclaim if he is to be faithful to Church teaching. Moreover, even to aver that *anything* touching people's lives is an "absolute" is to be open always to the charge of being callous and insensitive and lacking in compassion.[1] It has become popular, for example, to cite various bishops who are purportedly far more understanding and compassionate because they allegedly hold more liberal views about these various issues. Although erroneous, this is understandable, quite in keeping with the notion that political pluralism should equate to theological pluralism, so that political tactics should be quite as applicable to Church as to State.

It seems to have been an increasing awareness of this trend and others on the part of the Holy See that led to the publication of a document in October of 1986 that met with much consternation and resentment among some members of the homosexual community in the United States. This document, entitled "Letter to the Bishops of the Catholic Church on the Pastoral Care of Homosexual Persons," was issued by the Congregation for the Doctrine of the Faith, which is responsible for the preservation of Catholic teaching.

In December of 1975, the same Congregation had issued "Declaration on Certain Questions Concerning Sexual Ethics." The document stressed "the duty of trying to understand the homosexual condition" and noted "the distinction commonly drawn between the homosexual condition or tendency and individual homosexual actions."

The 1986 Letter observes, however, that during the eleven years since this Declaration had been published, great confusion had developed, and an "overly benign interpretation" had been given to the homosexual condition itself, "some going so far as to call it neutral, or even good."

While the Letter pointed out that a homosexual "orientation" is not sinful, it noted that special pastoral concern should be directed to those so oriented, "lest they be led to believe that the living out of this orientation is a morally acceptable option. It is not."

It stressed, further, that the inclination of the homosexual person, not sinful in itself, "is a more or less strong tendency ordered toward an *intrinsic moral evil; an objective* disorder."

There's the heart of it. The Church speaks of *intrinsic* morality, that which is *objectively* good or bad, not that which is voted or legislated as lawful or unlawful.[2]

1. My views on the true meaning of compassion may be found in Chapter II.
2. See my discussion in Chapter II on intrinsic morality and Natural Moral Law.

The 1986 Letter goes on to suggest some of the causes of confusion, such as new interpretations of the Bible, in which it is argued that the Bible ignores or tacitly approves of homosexuality, or that whatever happened in biblical times was "culture bound" and not applicable to contemporary life. The Letter rejects such interpretations.

Further, the Letter notes that there has been an unfortunate ignoring of the nature of the human person as made in God's own Image, and of "the divine plan of the loving and life-giving union in the sacrament of marriage. It is only in the marital relationship that the use of the sexual faculty can be morally good. A person engaging in homosexual behavior therefore acts immorally."

I am going to quote somewhat extensively from this Letter, since it spells out the formal teaching of the Church so clearly and expresses my own beliefs more articulately than I could. Moreover, the Letter is remarkably apt to the purposes of this book. Why? Because it explicitly distinguishes between and highlights the separate purposes of Church and State, their separate values and goals, and certainly their separate jurisdictions. This we find particularly in what it has to say about gay rights legislation and about the use of political tactics and pressures to affect the status of Church doctrine and to influence both the Catholic community and the body politic.

. . . Increasing numbers of people today, even within the Church, are bringing enormous pressure to bear on the Church to accept the homosexual condition as though it were not disordered and to condone homosexual activity.

. . . The Church's ministers must ensure that homosexual persons in their care will not be misled by this point of view, so profoundly opposed to the teaching of the Church.

The movement within the Church, which takes the form of pressure groups of various names and sizes, attempts to give the impression that it represents all homosexual persons who are Catholic. As a matter of fact, its membership is by and large restricted to those who either ignore the teaching of the Church or seek somehow to undermine it. It brings together under the aegis of Catholicism homosexual persons who have no intention of abandoning their homosexual behavior. One tactic used is to protest that any and all criticism of or reservations about homosexual people, their activity and lifestyle, are simply diverse forms of unjust discrimination.

The Letter is blunt about civil legislation.

There is an effort in some countries to manipulate the Church by gaining the often well-intentioned support of her pastors with the view to changing civil statutes and laws. This is done in order to conform to these pressure groups' concept that homosexuality is at least completely harmless, if not an entirely good thing.

"[The Church] is also aware that the view that homosexual activity is equivalent to, or is as acceptable as, the sexual expression of conjugal love, has a direct impact on society's understanding of the nature and rights of the family and puts them in jeopardy.

The Letter is equally blunt about "homosexual bashers."

It is deplorable that homosexual persons have been and are the object of violent malice in speech and in action. Such treatment deserves condemnation from the Church's pastors wherever it occurs. The intrinsic dignity of each person must always be respected in words, in action and in law.[3]

The Letter takes note of a common argument and rejects it.

It has been argued that the homosexual orientation in certain cases is not a result of deliberate choice; and so the homosexual person would then have no choice but to behave in a homosexual fashion. Lacking freedom, such a person, even if engaged in homosexual activity, would not be culpable.

. . . Christians who are homosexual are called, as all of us are, to a chaste life.

Then comes guidance for bishops.

. . . [T]his Congregation wishes to ask the bishops to be especially cautious of any programs which may seek to pressure the Church to change her teaching, even while claiming not to do so . . . For example, they may present the teaching of the Magisterium, but only as if it were an optional source for the formation of one's conscience. Its specific authority is not recognized. Some of these

3. As of the time of this writing, an increasing number of violent attacks on persons who are perceived as homosexual are being reported. I abhor such attacks, as does the Church, and consider them and all other forms of harassment and violence against homosexual persons to be totally reprehensible.

groups will use the word "Catholic" to describe either the organization or its intended members, yet they do not defend and promote the teaching of the Magisterium; indeed, they even openly attack it. While their members may claim a desire to conform their lives to the teachings of Jesus, in fact they abandon the teaching of His Church. This contradictory action should not have the support of the bishops in any way.

We encourage the bishops, then, to provide pastoral care in full accord with the teaching of the Church for homosexual persons of their dioceses. No authentic pastoral program will include organizations in which homosexual persons associate with each other without clearly stating that homosexual activity is immoral. . . . [W]e wish to make it clear that departure from the Church's teaching, or silence about it, in an effort to provide pastoral care is neither caring nor pastoral. Only what is true can ultimately be pastoral. The neglect of the Church's position prevents homosexual men and women from receiving the care they need and deserve.

Finally, the Letter expresses firmly the requirement that the Church may not in any way support anti-Catholic teaching or behavior, however compassionate may be the intention of its proponents.

All support should be withdrawn from any organizations which seek to undermine the teaching of the Church, which are ambiguous about it, or which neglect it entirely. Such support, or even the semblance of such support, can be gravely misinterpreted. Special attention should be given to the practice of scheduling religious services and the use of Church buildings by these groups, including the facilities of Catholic schools and colleges. To some, such permission to use Church property may seem only just and charitable; but in reality it is contradictory to the purpose for which these institutions were founded, it is misleading and often scandalous.

In assessing proposed legislation, the bishops should keep as their uppermost concern the responsibility to defend and promote family life.

Some will dismiss the Letter as only "one man's opinion." Those who understand the structure of the Church and the unique role of the Congregation for the Doctrine of the Faith will understand the foolishness of such a dismissal. Indeed, upon receipt of the Letter, bishop after bishop who had previously permitted various homosexual groups to hold special Masses in parish churches, in the course of which, in time, Church teaching came to be undermined, began rescinding such permission. (In every instance, the permission had been granted by the appropriate bishop in the first place in the hope that *legitimate* spiritual needs of homosexual persons would be met and that they could support one another by mutual efforts to *observe* Church teaching in their lives. The Letter arrived at about the time that the entire nature of many such Masses had changed, and they had become forums for rejecting Church teaching and calling for its change.)

I know that some members of the homosexual community think that I have been completely impervious to and unmoved by the diatribes in certain homosexual publications, the lampoons, some indescribably obscene and pornographic, the picketing in various places, the protests and disruptions in St. Patrick's Cathedral. Because I have acknowledged such rarely, and responded even less frequently, it is assumed that I consider their originators "non-persons," beneath my contempt. Nothing could be further from the truth.

I know some of them truly believe I hate them, and want nothing more than to make life miserable for them. It is unlikely that any denial on my part will convince them to the contrary. But at least I can put on the public record that this is totally untrue, and I bear them absolutely no malice. I cannot permit such protests as standing up in the Cathedral as I start to preach, and other disruptions of Masses, because of the sacredness of the Mass, and because of an obligation to other worshipers (plus my honest fear that these worshipers could lose patience and unfortunate conflicts could occur). It might help some to understand if I explain that I would take this same position in response to *any* protestors, whatever their cause. For example, while my support of unions is well known, I have made clear my abhorrence of using my Mass—or any Mass—as a forum for union protests, even if I agree with the reason for the protest.

To the Church, and certainly to me, personally, the Mass is *the* sacred act of our faith, the summary of all our most revered teachings and of all that we most cherish. Any disruption is a violation of the Mass itself, regardless of the target or purpose of the disruption. I was not in New York at the time, but I have been told repeatedly that a great sorrow for Cardinal Cooke was to feel he had to cause the removal of some women religious who had prostrated themselves in the center aisle of St. Patrick's Cathedral, during the Mass, to protest the war in Vietnam.[4] Neither the nature of the protestors nor the reason for their protest is the issue. The sacredness of the Mass *is*.

I have announced frequently that *all* persons, whatever their sexual orientation, are most cordially welcome at any Mass, and certainly my own. They are asked only to observe the normal courtesies and to confine protests to other times and places. I disagree completely with those who feel that the Church arbitrarily deprives them of the fullness of the practice of the Catholic Faith. I can and do, however, share their pain.

There is another group of homosexual persons to whom my heart truly goes out, and for whom I wish I could do more. They are non-protestors, but they have been led to believe that the Church has let them down. They are those described in the Holy See's Letter as believing that "God has made them the way they are," and that the Church has no right to penalize them for practicing homosexuality. They are simply oriented to persons of the same sex, they say, or have fallen in love with persons of the same sex as men and women fall in love with one another. They want to spend their lives together in a committed loving relationship, as do married heterosexual people. They feel they should have the same right to sexual exchange as do married men and women. They are deeply wounded that the Church answers that such behavior is unnatural and divinely forbidden, and that if they are to receive the Sacraments, they must *attempt* to lead chaste lives. They resent the fact that the Church's injunction to them is the same as it is to the heterosexual: Outside marriage (between a man and a woman) all sexual activity is sinful. They feel like men and women without a spiritual country, second-class citizens in a Church they basically love.

Life for these persons is especially difficult in the "anything goes" culture of sexual permissiveness. In a day in which many people treat heterosexual relationships as casually and meaninglessly as drinking a glass of water, there is that much more pressure on single people to do their "own thing," and not to be distressed merely because their "thing" is homosexuality.

What bishop does not suffer with such people? I cannot pretend that I think them to be wrong merely because my Church teaches they

4. At the time, Cardinal Cooke was Military Vicar for Catholics in the armed forces. It was not uncommon to protest the war by protesting his position.

are wrong. Honesty demands my saying clearly that I believe homosexual behavior to be contrary to Natural Moral Law, a violation of Sacred Scriptures and sinful. I do not for a moment believe church teaching fails homosexual persons. Truth never fails anyone. Nor do I believe we have failed them by not providing a meaningful ministry for them. I wish far more would take advantage of it. I believe it would bring them much peace.

I am speaking of what I believe to be a potentially wonderful program in the Archdiocese of New York. It has already provided a great deal of support to many, but is capable of helping far more. It is called "Courage." It was founded by Father John Harvey, a priest-psychologist who has devoted his entire life to a loving ministry to homosexuals. "Courage" is dedicated to the belief that chastity is a positive, constructive virtue, a powerful liberating force, and that it *is* possible, for heterosexual and homosexual alike.

A Mass is offered here in New York on Friday evening of every week, to give "Courage" members an opportunity to worship together and spiritually support and encourage one another in their respective efforts to practice chastity. All homosexual persons who want to try to observe Church teaching are welcome.

Shortly before the time of this writing, I expanded "Courage," so that now at least one priest and often a sister or a layperson is committed to ministry to homosexual persons in each of the eighteen geographical regions (vicariates) into which the archdiocese is divided. We will do *anything* we legitimately can to minister helpfully to homosexual persons. One thing we cannot do is change Church teaching, which we believe rooted in the Sacred Scriptures and in the Natural Moral Law.

I recognize human weakness (in whom more than in myself?). I know that both heterosexual and homosexual can slip and fall every day, a dozen times a day or more. The Church asks only that with God's grace we pick ourselves up and start all over again. The confessional exists not because we Catholics don't sin, but because we do.

I would be deeply grateful to have *anyone*, homosexual or heterosexual, tell me how I can minister more helpfully to homosexual persons *within the requirements of Church teaching*. I *know* there are laypersons, religious sisters, brothers and priests who consider me too "harsh" in this matter. They see me as a "hard-liner," lacking in compassion. I personally do not believe that compassion is true compassion which compromises truth. It always backfires on individuals and on society. It's quite like granting the "right" to suicide as the ultimate act of compassion.

There are many homosexual persons who go unnoticed—those who accept Church teaching and try to live it faithfully. "Courage" encounters many of them. Periodically one writes to me and pleads with me not to compromise Church teaching on homosexuality, despite the difficulties in their own lives.

I feel, too, for parents and loved ones of the homosexually oriented. So often parents feel guilty—or resentful that their son or daughter is maltreated by society and "rejected" by the Church. Their hurt is equally understandable. Perhaps most sorrowful of all, however, is the experience of husband or wife who learns that a spouse is either homosexual or bisexual. None of these are ever distant from my own mind, my heart, my prayers, as they and the rest of us try to grope our way along the pilgrimage of life in a bewilderingly complex society, a society that is crushed by pressures never known before.

What further can I say in this book to those I hurt because of my own belief in and attempted fidelity to Church teaching? I cannot bring myself to believe that they could ever have even a shred of respect for an archbishop, the primary teacher of Church doctrine in this or any other archdiocese, should he be unfaithful to what the Church holds and what he personally believes. Nor could they respect an archbishop who teaches or condones what he believes is ultimately damaging to homosexual persons themselves, simply for his own popularity, or so that he may be perceived as compassionate. Popularity is a heady intoxicant, but as every intoxicant, it can destroy the life of one who thirsts for it above all else.

It is admittedly one thing, however, for a bishop to insist upon Church teaching for Catholics. Most people expect him to do so, even if some believe he interprets it too strictly, or others too loosely. For a bishop to take strong stands on proposed *civil* legislation that affects people of every religious persuasion is something else again.

I refer to the position taken by the Archdiocese of New York in regard to the gay rights legislation strongly supported by Mayor Koch and finally passed by the City Council in 1985. Whereas my predecessor, Cardinal Cooke, had strongly rejected such proposed legislation, and had worked quietly to prevent its passage, the climate had changed by the time I arrived in New York. Such legislation was being passed in a variety of cities. Political activism on the part of some sectors of the homosexual community had increased significantly, and, very importantly, the composition of the City Council had changed dramatically. The probability of preventing passage of legislation was virtually nonexistent.

As a *citizen* in a highly visible position, I felt an obligation to the entire society that silence could not satisfy. I had to object to legislation I believed to be morally wrong. As *Archbishop*, I knew that silence would signify consent to the legislation, and gravely confuse the Catholics who are my direct responsibility. This time, Brooklyn's Bishop Mugavero, as well, was opposed to such legislation. (We had respectfully differed with one another, on Executive Order 50, as noted earlier in this book.)

This is an excellent example of the complexities of Church-State relationships when it comes to the formation of public policy. I see the churchman's responsibility primarily in terms of the moral dimensions of any policy. I do not believe in a "human right" to practice homosexual behavior. I believe that constituting such behavior as either a "civil" or a "protected" right can have a severely damaging effect on society at large, in the long run, adversely affecting marriage, family life and young people in a particularly grave way. I see it, further, as one of the many efforts to impose a national religion of civil rights on our entire society.

Nonetheless, amid great public clamor, vituperative exchanges and near-physical combat hardly observant of Marquis of Queensberry rules, the gay rights legislation passed.

Much of the rancor still borne by some members of the homosexual community, I believe, is traceable to my resistance to the passage of what they believe to be minimally just legislation. I recall, indeed, even being boycotted by some Broadway personalities. At least the information given me was that a charitable benefit, "Broadway's Salute to Archbishop O'Connor," was boycotted because of my stand on such legislation.

An archbishop does what he believes he should do. He lives with the aftermath, perhaps for the rest of his life. There is no such thing as a free lunch.

So Solomon would be welcome in New York, from my perspective, should he ever be able to join me or replace me. I would give a great deal to be able to watch him in action. And I'll bet he'd get a lot of invitations from my brother bishops throughout this testy, lovable land.

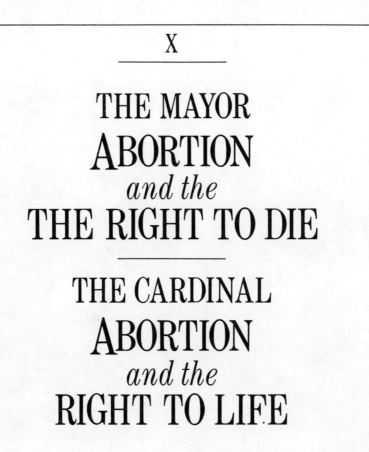

THE MAYOR
ABORTION
and the
THE RIGHT TO DIE

THE CARDINAL
ABORTION
and the
RIGHT TO LIFE

THE MAYOR

Of all the complex topics that confront us today, perhaps the most controversial area of debate concerns birth control and abortion. Because it is such a painfully intimate and emotionally charged subject, it seems appropriate that I begin this chapter by sharing with you a personal story.

My mother died in 1961. Some years before her death, she told me that during her lifetime she'd had a number of abortions. She went on to say that when she found out she was pregnant with her third child, she didn't want to complete the pregnancy. Her reasons were economic. Our family was suffering in the Depression. My father had lost his business. We were very poor. The prospect of another mouth to feed posed serious problems. In those days, however, abortions were readily available only to wealthy women and those willing to risk death at the hands of back-alley butchers. My mother told me that she tried to induce a miscarriage by jumping off chairs and trunks. It didn't work. When she finally accepted that the child was going to be born, she worried that she might have injured the fetus. As it turned out, that child was my sister Pat. Not only was she not injured, she went on to become one of the most remarkable women I've ever met.

I understand why my mother felt the way she did. Nevertheless, I'm glad she failed in her attempt at self-induced abortion. I thank God that Pat is here. She went on to have three terrific sons and to make her mark in the fields of education and civic leadership. I couldn't have asked for a more wonderful and loving sister. It would have been a tragedy if she'd never been born.

My mother's story often came to mind during my years as a congressman. The national debate over legalized abortion had reached the boiling point. In 1970, New York became the first state to make unrestricted abortion permissible under law. The effort to pass this bill had been marked by years of emotional and acrimonious argument. Those supporting the new law were being called murderers of unborn children. Those who opposed abortion were sometimes labeled as oppressors of women, who inflicted unwanted children on families unable to care for them.

It was not by accident that passage of the open-abortion law in New York coincided with the rise of modern feminism. Women's groups were flexing their political muscle and telling legislators that women had the right to control their own bodies. There could be no real argument about the fact that the right to a safe abortion was something that a great many women wanted. When the New York law went into effect, women from other states and countries came here to have abortions. Discussing the theoretical rights and wrongs of abortion is important, but experience was demonstrating that abortion on demand was something that a great many women wanted. And they didn't want to be forced to travel to New York to get it.

The success and popularity of the New York law strengthened the hand of abortion activists across the country. In 1973, the United States Supreme Court—responding to the logic and legal briefs of the pro-abortion lobby—ruled in *Roe* v. *Wade* that anti-abortion laws were unconstitutional. Overnight, a social revolution of tremendous moral, ethical and demographic impact swept the nation. Just a few years before, abortion had been one of the most serious crimes on the lawbooks. It was a subject polite people rarely discussed. Now it was freely available in neighborhood clinics and doctors' offices from coast to coast.

Anti-abortion activists—sometimes known as "right-to-life" people—realized they were losing in both the courts and on the streets. They stepped up their campaign to make abortion illegal once again. I remember right-to-lifers coming to see me at my congressional office in Washington. I did not consider myself to be "pro-abortion." I was an advocate of free choice. Abortion, I believed, was a matter of individual conscience. From the right-to-lifer's point of view, however, "free choice" was the same thing as "pro-abortion." They lobbied very hard to get me to change my mind and support federal legislation outlawing abortion in the United States.

Some of the right-to-lifers engaged in tactics that were—to say the least—counterproductive. Some of them would march in picket lines carrying horrible pictures of aborted fetuses, and other bloody results of abortions. The pictures were disgusting, and so were the tactics. Instead of inspiring horror at abortion, they prompted many of us in Congress to question the motives and character of the right-to-lifers themselves. It was an outrageous attempt to batter people emotionally, and bully them into supporting the beliefs of the right-to-life groups.

I think the right-to-lifers eventually came to see that certain aspects of their strategy were having the opposite result of what they intended. They recognized that a change of tactics was called for. I remember one leader of the right-to-life movement—a nurse named Jean Head—used to bring me roses. Instead of issuing shrill threats and accusations, she would discuss with me her determination to make abortions illegal. Her approach to the subject was very intelligent and reasoned. She believed that a fetus is a human being from the moment of conception. My position was—and still is—that although at some point prior to birth the fetus becomes a human being, we don't know exactly when that point is reached. The developing fetus progresses through many stages. At some stages it is more animal than human, but eventually it does become a human being, with the rights of a human being.

Jean Head listened patiently to my side of the issue. And I must say I was impressed by her willingness to talk about such a high-powered subject in such a calm and considerate manner. I said to her, "Ms. Head, you bring me roses, even though you disagree with me. But if I changed my position, and came out against abortion, those who support me now would not bring me roses. They would bring me cactuses. They would be totally enraged by my point of view, and would become crazed with anger. So I want to commend you for defending your position in such a responsible and courteous way."

We tend to forget that when abortion was illegal, it was pro-abortionists who took to the streets and pressured legislators to change the law. They told horror stories about women who died while trying to abort themselves with coat hangers, and about the sordid and dangerous conditions under which illegal abortions were performed less than twenty years ago. Their message was that abortions are going to take place anyway. It makes more sense for everyone to have abortions performed safely, instead of making such procedures the exclusive privilege of the rich.

This is an issue in which compromise is difficult, if not impossible. Many right-to-lifers consider abortion to be murder. They don't want to be part of a society that condones such a practice. On the other hand, those who advocate a woman's right to abortion believe just as fervently that no one should have control over what happens inside someone else's body. They believe children should be born to parents who want them, and cite disturbing statistics to show that children born to mothers unable or unwilling to properly care for them are more likely to suffer abuse and neglect. And what of women who are victims of rape or incest, or who are told that they will bear a mentally or physically deformed child? In such cases should we compel a pregnant woman to bear a child she doesn't want? I say no.

Given the passions that rage on both sides of the issue, it is not surprising that acts of violence have been associated with efforts to halt the work of abortion clinics. In October 1986 a bomb exploded at an abortion clinic on East Thirtieth Street in Manhattan. Two passersby were injured. Two weeks later, three sticks of dynamite were discovered at an abortion clinic in Queens, after a telephone threat was received. A month later a bomb went off at an abortion clinic on East Twenty-third Street in Manhattan. Four days after that another bomb—fifteen sticks of dynamite—was defused at a Planned Parenthood center in Manhattan. According to police, if the bomb had exploded it would have killed a real-estate agent who'd been handcuffed to a pipe by the bomber.

It was clear that the bombings and attempted bombings were the work of one person or group. I denounced the bombers as terrorist fanatics and called for the FBI to join the investigation. Alfred F. Moran, executive director of Planned Parenthood in New York City, said that while he didn't think the Catholic Church was in any way responsible for anti-abortion terrorism, he did believe that the Church and others who opposed abortion were playing an indirect role in the violence by "labeling women as baby killers, and calling abortion murder.

"That rhetoric incites the less stable elements of the right-to-life movement," Moran said. He went on to cite more than ninety bombings or attempted bombings that had taken place at abortion facilities across the nation since 1977.

Cardinal O'Connor was understandably distressed by Mr. Moran's statement. His Eminence said that he did not engage in any such rhetoric, nor did responsible members of the pro-life movement. He called the bombings "a heinous crime." Later, Cardinal O'Connor played a key role in helping to bring the violence to an end. He used his position of moral leadership to help persuade the bomber to surrender to authorities.

But the apprehension of individuals who use violence to express their opposition to abortion does not lessen the intensity of the debate. A woman still has a right to an abortion, but the right-to-lifers have been steadily chipping away at the legal foundation of abortion law. In 1972, the New York State Legislature voted to rescind its pioneering abortion statute, but the bill was vetoed by Governor Nelson Rockefeller. In 1976, the Legislature voted to require parental consent for minors seeking abortions. The law was vetoed by Governor Hugh Carey. In 1977, Congress passed the Hyde Amendment— later upheld by the Supreme Court—which restricts the use of federal funds for abortions. This law has had the effect in many states of making abortions unaffordable for poor women. Only New York and a few other states now reimburse the costs of an abortion under Medicaid.

Clearly, the abortion debate is far from over. "Pro-life" and "pro-choice" forces are engaged in a fierce and ongoing struggle to shape the law of the land. Each side is firmly and sincerely committed to its cause. Each believes the other to be ill-advised or worse. The level of accusation and acrimony shows no sign of abating. We find ourselves in a strange and curious moment in history. The world population is soaring. And yet industrialized nations such as the United States, Japan and the countries of Europe are experiencing a rapidly falling birthrate. Military experts say the number of births in West Germany is so low that by the year 2000 the Germans will fall far short of meeting their manpower commitments to NATO.

In Japan, demographers are worried about the consequences of large numbers of older, retired citizens who will have to be supported by a much smaller working-age population. In China, where the population now tops one billion, strict birth control and forced-abortion policies are limiting couples to one child. As a result, the Chinese are facing a future in which family life will be radically altered. Everyone will be an only child. The adults of tomorrow will have no brothers, sisters, aunts, uncles or cousins.

How did the world get into such a strange and unbalanced situation? The wealthiest nations—which could easily feed and house larger populations—are faced with declining birthrates. Third World nations, meanwhile, have rapidly growing populations that are tragically afflicted by widespread hunger and poverty. Clearly, we need a better understanding of international population problems.

A look at the history books shows that world population levels have increased from an estimated 500 million in 1650 to more than 5 *billion* today. Some scientists predict that world population may well reach 10 billion in the twenty-first century. For many reasons, this forecast is alarming. First, it's entirely possible that our planet cannot support such a large number of people. It's not only a question of how we're going to feed and shelter 10 billion people. World ecology may be fatally disrupted by side effects of the industrial growth needed to support this population. Scientists warn that the ozone layer has already been dangerously depleted by the introduction of chlorofluorocarbons into the atmosphere. Even if production of these chemicals is stopped immediately, the ozone layer—which helps block ultraviolet radiation from the sun—will continue to shrink for decades to come, with possibly calamitous effects on both human health and environment.

There are other danger signals that we're reaching the global limit of industrial growth. Sewage disposal is becoming an increasingly difficult problem to solve. Sewage treatment is part of the answer, but the treatment plants themselves create huge amounts of sludge, which must in turn be disposed of. New York City has been dumping its sludge 106 miles out to sea, but we are now under legal pressure to end all such dumping by 1991. Also, we still have to find ways to deal with acid rain, smog, nuclear waste, and the gradual but steady warming of the atmosphere that comes from burning huge quantities of fossil fuels.

Some people say we shouldn't worry about overpopulation, because new scientific knowledge will save us from the negative consequences of today's technology. Personally, I doubt that we can safely trust our future to science alone. The twentieth century has given us countless examples of the atrocities that can result when morally aberrant people get control of modern technology. However, this doesn't mean we can't make better use of our ability to understand the world and our place in it. In particular, I think we have to make a concerted effort to stabilize world population levels by using our extensive medical knowledge of birth control in a rational and responsible way.

Some experts believe the techniques of birth control are not a recent discovery. Birth control seems to have been widely and effectively practiced at least as far back as ancient Greece and Rome. According to one scholar, "The existence of contraceptive methods [in ancient times] is established by the Old Testament, by the Talmud, by Aristotle, by Pliny, and by physicians. . . . A very wide range of possible techniques was known."[1] Apparently, available evidence indicates family planning was very much a part of society in later times, as well. Other scholars agree. In the eighth and ninth centuries A.D. women in Germany had an average of 2.36 children. In central Italy, during medieval times, the figure was 2.44 children. Higher mortality rates are often cited as the reason for these low numbers, but the effective use of birth control, researchers say, must also be considered part of the reason why population rates were so stable. Today we seem to be returning to traditions that existed many hundreds of years ago, before a prohibition against birth control was enforced by civil and religious authorities. The birthrate in America continues to fall. Although the specter of overpopulation still haunts the world, experience shows that government policies that encourage smaller families can not only succeed, they may even succeed too well.

In the early 1970s the island nation of Singapore was worried it would soon run out of room if population growth wasn't curbed. Government leaders adopted a rigorous program calling for a maximum of two children per family. The tax system was amended to discourage large families. The program worked. Less than fifteen years later, the birthrate in Singapore had fallen dramatically. In 1957, women in Singapore were having an average of 6.4 children each. By 1985, the average was 1.6, well below replacement level. Prime Minister Lee Kuan Yew warned that if the trend continued, Singapore would not have enough people to meet the needs of its armed forces. Economic growth could be severely hampered. So the government reversed itself and began a hard-sell campaign urging its citizens to have more children. The tax system was amended once again, this time to encourage larger families.

1. John T. Noonan, *Contraception* (Cambridge, Mass: Harvard University Press, 1966)

Other Asian nations, such as Taiwan and South Korea, have also seen a sharp drop in birthrates. So we know that overpopulation can be avoided by encouraging family planning. I believe family planning should be an important part of social policy in America. A key element in the success of such a policy must be the strengthening of a sense of responsibility in our citizens—both moral and social responsibility. We know that children should be raised in an atmosphere of love and support, and that both the father and mother have vital roles to play. We must do a better job of instilling an awareness of moral and social responsibility in our young people. Self-control and birth control go together. Ideally, children should be born to parents who want them, and who are ready and able to care for them properly. This ideal may be difficult to achieve, but it should be our goal nonetheless.

The place of birth control in our society is firmly established. What about the related, but far more painful, question of abortion? On many levels, the subject of abortion makes me uncomfortable. I think that's true of most people. We're all glad that we were conceived and born, and we don't like to think of ourselves as denying the gift of life to others. But for those who are not ready to have children, pregnancy can present agonizing choices. Is it better to have an unwanted child, or bring the pregnancy to an end?

There are as many answers to that question as there are people who ask it. Personally, I don't think abortion on demand is a good idea. On the moral level, I think abortion should be limited to cases of rape and incest, and to cases where the fetus is not developing normally or the mother's life is endangered by the pregnancy. I don't think abortion should be used as a routine form of birth control.

Neither do I think that abortion should be outlawed by a constitutional amendment. Let me sum up my position by telling you something that happened during one of my frequent "Town Meetings," in which residents of a particular community are given an opportunity to address their concerns directly to me and other city officials. The year was 1981, a mayoral election year in New York City. A Town Meeting had been convened in the gym of the Holy Child Jesus Church in Richmond Hill, Queens. A crowd of six hundred people was present. A woman asked me to define my position on abortion.

I hesitated before answering. Standing nearby were a number of priests and high-ranking clergymen from other parts of the city. I didn't want to offend them or abuse their hospitality. So I answered, "I think you know my position . . . what's the sense of arguing?" But other parishioners would not let the matter rest. They demanded that I be specific. I said, "My position on abortion is that it's a matter of personal conscience."

I expected boos, but there weren't any. Maybe it was because those who disagreed with me had too much respect for me and my office. At any rate, the vast majority of the crowd agreed with what I said and applauded loudly.

There is no subject more sensitive or painful than abortion. I understand the feelings of those who wish to eliminate it by law. But, reluctantly, I cannot agree with them. The attack must come from a different direction. It's a moral question that can't be effectively fought on the legal front. I believe *Roe* v. *Wade* will, and should, continue as the law of the land. That, however, doesn't put the moral controversy to rest.

The future of our nation depends on our ability to inculcate a strong sense of morality in our young people. That moral sense should be based on philosophical, ethical and religious teachings, which are the underpinnings of conscience. The way to oppose abortion is by challenging the conscience of those who advocate it. If the battle cannot be won at the level of conscience, it cannot be won.

The call came in the middle of the night. . . : a 20-year-old girl named Debbie was dying of ovarian cancer. . . . As I approached [her] room I could hear loud, labored breathing. I entered and saw an emaciated, dark-haired woman who appeared much older than 20. She was receiving nasal oxygen, had an IV, and was sitting in bed suffering from what was obviously severe air hunger. The chart noted her weight at 80 pounds. . . . She had not eaten or slept in two days. She had not responded to chemotherapy and was being given supportive care only. It was a gallows scene, a cruel mockery of her youth and unfulfilled potential. Her only words to me were, "Let's get this over with."

I retreated with my thoughts to the nurse's station. . . . I asked the nurse to draw 20 mg of morphine sulfate into a syringe. Enough, I thought, to do the job. . . . Debbie looked at the syringe, then laid her head on the pillow with her eyes open, watching what was left of the world. I injected the morphine intravenously and watched to see if my calculations on its effects would be correct. Within seconds her breathing slowed to a normal rate, her eyes closed, and her features softened as she seemed restful at last. . . . [W]ithin four minutes the breathing rate slowed even more, then became irregular, then ceased.

It's over, Debbie.

When I read these words in *The Journal of the American Medical Association*, I was horrified. I was outraged. Assuming that this incident actually took place—and I have to so assume, or else why would so distinguished a journal publish this?—I can only conclude that the author, who describes himself as a gynecology resident "rotating through a large, private hospital," is a murderer. He should be identified and he should be prosecuted to the extent the law allows. Despite my importunities and the efforts of the appropriate authorities, a judge dismissed a grand-jury subpoena demanding the identity of the anonymous doctor.

Whatever his motivations, what he did was wrong. I don't believe that any physician has the right on his own to take the life of a patient no matter how painful that life may be. Doctors may be gods to their patients, but that doesn't give them the right to play God and determine unilaterally when and how to terminate a life, no matter how compassionate the roots of such a decision may be. Theirs is to heal and, where healing is not possible, to assuage, to comfort, to ease. And most do just that.

Regrettably, neither the United States attorney general or the district attorney of Cook County, Illinois, was able to identify and prosecute Debbie's killer. The attorney general said his office had no jurisdiction. The Cook County D.A. was frustrated by a court ruling protecting newspapers and periodicals such as the *AMA Journal* from revealing their sources, or, as in this case, submitting to an investigation of an anonymous writer's identity. This, to me, is a perversion of justice. A murderer has confessed his murder—indeed he has boasted of it—and is let loose to do it again. A modern-day Jack the Ripper goes undetected, not because he can't be found but because a judge won't let prosecutors find him.

In New York City, we have the largest municipal health-delivery system in the nation. We have eleven acute-care hospitals, five long-term inpatient facilities, over forty health and outpatient clinics. Our hospitals admit over 240,000 patients a year. Our emergency rooms treat over 1.2 million people annually. Our clinics log nearly 4 million visits each year. People come here from overseas and out of state to get treatment, like dialysis, that may be unavailable to them back home. We accept the supreme burden of caring for those whom no one else will care for: the indigent, the homeless, the abandoned. We can do no less. It is the obligation of our hospitals—our private as well as our municipal facilities—and our community of physicians to heal, to help preserve life. This is in accordance with the Hippocratic oath. Patients, of course, can exercise their right to refuse medical treatment, even at the risk—and sometimes with the intention—of dying. Many patients have living wills stipulating that no "extraordinary" or "heroic" measures be taken to prolong their lives in the event of, say, a stroke or other catastrophic or terminal illness. The law compels us to honor their wishes. If and when we are in doubt about what these wishes might be, our physicians, unless otherwise instructed by the courts, err on the side of treatment.

The Hippocratic oath aside, I believe that a fully competent patient retains the right to decide to end his or her life rather than to live on in pain or indignity. (In New York State, this right has been affirmed by law since 1914.) Such a decision, of course, must be based on informed judgment and should be made after discussion with the attending and/or the family physician. This is not "mercy killing"; this is not what the Chinese call "peace and happiness death." It is, rather, the exercise of a right.

It is my belief that a person in certain extreme medical circumstances—a terminal patient in the terrible final stages of cancer, for instance—has the right to refuse all medical attention and to decline food and water. I believe also that if a patient is not competent to make such a decision—a stroke victim who is all but brain dead, for example—a legal guardian, with the consent of the court of appropriate jurisdiction, should be allowed to determine for this patient on the use of extraordinary measures. Where there is a living will stipulating a person's wishes in the event he or she is incapacitated and unable to give voice to his/her wishes, there can be no uncertainty.

I do not believe that the Cardinal and I are in disagreement in this regard. The Church teaches that each person has a duty, but not an absolute obligation, to preserve his or her own life. But there is no obligation to use extraordinary measures made available by advances in medical technology to sustain life. As technology provides medical options unknown to earlier generations, complex questions relating to those options arise; as the recent report of the New York State Task Force on Life and the Law points out, it is no longer clear that all available means must be used to maintain life. Any benefit of extending life, often for only a short time, a time suffused with suffering and disability, must be weighed against an earlier, more peaceful, death. While I am hardly a biblical scholar, I do not believe that this position conflicts with an interpretation of the Halakhah: Although it is forbidden to shorten the life of a person even in the process of dying, an action that does not hasten death but rather removes a device that sustains life artificially is permitted.

Who doesn't remember—assuming, of course, that you were old enough to understand the headlines—the Karen Ann Quinlan case? As a result of an automobile accident, this twenty-one-year-old New Jersey woman was rendered comatose. Her condition was irreversible. Her father asked to be appointed her legal guardian so as to authorize her removal from the mechanical respirator which was thought to be keeping her alive. The ensuing court battle, which attracted international attention, set a landmark legal precedent: The New Jersey Supreme Court affirmed the right of a terminally ill patient to refuse certain medical treatment as part of the individual's right to privacy. (The respirator was removed. Karen Ann did not, as was expected, die. She lingered, comatose, for another nine years before passing away in 1985.)

In a less celebrated case in New York, Brother Joseph Fox, a Roman Catholic cleric, lapsed into a coma and was placed on a respirator. The director of the religious society to which he belonged initiated proceedings to obtain judicial approval to withdraw the respirator, a request that was contested by the hospital. The New York State Court of Appeals agreed with this request, based on "clear and convincing evidence" that Brother Fox had in fact expressed his wishes about life-sustaining treatment before becoming unconscious. This decision, which stipulated a clear prior decision of the patient, represented a departure from the approach taken by most other states. In another case involving a clergyman, an eighty-three-year-old monsignor named Thomas O'Brien, disabled by a stroke, kept pulling out a nasal feeding tube. Ruling him "not competent to make profound decisions," a judge ordered the surgical implantation of a feeding tube in Monsignor O'Brien's stomach. He died before the case could be argued further.

These cases, heartrending and wrenching though they may be, confront what is a difficult issue—with all the nuances and particulars of each specific situation—of the right of the individual, facing death, to determine his/her path. But the taking of life without consent is another matter.

Consider the case of Roswell Gilbert. On March 4, 1985, this retired engineer shot to death his terminally ill wife of fifty-one years. "I couldn't allow my lovely lady . . . to descend into a hell of suffering and degradation," he explained. Emily Gilbert had been living in continual pain from spinal bone fractures caused by osteoporosis, a debilitating and incurable bone disorder, and from Alzheimer's disease, the degenerative disease of the mind. Gilbert claimed that he acted out of love when he fired two bullets into his wife's head. "I want to die. Please kill me," he said were her last words to him.

Now, I know this must have been terribly painful for Mr. Gilbert. I have no doubt, from what I know of this case, that he loved his wife very much. But while he does not believe that he committed a crime—he has said that "justice is on my side but the law is on somebody else's"—his action simply cannot be condoned. It is beyond what is considered acceptable by our society.

No question concerning the ending of life is easy. When my mother developed cancer in 1960, and when I was told she had only ninety days to live, we did everything we could for her. But we didn't—we couldn't—tell her that she was dying.

My mother was sixty-two at the time. I remember visiting her one day—I wasn't living at home then—and she was all packed. She told me she was going into the hospital the next morning. "I have a gallbladder condition," she told me. "I was at the beach and I felt as I had for many years a discomfort. The doctor always told me that it was my gallbladder and that it could be handled with pills, but I knew that there's something wrong."

Her doctor had set surgery to remove her gallbladder the next day. I convinced her not to have the surgery at her doctor's hospital—it was a small proprietary hospital. My mother was very strong-willed, but she didn't fight it. I made inquiries, and we took her to Brooklyn Jewish, which was a good hospital. "Nothing serious," the doctor there told my father and me. A half hour later, after the surgery, he came down and said to my father, "I opened her up and four quarters of her abdomen are filled with cancer. There's no way of operating. I just sewed her back up. And I'm telling you that it would be wrong to take her to different quacks. They'll all have special cures. Don't do it. In fact, you shouldn't even have her X-rayed because X rays will not help her. They will only torture her. So just take her home, make her comfortable, and she will die in ninety days."

So we took her home. But she was in great pain. The local doctor we had come in twice a day couldn't do very much for her. She was suffering. She was jaundiced. She couldn't defecate; she had to have suppositories. But she didn't know she was dying.

We went back to her surgeon. We told him we just couldn't sit by and allow her to die. We had to do something. Even though he said X rays wouldn't help, we told him we had to try. And he gave us the name of a clinic in Brooklyn. We took her there. We told the doctor that she didn't know that she had cancer. But she knew. And I remember to this day that she reached out and she put her hand on mine and she said, "I didn't know I was that sick."

Of course, the treatment was useless.

Then a cousin called up and said, "I know your mother is suffering from cancer." Like all families in those days, you never told anybody about cancer, but it always got out. Cancer was something you just never talked about. My cousin told us about this doctor—Revici is his name—who had his own hospital and who, she said, had a "special medicine, and I know people who have been treated by him and who have been cured." So we took her there, to Trafalgar Hospital on East Ninetieth Street. Dr. Revici himself examined her. He told us he could eliminate the cancer, "but she has to come to my hospital right away." Now that was a godsend because hospitals in those days did not take terminally ill patients: If there was no hope for recovery, a hospital just would not take you. You had to die at home.

When he said he would take her, we were relieved. I couldn't spend all the time I was spending with her. My father couldn't; he had his fur business. We couldn't afford someone to come in every day to tend to her, in addition to the doctor who was getting paid and not helping much. It was awful. So I could have kissed his fingers. To us Dr. Revici wasn't a quack: Would a quack get paid by Blue Cross? And all he was charging was $25 a day for his medicine—what his patients thought was a magic elixir.

My mother had a right to die—earlier than they allowed her to die. I visited her every day. One day she was sitting up in bed. She was in terrible pain. "Why don't they let me die?" she was screaming. "Just let me die." So I said, "Mother, you're not going to die. You're not going to die. You're going to get well. We wouldn't let you suffer if we didn't know you're getting better." And because we still tried to hide the truth, this prevented our having a heart-to-heart talk. It was absolutely stupid that we were never able to discuss with her the truth about her condition. Never. And that meant that every single conversation we had with her was a fraud. I will always regret this. Today it's different, at least I think it's different: Doctors, out of fear of malpractice, do tell their patients—and more families do now talk honestly about impending death.

I remember telling the doctor—it was Revici's assistant—"Doctor, why don't you let my mother die? She wants to die." And he said, "Listen, if I thought that I couldn't cure your mother I wouldn't do this." He was doing a surgical procedure called a cutdown, because she had run out of veins he could tap for the IV. She died a few days later—five days short of three months. She died because her strength ran out. I certainly don't advocate that she should have been put to death, and no doctor would have so consented. But all around it was a painful episode. And the final indignity: Her diamond engagement ring was stolen from her finger after she died and lay upon her hospital bed.

This issue again attained personal relevance this past summer. When I suffered my stroke—the doctors called it a trivial event but, believe me, to me it was major—I got to thinking about my mortality. I remember saying to myself, "Dear God, if I'm going to be paralyzed or left speechless, I'd rather die." Can you imagine me, speechless? Thank God there was no paralysis of any kind. Or as the doctors say, "No deficit."

I thought about Steven McDonald, the young police officer who was so cruelly paralyzed by a bullet fired in haste. I thought about his courage and his family. Each of us has different strengths and each of us looks at life differently. What Steven McDonald is doing is superhuman. He has in fact dedicated his life to encouraging others to survive their infirmities. He is now part of a group that goes out and instructs other cops and firefighters who have been severely injured.

If, God forbid, I were ever placed in a condition of similar disability, or worse, I could not do what Steven McDonald has done. His lust for life is extraordinary, and he deserves our highest praise. Were it not for his example, I would know with certainty that, put in the same situation, I would have given up long ago. Compared to him I'm a coward.

THE CARDINAL

Was Tyrone Power's name in the movie really Captain *Holmes,* or am I unconsciously associating him with the name of a man who was such a strong forerunner of the captain's pragmatism, famous Supreme Court Justice Oliver Wendell Holmes, Jr.?

Abandon Ship was the movie. It was produced way back in the 1940s, but could have appeared yesterday.

The ship has sunk. Too many crew and passengers are packed into a single lifeboat. A storm is brewing. Captain Holmes decides the overloaded lifeboat can't survive and that he will have to order some occupants over the side in life jackets. Those least capable of enduring the long trip to the coast of Africa, or those unable to take turns rowing, will go first. He chooses a sick woman, an elderly husband and wife, a sailor growing weak. Passengers and crew refuse to put them overboard until Captain Holmes points his gun at their heads. Some twelve people are abandoned. The very next day, the remaining passengers and crew are discovered by a passing ship. All are saved except the twelve driven overboard. The movie ends, leaving it clear that they, too, would have been saved had the captain not made his decision.

The film was one of a number synopsized for a film anthology under the general title *Searching for Values.* It is still vivid in my memory, however, because it addresses so simply and starkly the question, The Right to Live: Who Decides?

High schoolers of my day were force-fed *Autocrat of the Breakfast Table.* (Years later I found it as difficult to teach as I had found it to read as a youngster.) Its author was the eminent physician of the nineteenth century, Dr. Oliver Wendell Holmes, Sr. Dr. Holmes wrote that "medicine, professedly founded on observation, is as sensitive to outside influence, political, religious, philosophical, imaginative, as is the barometer to the atmospheric density."[1]

Dr. Holmes's famous Supreme Court justice son was to say substantially the same thing about law that his father had said about medicine.

He opens his famous work, *The Common Law,* with the words: "The life of the law has not been logic; it has been experience." And he goes on.

> The substance of the law at any given time pretty nearly corresponds, so far as it goes, with what is then understood to be *convenient.* . . . The very considerations which judges most rarely mention, and always with an apology, are the secret root from which the law draws all the juices of life. I mean, of course, considerations of *what is expedient for the community concerned.* [2] [Emphasis added]

We spoke earlier in this book of the moral philosophies that have shaped us as a people, with the Founding Fathers influenced particularly by Natural Moral Law, rooted in *absolutes.* We mentioned, as well, Pragmatism, Social Darwinism and Utilitarianism, all rooted in the *relativity* of values. Shorthand: *expediency.*

Justice Holmes's approach to law, enormously influential ever since, combined all three of these relativistic philosophies and explicitly excluded absolutes. For Holmes, nothing was *intrinsically* right or wrong. There was no such thing as a moral law that runs through all of nature.

A landmark case came before the Supreme Court in 1927, *Buck v. Bell.* The Court held that compulsory sterilization was constitutional. Justice Holmes wrote the court opinion. "It is better for all the world, if instead of waiting to execute degenerate offspring for crime, or to let them starve for their imbecility, society can prevent those who are manifestly unfit from continuing their kind. . . . Three generations of imbeciles are enough."[3]

1. Quoted in *Encyclopedia of Bioethics* (New York: Macmillan Publishing Company, Inc. 1978), Vol. 4, p. 1405
2. (Boston: Little Brown, 1881), pp. 35–36
3. *Encyclopedia of Bioethics,* Vol. 4, p. 1614

What kinds of things does such reasoning lead to? In 1961 the attorney general of Oregon listed persons who could be compulsorily sterilized. They included:

Feeble-minded, insane, epileptic, habitual criminals, incurable syphilitics, moral degenerates or sexual perverts, who are, or, in the opinion of the institution heads, are likely to become menaces to society . . . [and] persons convicted of committing or attempting to commit the crimes of sodomy . . . or . . . an act of sustained osculatory relations with the private parts of any person, or permitting such relations."[4].

That's rough stuff. It's rooted in Pragmatism (the philosophy that if a thing *works*, it's "good"), Social Darwinism (the survival of the fittest), and Utilitarianism (the greatest good of the greatest number). It's also rooted in scientific ignorance. And it's all very relative. It's at the heart of an insidious usage of an otherwise valid concept of "quality of life." In this usage, we tend to judge the worthwhileness of the mentally retarded, the hydrocephalic, those with Down syndrome, the brain-damaged, the blind, the crippled, the cancer-ridden, the terminally ill and a whole host of other categories of people. It is the "meaningful life" mind-set that has gained incalculable support in our society, and which is leading us with remarkably increasing rapidity to the inevitable, some kind of legislatively or juridically determined agency to determine the right to life: Who is to live? Who is to die? Who decides?

State after state has already established mechanisms to guide its chief executive, its legislature or its courts. Frequently called Ethics Panels, or by some similar title, most of them are tasked to deliberate issues of "brain death," euthanasia,[5] living-will legislation, "death with dignity," who can remove life-support systems when, what constitutes extraordinary means of sustaining life, whether basic food and hydration can be withdrawn, and so on.

Understandable reasons are presented for such deliberations: advancing medical technology, the number of people living to significantly older ages, spiraling medical, hospital and nursing-care costs, and questions of what constitutes "meaningful life," or "quality of life."

---

4. *Encyclopedia of Bioethics*, Vol. 4, p. 1614
5. Euthanasia is defined in the *Modern Catholic Dictionary* as "literally 'easy death,' the act or practice of putting people to death because they or others decide that continued life would be burdensome." (New York: Doubleday, 1980)

Perhaps no field of speculation has developed more rapidly, so rapidly that the likelihood that it has penetrated our national consciousness—or conscience—is remote. Coupled with increasingly dire predictions about overpopulation and with ever-intensifying emphasis on "privacy" (meaning total control over one's own body), we may well be on a downhill sleigh ride extremely difficult to stop, or even slow down. My good friend Joseph Cardinal Bernardin introduced into the pro-life lexicon the valuable concept: "Consistent Ethic of Life." Life is of one piece. Assaulted in *any* way it is open to assault in a thousand other ways. I believe we must now add to the lexicon "Consistent Ethic of Death." It was prophesied with the passage of *Roe* v. *Wade*, in 1973, that once we legitimized killing of the unborn, ultimately no life would be safe—"hopelessly" retarded, blind, wheelchaired, cancer-ridden, elderly, or simply those who eat food, drink water or occupy crowded space! Easy recourse to death to resolve problems related to the unborn consistently leads to easy recourse to death to resolve a host of other problems.

Traditionally we have turned to juries and courts to determine innocence or guilt, with the power, in certain types of cases, to assign a death sentence to those found *guilty*. Is it conceivable that we will soon be turning to juries and courts on a routine basis to assign death sentences to the *innocent*? We are already turning to the courts with increasing frequency in cases of diagnosed terminal illness to determine whether life may in fact be terminated, or must be sustained. Note, for example, the 1988 case of Mary O'Connor, in New York, a seventy-seven-year-old stroke victim, still conscious, whose family requested that all hydration and food be withheld. The case went to court and the family's request was granted. (Ultimately this decision was reversed by the highest court in New York State.) And the famous 1987 case of Nancy Ellen Jobes, in New Jersey, a pregnant thirty-two-year-old woman who, as the result of a car accident, had surgery to remove her dead unborn baby and suffered a loss of oxygen and blood flow to the brain. Ms. Jobes had been living in a nursing home for seven years when the family requested the removal of her feeding tube. That request was granted by the court. Such cases have become legion.[6]

6. In 1987, CBS's 60 *Minutes* estimated that some twenty thousand deaths annually in Holland are at the hands of doctors engaged in euthanasia. Others lower the estimate to five thousand to eight thousand deaths annually. In any event, cardiologist Dr. Van der Does calls it "a point of no return." He says: "Once you say euthanasia is permitted in certain cases, I don't think it will be possible to stop somewhere along that track." This seems to me another example of the Consistent Ethic of Death.

Am I stretching things? I don't believe so. Indeed, I am so convinced of what is happening that I personally wonder whether the principal argument regarding *abortion* is any longer the question of whether or not the unborn is *human.*

For years many of us have believed that those who support abortion as a legitimate choice would not do so if they really believed the unborn to be actually a human baby. We have believed that people have become so confused about medical, scientific and legal arguments, and so misled by pro-abortion propaganda that all they need are pictures of aborted babies, or scientific evidence that an unborn is human, and they will totally reject abortion. We have considered it a fair-minded assumption that Americans are automatically revolted by the very thought of killing an innocent human being, much more so a baby. Some Americans, yes, certainly. Thus, the extraordinary work of people like Dr. Bernard Nathanson and his wife, Adele, in showing films of actual abortions, is saving a lot of babies, and "converting" a lot of people.

But I fear that the issue of whether or not the unborn is human may no longer be the primary question. We have begun more and more to substitute the question: "Who has the *right* to live, the *right* to die—born, unborn, guilty or innocent?" Who decides?

This is today's reality. I believe we should be facing up to it and fear we are not doing so as a people. Legislatures and courts are coming up with piecemeal determinations of who has the right to live, who has the *right* to die. The Hemlock Society has been arguing the right to suicide for years. Its persistence is beginning to pay off beyond its dreams. As I see it, the national trend is toward favoring suicide on the basis of "quality of life," or "meaningful life."

In various states an argument is being waged as of this writing, concerning the appointment and authority of "proxies." Under what circumstances can a patient-appointed or a state-appointed proxy declare that all life support should be removed from a patient? Who can avoid shuddering at the variety of goals that could motivate a proxy? Agatha Christie would have a field day. And what power to the State!

The question of whether the unborn will live or die seems hardly answerable any longer merely by proving the unborn's personhood. The unborn, like the ever enlarging group of other innocents are being subordinated to a "quality of life" requirement and to an all-pervasive concern with "privacy" rights. Humankind is close to preempting from its Creator the right to determine who shall live and who shall die.

I have long had a special, but by no means exclusive concern about the unborn. Thanks to various propagandists, there are those who have been misled to believe that I developed my concern only very suddenly during the 1984 presidential election campaign, in order to influence the outcome of the election. During that campaign the "single issue" allegation was given new impetus, and became a useful slogan to discredit the pro-life movement. It became even more useful politically, however, to discredit those who were allegedly single-issue voters—but only if the issue was abortion.

The fact never ceases to amaze me. As noted elsewhere in this book, I have testified on several occasions before congressional subcommittees concerning certain critical issues of public policy. In addition to such congressional testimony, I have given innumerable public addresses, preached countless sermons, appeared in endless numbers of radio, newspaper, periodical and television interviews, concerning Nicaragua, housing, hunger, the defense budget, weapons procurement, tax structures, the economy, Ethiopia, Ireland, El Salvador, and a variety of other critical issues. I have repeatedly argued in behalf of labor and just wages, and have directed that no activity under the cognizance of the Archdiocese of New York—hospitals, schools, cemeteries, etc.—use substitute labor to break strikes. In other words, I have publicly argued a broad spectrum of critical public-policy issues, social issues, with a particular emphasis on quality of life for the poor.

Some people have disagreed with me vehemently on some of these issues but I have not *once* been told that in addressing any one of *these* issues, I have "crossed the line between Church and State." I have not *once* been told that I am creating divisiveness in our society. I have not *once* been told that I have interfered in the political process or attempted to influence a political campaign, and I have certainly not *once* been told that I am a single-issue bishop because of my position on any one of these issues. In fact, most of what I have said has never been reported. It hasn't been considered "controversial" enough to report.

On the other hand, when I have pleaded on behalf of the life of the unborn, I have been accused of being indifferent to the problems of the poor, the homeless, the abused child or mother, or the dangers of nuclear war, or whatever, because in a particular address I have focused on the life of the unborn. Yet I have never once talked to any audience about any of these other issues and been accused of being indifferent to the *unborn* for not mentioning *them.*

Why is this? Can it be that strong talk concerning the unborn hurts our consciences, so we don't want to hear it? Can it be that the unborn is simply not a priority for too many of us? Have our insights into the sacredness of human life become blurred? Are we victims of the fallacy of exaggerated "pluralism" in which the only sin is moral certitude? *Everything* has to be up for grabs? No one can be morally certain about *anything*?

The single-issue attack is made in two different ways. As I noted above, some argue that pro-lifers are concerned only about the single issue of the unborn, and are allegedly uninterested in or even callous about the "born," whether unwanted or abandoned children, single parents, or anything or anyone else except the unborn. This attack treats pro-lifers as devoid of compassion, totally insensitive to the problems and pressures that pro-choice people purportedly understand and respond to.

The other single-issue attack is on those allegedly guilty of damning everyone for public office who is not pro-life, and urging people to vote for anyone of any party who *is* pro-life. To prove the allegations the accusers point to various paragons of public service who are opposed to nuclear-weapons systems, racism, sexism, poverty, homelessness, and other national ills. These doughty souls should be examined, it is averred, on their shining records in those particular *important* endeavors, and not penalized because they recognize a woman's right to her own body and the right of the poor to have abortions as readily as the rich. The thrust of the argument, of course, is that the anti-abortionist appreciates none of these virtues and is clearly willing to choose a madman or madwoman who would push the nuclear button on the slightest provocation. Or will choose someone who hates the poor and wants them homeless. Or someone who hates blacks and Hispanics and Filipinos and women.

It's all a caricature of course. Perhaps there *are* pro-lifers who might vote for a nitwit, or an incompetent, or an utter fool, or a racist, sexist, or whatever only because he or she is pro-life. There are also non–pro-lifers who might write Mickey or Minnie Mouse into the ballot. Such in either category are trivial in number.

The reality is quite the opposite of the caricature. Anti-abortionists look for candidates with anti-abortion records, as anti-racists look for anti-racist candidates, anti-nuclear voters look for anti-nuclear candidates, and so on. But more. The average anti-abortionist is trying to encourage candidates to *be* all the good things, and to *do* all the good things elected officials should be and do *plus* being actively opposed to abortion.

We have a right to expect our public officials to have the professional competency, the ingenuity, the personal integrity to design and promote, through responsible legislation, a state of affairs in which every human person is safeguarded. We expect them to preserve the magnificent tradition of our nation which teaches that the weakest among us need the strongest protection and that all of us are created equal and endowed by our Creator with the inalienable right to life. Let's be honest: A great weakness of the unborn is that they can't lobby and they can't vote. They have nothing to offer but their lives.

In regard to accusations that pro-lifers would vote against the most highly qualified candidate "merely" because he or she is pro-choice, I could argue that many voters, including a number of radical feminists and pro-choicers will vote against *any* anti-abortion candidate, no matter how brilliantly qualified, for the sole reason that he or she actively opposes abortion. Is that, or is it not, single-issue voting?

How many blacks would or should vote for a segregationist? (How many whites *should*?) How many women would or should vote for a candidate who promises a restriction on women's salaries? (Should anybody?) Need we multiply examples? How long has it been since a candidate for the presidency has not *hoped* for a single issue on which he can attack an opponent?

The political pundits during the Bush-Dukakis campaign spelled out the alleged strategy of each candidate quite publicly for all of us. Governor Dukakis would emphasize jobs, jobs and more jobs. Or reduced defense expenditures. Or improved foreign relations. Or whatever would defeat Vice-President Bush. The vice-president would hammer away on a world at peace, or a strong defense, or a Reagan heritage, or whatever would defeat Governor Dukakis.

What kinds of single issues did we see each candidate jump on? Governor Dukakis failed to contact Jesse Jackson before he announced his selection as running mate. Immediately it was alleged that Governor Dukakis was obviously insensitive to blacks. Great issue. Grab it. Run with it. See if it plays in Peoria.

Vice-President Bush tells a television interviewer he jumped out of a burning airplane in combat. A purported eyewitness says there were no flames. Issue: single. The eyewitness claimed that George Bush was no hero, that he lied, that he panicked under combat. Don't worry about the truth. You've got your issue!

Then, suddenly, every other single issue is swept off the front page. The vice-presidential nominee, one J. Danforth Quayle, is suddenly discovered to have spent six of the Vietnam years in the National Guard, instead of serving as a foot soldier in Vietnam. Instantly, all other qualifications or disqualifications were ignored. The single issue became the nature of National Guard Service and/or George Bush's judgment in selecting Mr. Quayle. One Democratic campaign worker, for example, was quoted as jubilantly telling Mr. Dukakis when the Quayle selection was announced: "It's all over, we've won!"

It's called politics. It's the way the game is played. No one in living memory, I wager, ever heard any issue called a single issue or any voter a single-issue voter before the abortion issue burst on to the political scene. Yet we have been, in fact, a nation of single-issue voters for generations. How often have we been told that Richard M. Nixon lost a television debate to John F. Kennedy, and an election, to boot, because he hadn't shaved before the show! Now *there's* a single issue.

My father once voted for Socialist Norman Thomas because of a single issue: He was fed up with the other candidates.

As one pro-lifer, I return now to the first allegation: callousness about everyone but the unborn.

How does one get at this allegation? There are so many marvelous works of charity going on in the Archdiocese of New York that have nothing to do with the unborn *per se* (although I must add, all such work *is* based on the sacredness of every human person). The magnificent works of Catholic Charities were built by my predecessors, so I can speak of them without boasting. What follows is illustrative of the kinds of issues the Church in New York is sensitive to and the way in which we attempt to best use our limited resources to address these issues.

Cardinal Hayes, Archbishop of New York from 1919 to 1938, was called the Cardinal of Charities. The largest Catholic health-care system in the country was advanced during his tenure. (It was actually begun by Archbishop Hughes as far back as 1850.) Nursing homes, youth activities, much of the infrastructure on which later archbishops could build came into existence. Cardinal Spellman, so often impugned as the "power" in the "powerhouse" called the Archdiocese of New York, gave himself, in fact, to establishing new homes for helpless children. Cardinal Cooke, gentlest of all men, was virtually a riverboat gambler when it came to hospitals. A graduate of the School of Social Service of Catholic University in Washington, he was as expert and enterprising a "social worker" as ever visited the five-story walk-ups in the Bronx. During his years as chairman of the Pro-Life Committee of the National Conference of Catholic Bishops, worrying first about the unborn never distracted him from a broad spectrum of the works of justice.

It was Cardinal Cooke who took a chance to begin the rebuilding of the South Bronx. It was Cardinal Cooke who risked millions of Archdiocesan dollars to bail out Catholic hospitals on the verge of bankruptcy, because they were in poor communities and he would not permit the poor to be deprived of their services. St. Clare's Hospital, now a national model for treatment of persons with AIDS, would have long since closed its doors, had Cardinal Cooke not come to its rescue before AIDS was even heard of by most people. It was (is) the only Catholic hospital available to the poor in its particular West Side section of New York. What had been Flower Fifth Avenue Hospital became the Terence Cardinal Cooke Health Care Center, one of the finest facilities in the United States for paralytics and other helpless people. It recently opened a crucially needed nursing-care center for patients with Huntington's disease. (As of this writing, it is one of the few such facilities in the world.) Even more recently it opened a long-term nursing-care center in New York for persons with AIDS, perhaps the first in the United States.

In the meanwhile, homes for the aged, soup kitchens, housing projects, pregnancy centers for women from every walk in life and an almost endless variety of similar facilities were coming into being day after day.

This is the spirit of concern for every human person that gave birth to the maternity shelter at the New York Foundling Hospital under the care of the Sisters of Charity and connected with St. Vincent's Hospital. It is the same spirit that motivates Rosalie Hall, operated by the Misericordia Sisters and attached to Our Lady of Mercy Medical Center. Young women go to these shelters, most single, most minorities, very many with no skills, no jobs. They remain during their pregnancy and are taught basic, income-earning skills. Their medical and hospitalization needs are taken care of as well as the support of a caring staff. The sisters are deeply saddened when any young woman feels she must have an abortion. Not infrequently a resident has had a previous abortion. She is treated with the same gentle love as the others.

Many women, young and older, particularly in areas outside the city, seek abortions out of confusion, fright, shame and isolation, not knowing where to turn. In October of 1984 we began advertising widely that any woman, of any religion or none, married or single, of whatever color or ethnic background, could call a hotline number, come in person, or be visited by a social worker at any location requested, regardless of distance. In complete confidence and at absolutely no cost to those in need, any such troubled girl or woman can receive counseling, medical care, hospitalization, shelter, delivery of the baby, arrangements for adoption if she desires or assistance to keep the baby herself. Since its inception, thousands of calls have been received on the hotline and requested services rendered. To take care of homeless pregnant women and women with newborns, shelters have been established (following costly investments to renovate facilities and bring them into compliance with fire and safety codes) to help this very vulnerable group of women and children until permanent housing can be located.

Tucked away in Garrison, New York, the Franciscan Sisters of Peace administer the Nazareth Life Center, another shelter for women facing an unplanned pregnancy in suburban counties. The sisters who live and work tirelessly at this center are inspired by the gentle spirit of St. Francis and their deep commitment to help women bring life into this world. Nazareth is a beacon of hope and loving care, and the volunteers who assist the sisters are full partners in the pro-life mission.

One of my favorite projects is carried out by the Archdiocesan Office of Christianity and Family Development. It's called Project

Rachel.[7] Little pain is so poignant as the pain of those who regret having had an abortion.[8] Sometimes it's simply the crushing grief of having given up flesh of their flesh, blood of their blood. Sometimes it's a shattering sense of guilt, born of the belief that they have killed an innocent child—their own. Sometimes they live for years with shame, in secrecy, never having told husbands, or parents, or fathers of their babies what they have done. Project Rachel offers counseling, spiritual, psychological or psychiatric care, confession and absolution for Catholics who desire it. It is named for Rachel of the Old Testament who wept inconsolably over the loss of her children.

There are some, I am sure, who doubt the emotional (and spiritual) impact abortion can have on a woman. But countless numbers of women who have had abortions are looking for help, and a substantial number call the Archdiocese. Several hundred sisters and laypersons as well as some fifty priests in the Archdiocese have received special training to counsel these women. The priests are specially prepared to administer the Sacrament of Reconciliation to and to counsel people who have been involved in an abortion. Those who have come for help include not only women who have had abortions, but fathers of not-to-be-born children, grandparents, close friends and even medical personnel. Countless pieces of countless lives have been picked up and put back together. People become whole again. Lives are renewed. There is never any censure for the woman who has had an abortion, only caring, only gentleness and love.

Neither these nor the many other Archdiocesan "life support" programs that could be described could be possible today were it not for the vision and the caring of my predecessors. The question that must be asked, then, is whether I have at least continued my predecessors' activities, or have been so preoccupied by the single issue of abortion that everything else is being neglected, and all resources being drained off these other activities. It's a fair question. If so, then indeed I must be faulted, but I would say that the fault would be due to my laziness or incompetency or lack of vision, and not to my "obsession" about abortion. Indeed, I am probably not doing nearly what I *should* be doing about abortion.

7. *Project Rachel* is the service mark of the Archdiocese of Milwaukee. The program operating in New York is based on the model of Project Rachel operating in other dioceses.
8. A beautiful little booklet that has proved exceptionally helpful in the healing of those who have been involved in abortions is *Abortion and Healing: A Cry To Be Whole* by Michael T. Mannion (New York: Sheed & Ward, 1986).

That I *am* a single-issue man, however, I do not deny for a moment: The issue is life. I *am* obsessed, not about abortion, or about the unborn, but about life at every stage of its existence, from the moment of conception to the ultimate burial of a body and beyond. My theology and my vocation commit me to a profound concern about life *after* death, as well as before.

I wonder if Mother Teresa of Calcutta is thought of as a single-issue woman. Surely no census could ever count the poor and broken bodies she and her sisters have picked up all over the world, the poor and broken souls they have helped mend, the countless numbers they have nursed until they have died in dignity, knowing that whatever their lives or their beliefs, God loves them. Yet when Mother Teresa gave her address in Stockholm upon receiving the Nobel Peace Prize for that very same "multi-issue" work, her theme was: "The greatest obstacle to peace in the world is abortion."

I believe that as firmly as does Mother Teresa. Must one have a religious faith to believe it? Must one see a connectedness in all human life? Is there a mystique about it hidden from the nonbeliever? Or is it enough to be convinced that if the infant in the womb is not safe, then ultimately no one is safe? Is it sufficient to be convinced that if we become callous as a people to the putting to death of millions of unborn infants, then we ultimately lose a sense of the sacredness of human life itself, and become contemptuous of the life of the individual?

Is it too dramatic to ask if one day, whether we will it or no, someone will be appealing to judge or jury that, in whoever's best interest it would seem to be, *we* be judged as no longer living "meaningful lives"? Will there one day be those encouraging *us* to make that decision for ourselves, because *we* are a problem for others?

Why are we caught up in this dilemma: Right to live, right to die; who determines which? I believe it is in large measure because our judicial or legal philosophy underwent such a radical departure in the hands of Justice Holmes, aided by many others. That departure was away from all moral absolutes, in the direction of sheer relativism. This was to come to mean that we would no longer speak of life itself as *intrinsically* good. The "quality" of life would become the criterion of its goodness or badness. We would no longer speak of the right to life of the innocent, but only a right to a "meaningful life." And in certain circumstances, the "meaningfulness" of one life would have to be weighed against the "meaningfulness" of another. Each individual life would have to be measured against another individual life, to see which should be given priority. Ultimately some arbiter would have to judge this. Essentially, this is what the Supreme Court did in *Roe* v. *Wade*, in 1973.

So we come full circle once again to the question of values. The State has already done in respect to the unborn, and is in process of doing in respect to children and adults, what the Church refuses to do: give priority to one innocent life over another. The State has tended to abandon what is to the Church an essential value: the intrinsic worth and dignity of every human person.

While I believe Justice Holmes and others of his legal bent distorted our constitutional heritage in abandoning moral absolutes, I can certainly not fault him or the State as such for a fact we noted before, here once again clearly revealed: that Church and State differ sharply in essential purpose. While both have obligations to the here and now, only the Church has positive obligations to the "hereafter."

I believe this reminder important because the law is a great teacher, the foremost teacher, perhaps, in our land. Whatever our infractions, we are basically a "lawful" people. From early childhood we are taught what is lawful, what is unlawful. Television police arrest people for stealing and television judges put them in jail. When television drivers run red lights, sirens blow, the chase is on, and when the cops catch up with them, tickets are handed out.

It is safe to say that for many youngsters growing up today, attending schools where the teaching of both moral and religious values is forbidden (by *law*), virtually the only right or wrong they learn is what is *legally* right or wrong. But the law authorizes abortion. The teaching is clear. As years pass, it is not only clear, it is taken for granted.

And what is being taken for granted with an increasing sense of routineness, in my judgment, is that the value of life is proportioned only to the *quality* of life; that there is "meaningful" life and "meaningless" life; that there are prior rights to life and subordinate rights to life.

It is one thing to argue about whether or not the unborn is a human person. It is quite another thing to say it doesn't matter. The rapid development of the principle of "prior rights" and the prospective establishment of umpires whose calls mean life or death surely has to be gravely disturbing to us all, regardless of where we are on abortion.

Let me emphasize this notion of prior rights by what is to me a horrifying news story I read while working on this book. The AP report, datelined London, read: "Success-hungry women track and field competitors are improving their performances by deliberately becoming pregnant and then having abortions." The report went on to say that this development had followed a discovery that "muscle power increases greatly during the first months of pregnancy."[9]

Surely we can all see the warning. The unborn can't begin to "compete" with an athlete who considers it her prior right to use the unborn so that she herself can compete more effectively with others. I can't imagine our not being horrified by this kind of thinking, whatever our general positions on abortion. If nothing else, the report makes clear that once we have become accustomed to abortion as a common occurrence, and see it as a woman's right, taking priority over all other rights, there is really no limit to what may happen—always in the name of "rights."

I want to say one more thing about the State and the question of values. The law may be the law, at any given time. In my judgment, that fact does not relieve the executive, the legislative or the judicial branch of government from pursuing actively any changes in the law they believe should be made. If, after all, one is a true Holmesian, relative about both morality and law, one need but be reminded of his dictum: "The prophecies of what the courts will do in fact, and nothing more pretentious, are what I mean by the law."[10]

If one argues commitment to moral absolutes, however, and to the intrinsic value of every human person, it seems to me that one is morally bound to try to effect a change in the law concerning abortion. To argue that one's constituents, or a majority of the people, favor abortion laws is only to argue with Holmes that law is a matter of *convenience*. To argue that poor women must not be deprived of the "right" of rich women to have abortions is to argue circularly that there can be a right *against* life. Then one is, again, not a moral absolutist, but a Holmesian relativist.

Finally, to argue that one cannot end abortions by law is to argue

9. *Daily Times*, Delaware County, Pa., May 19, 1988
10. *The Path of the Law*, quoted in Bergen Evans, *Dictionary of Quotations* (New York: Avenel Books, 1978), p. 378

that one cannot "end" traffic injuries by seat-belt requirements, or teen drunkenness by age restrictions. Nor will it do to say simply that we cannot legislate morality. We legislate *behavior* every day. Our entire society is structured by law. Of course one never ends *any* violations of law by law alone. It's a sad view of law, however, to consider it so poverty-stricken that its effects are negligible. Moreover, all distorted reports to the contrary, before 1973 every piece of verifiable evidence available demonstrates that abortions of *any* kind—following rape, incest, whatever—were a fraction of a fraction of what they are today. The law has been a powerful impetus in helping to generate an abortion mentality. Would a change of law change that mentality? Not immediately, but give it the same fifteen years as between 1973 and today. In those fifteen years, more than 20 million unborn have been put to death, incredibly, more than in all the wars our nation has ever fought.

Law is intended, after all, to protect us from one another regardless of private and personal moral beliefs. The law does not ask me if I personally believe stealing to be moral or immoral. The law does not ask me if my religion encourages me to burn down houses. As far as the law is concerned, the distinction between private and public morality is quite clear. It is obviously not the right of an elected official, or legislator, or the law itself to impose *beliefs*, but they are all expected to monitor *behavior*. There is no law that requires a drug pusher to believe he is destroying human life. Even if people *want* his drugs, the law forbids drugs on demand. The law says nothing of the personal beliefs of the rapist, the arsonist, the thief, the murderer, the kidnapper or the game poacher. The law simply says: You will not do these things *regardless* of your personal moral, spiritual or religious beliefs. Basically, when I violate other people's rights, I am involved in a matter of public morality, subject to penalty under law.

The National Conference of Catholic Bishops testified before the Senate in 1981, "We have no intention of asking the government to take over our own task of teaching moral principles and forming consciences." The testimony went on to argue, however, that the law has a critical teaching function. On this basis, too, we would appeal to those in public life who could do so much to help achieve modifications in the current laws.

It is one of our proudest traditions that bad laws can be changed. There is no better example than the slave laws. And while many blacks still suffer in our country and are still far from enjoying all the human and civil rights due them by both moral and civil law, the reality is that if the 1857 Supreme Court decision in the famous Dred Scott Case had been allowed to stand, they would still be legally slaves, noncitizens, forever unable to become citizens. In 1857, it was not enough for people of goodwill to call slavery wrong; it was absolutely essential that they call the *law* wrong and work to change it.

Constitutional Law Professor Edward S. Corwin quotes President Abraham Lincoln on Supreme Court decisions:

> The candid citizen must confess that if the policy of the Government upon vital questions affecting the whole people is to be irrevocably fixed by decisions of the Supreme Court, the instant they are made in ordinary litigation between parties in personal actions, the people will have ceased to be their own rulers, having to that extent practically resigned their Government into the hands of that eminent tribunal.[11]

In an evening radio message on February 6, 1988, the Mayor excoriated the White House for depriving poverty-stricken women of funds for abortion:

> In 1973 the United States Supreme Court decided that a woman has a constitutionally protected right to make an informed choice between childbirth and abortion. It's her body, said the Court, and thus her right to choose. That's the law of the land and that's the way it ought to be.[12]

"That's the law of the land," says the Mayor, "and that's the way it ought to be." Is the Mayor saying: "Because that's the law we have to observe it"? Or is he saying: "That's the law and I agree with it"?

How frequently has the Mayor argued that various laws should be changed? He justifiably describes changes in the law he sought as a congressman. In New York, he consistently pursued and ultimately won gay rights legislation, a dramatic change in then existing law. His own books reveal the pride he takes in being a law-changer. I must assume, then, that the Mayor does not believe abortion laws should be

---

11. Edwin S. Corwin, *Court over Constitution: A Study of Judicial Review as an Instrument of Popular Government* (Princeton, N.J.: Princeton University Press, 1983), p. 73
12. Certain later Court decisions broadened the notion of privacy beyond the 1973 decision, but none have made it an absolute right. In any event, the Mayor refers explicitly to 1973.

changed. If he does, it would help for him to say so, and work to change them. After all, the law prior to 1973 was radically different. Mayor Koch himself says elsewhere in this book: "We tend to forget that when abortion was illegal, it was pro-abortionists who took to the streets and pressured legislators to change the law."

There are millions of people of intense goodwill on both sides of the abortion argument. They have a right to hear reasoned presentations from varying perspectives. Such presentations may be passionate and emotional, but still "reasonable" given their respective starting points. Both political and ecclesiastical leaders have an obligation to clarify, not to obfuscate. Granted that we can all get carried away on occasion in the heat of debate, or say things under pressure or in difficult media interviews that we might later prefer not to have said. That's quite different from a calculated, contrived program of confusing the issues for our own ends.

A famous editorial in the journal of the California Medical Association back in 1970 made the point clearly and bluntly that it would be essential to generate ambiguity if abortion were to become acceptable.

Since the old ethic has not yet been fully displaced, it has been necessary to separate the idea of abortion from the idea of killing, which continues to be socially abhorrent. The result has been a curious avoidance of the scientific fact which everyone really knows, that human life begins at conception and is continuous whether intra- or extra-uterine until death. The very considerable semantic gymnastics which are required to rationalize abortion as anything but taking a human life would be ludicrous if they were not often put forth under socially impeccable auspices. It is suggested that this schizophrenic sort of subterfuge is necessary because while a new ethic is being accepted the old one has not yet been rejected. [13]

This editorial was not written to *oppose* abortion. It was simply an exceptionally frank warning to doctors that they had better "get with" the new ethic and gear up for the brave new world of abortion ahead of them. Precisely as the editorial pointed out, some real semantic gymnastics or, in plain words, "double-talk," would be required to make people forget that abortion is the taking of human life. But

13. "A New Ethic for Medicine and Society," *California Medicine*, 113:67, 1970

those determined to make people forget were prepared to supply the new language required.

This is one reason we in the pro-life movement feel saddened when accused of "imposing our view." We perceive, on the contrary, that individuals and organizations determined to legalize abortion and abortion funding are not only committed to imposing *their* views, but to changing traditional life and death language to make those views seem rational and humane. The "unborn child" has become the "fetus." A dead child following successful abortion has become "fetal waste." The child still living after unsuccessful abortion but not expected to live has become "fetus ex utero." And in an amazing subsection of regulations issued by the United States Department of Health, Education and Welfare[14] on June 30, 1974, one can interpret the definition of pregnancy itself to include abortion! If in the new "Thinkspeak," abortion is only the excising of fetal tissue, and not the killing of a baby, what will we call infanticide, or the killing of an infant?

These language changes are seen clearly for what they are when we are reminded that, for some thirty years prior to the 1973 decision of the Supreme Court, the Department of Health, Education and Welfare (HEW) had interpreted the Social Security Act to mean that a pregnant mother on welfare received aid for herself *and* her unborn child, as her dependent. One year after the 1973 decision, the Supreme Court decided that "child," as used in the Social Security Act, does *not* include the unborn. One must ask, where was the protest on the part of those who argue in favor of the poor, particularly those who demand that abortions be funded for the poor. Indeed, state courts had always treated the unborn child as did HEW prior to that decision, in that fathers were required to support unborn children as well as those already born. It is interesting that the Supreme Court reached its decision despite the fact that nineteen of twenty-five federal courts that heard litigation of the meaning of "child" before the case went to the Supreme Court held that "child" as intended by Congress in the Social Security Act included the unborn.

For centuries common sense had prevailed as had commonsense language. A pregnant mother convicted of murder, for example, could not be executed, because her unborn *child* was innocent of her crime.

14. Now Health and Human Services (HHS)

Margaret Sanger, famous leader of Planned Parenthood in its early days in the United States, fought against abortion as "barbaric" and as "the killing of babies," not simply "fetuses." A Planned Parenthood 1962 pamphlet to reduce teenage pregnancy by encouraging contraception was quite straightforward in telling young girls: "An abortion kills the life of a baby after it has begun. It is dangerous to your [the mother's] life and health. It may make you sterile so that when you want a child you cannot have it. Birth control merely postpones the beginning of life."[15] The pamphlet was withdrawn. I am told that when asked in 1982 about this statement, representatives of this same organization replied that this brochure was written in 1962 when abortion was *illegal*. So the *law* determines what we believe!

I have read Mayor Koch's statement to the effect that nasty, horrible, bloody pictures of the aborted really alienate people, rather than move them to compassion or to counteract abortion. I have heard that argument before. I have also heard that nasty, horrible, bloody pictures of the war in Vietnam on living-room television sets during the dinner hour turned the American people *away* from supporting the war.

Will the Mayor and I and people like us ever come to a mutual understanding on these "life issues"? At the moment, the Mayor's position can perhaps fairly be said to represent the position of the State, since the "law" is on his side, even if he may interpret it too loosely, in my view. And I believe that my position fairly represents that of the Church, even though some might say—and I disagree—that I interpret it too strictly.

That we cannot continue as a nation to *drift* in regard to these issues, however, should be frighteningly clear to both Church and State. The Happy Warrior, Senator Hubert Humphrey, had it exactly right:

> The moral test of government is how it treats those who are in the dawn of life, the children; those who are in the twilight of life, the aged; and those who are in the shadows of life, the sick, the needy and handicapped.

It was mathematician-philosopher Blaise Pascal who said: "The heart has its reasons that reason never knows."

15. Planned Parenthood Federation of America pamphlet, "Plan Your Children for Health and Happiness" (1962)

In the Archdiocese of New York we encourage every girl, every woman, offering her baby for adoption, to write a letter to the baby that the baby may read years later, and/or to the adopting parents of the baby that she is offering for adoption. In either event, anonymity is preserved of course.

Here is one of the letters.

Dear Parents of Moses,

I've spent the past two days being quite heroic, cheerful, level-headed, about the birth of this wonderful new person. When he was born my only thoughts were, "Thank God he's alive and so happy. He hadn't joined the ranks of the prolific number of aborted fetuses." Now it's Tuesday, late in the evening, and my tears are finally flowing. Not because I have any doubts about the quality of life he is sure to have with you but because of the sadness of parting with this tiny, perfect creature whom I have delighted in these past two days and the past nine months. I know that he should be with you.

I'm calling him Moses because he lives. Twice I scheduled abortion appointments and decided it wasn't his fault or folly that he had been conceived. I knew he would be beautiful, healthy, and in some way a very welcome addition to this earth. I feel that I am placing Moses in his reed basket and sailing him down the Nile, his Nile, your Nile, mine. I know that he and I will not share life together on a day-to-day, face-to-face basis, but we do share other dimensions. That of time and another subtle dimension because he grew within me for nine months.

I am told that Moses has 20-some cousins already—fantastic. I feel as though my family is expanding to include you and all your relatives. Please let him know he was given out of love, he was conceived in love, and I feel so good and sure that your love is now what he mostly needs. He is my greatest gift to the world.

Congratulations,
Mary

Mother Teresa of Calcutta would call this "something beautiful for God." But how beautiful as well for the natural mother herself—what pain it helps relieve, what wholeness it helps restore. How beautiful for the adopting parents. Above all, how beautiful for the baby who will one day learn that he or she, far from being rejected, was loved so very deeply and owes life itself to such loving sacrifice.

INDEX

"South Bronx Churches," 215
"South Bronx People for Change," 215
South East Bronx Community
    Organization (SEBCO), 195,
    199, 215
South Korea, 322
Soviet Union, 32, 70, 71, 137, 171
Special Services for Children, 105, 127
speech, freedom of, 82, 139, 167
    see also First Amendment
Spellman, Francis Cardinal, 21, 340
Stalin, Joseph, 137, 274
Starr, Roger, 211, 218–219, 285
"Statement on School-Based Clinics"
    (Roman Catholic Bishops), 182n
Staten Island Advance, 139, 144
sterilization, 332–333
Stevenson, Adlai, 72
Stonewall bar, 103–104, 294
"Strategies for Ministry in the Urban
    Struggle," 213–214
street vendors, regulation of, 17–18
suicide, 182, 231, 252, 335
Sullivan, Rev. Leon, 32–33
Supreme Court, New Jersey, 326
Supreme Court, New York, 97, 122,
    123
Supreme Court, U.S., 34, 85, 98, 105,
    123, 168–173, 179, 260, 332,
    347
    abortion and, 316, 319, 344, 349
    "separate but equal" ruling of,
    257–258, 266–267
synagogues, 37–38, 72

Taiwan, 322
Tanenbaum, Rabbi Marc, 27, 37
tax credits, private schools and,
    167–168
Taylor, Mary Gay, 135
Taylor, Rev. Gardner, 170
television, 135, 139, 141–142, 145,
    152, 158
Ten Commandments, 40–42, 86, 179
Ten Year Plan, 192–200, 202
Terence Cardinal Cooke Medical
    Center, 253, 286, 340

Teresa, Mother, 20, 225, 226, 248, 249,
    343, 351
tests, public-employment, 265–266
Theobald, Archbishop of Canterbury,
    46
Thomas, Norman, 339
Thomas Aquinas, Saint, 76, 286
Time, 74
Times Square, clean up of, 24
Toohy, Monsignor William, 111
totalitarianism, 137–138
Toussaint, Pierre, 249
transcendent needs, 47–48
Trojan Horse, 113–114, 118, 120, 124,
    125, 128–129, 130, 172
Truman, Harry S., 23, 72
Trump, Donald, 159
Trump (Trump), 159
Tuchman, Barbara, 113, 177
Tweed, William Marcy (Boss), 30

unemployment, 62, 145, 284–285
unions, 307, 336
United Nations, 136
Universal Studios, 274
Urban Development Corporation, 211
Ursula, Sister, 272
Utilitarianism, 332–333

Vallone, Peter, 98, 296
value-free judgments, impossibility of,
    74–75, 78
values:
    education and, 31–32, 106–107,
    165, 178–179, 181–183, 229,
    245
    Natural Moral Law and, 77–78, 81,
    83–89, 309, 332
    universal, Church-State relationship
    and, 40–42, 61
    see also morality
Van der Does, Dr., 334n
Vatican, 16, 18
Vatican II, 49–51, 78, 86
Vietnam War, 65–66, 137, 308, 339,
    350
Village Independent Democrats, 259

ABOUT THE AUTHORS

John Cardinal O'Connor, who has degrees in Advanced Ethics, Clinical Psychology, and Political Theory, served as a Navy Chaplain for twenty-seven years, retiring with the rank of Rear Admiral in 1979. He was appointed Archbishop of New York in 1984 and elevated to Cardinal by Pope John Paul II in May 1985. He is the author of a number of works including *A Chaplain Looks at Vietnam* and *In Defense of Life*. Mayor Edward I. Koch, a lawyer, is a former five-term Democratic congressman from Manhattan. He has been Mayor of New York since 1978. He is the author of *Mayor*, a number-one best seller, and *Politics*.